Television Programming for News and Public Affairs

Frank Wolf

The Praeger Special Studies program—
utilizing the most modern and efficient book
production techniques and a selective
worldwide distribution network—makes
available to the academic, government, and
business communities significant, timely
research in U.S. and international economic, social, and political development.

Television Programming for News and Public Affairs

A Quantitative Analysis of Networks and Stations

PRAEGER SPECIAL STUDIES IN U.S. ECONOMIC, SOCIAL, AND POLITICAL ISSUES

Praeger Publishers   New York   Washington   London

PRAEGER PUBLISHERS
111 Fourth Avenue, New York, N.Y. 10003, U.S.A.
5, Cromwell Place, London S.W.7, England

Published in the United States of America in 1972
by Praeger Publishers, Inc.

Library of Congress Catalog Card Number: 72-82780

Printed in the United States of America

In Loving Memory of

C. M. S.

"Under modern conditions in television, network managers and national advertisers, in large measure, choose and disseminate, through affiliate-licensees, raw materials which greatly affect the formation of public ideas and attitudes. The sum of these choices may well be vital to our freedom and progress. Hence, the policies and practices which govern such choices are of importance to the public interest."

Television Network Program Procurement, U.S. Federal Communications Commission, Office of Network Study, Second Interim Report, Part II (Washington, D.C., 1965), p. 23.

In executing even a modest research project debts are incurred, debts whose mere acknowledgment is insufficient. The project would not have been undertaken without the support and encouragement of Professor Harvey Mansfield and Professor Wallace S. Sayre. Progress would not have been possible without the generosity of Professor Fred W. Friendly and Federal Communications Commission (FCC) Commissioner Nicholas Johnson.

This book would never have reached the printing press without the interest taken in the project by Professor W. Philips Davison. The financial support provided by a research grant from the National Association of Broadcasters (NAB) at an earlier stage in the research was also most helpful, although the NAB has no responsibility for its conclusions or limitations.

Two students, John Gaskill and Joanne Cincotta, were also very helpful in collecting and analyzing data. Mary Heister, the librarian at TV Guide in Radnor, Pennsylvania, was most generous with her time and expertise, as was the staff of the Television Information Office of the NAB in New York.

Those many busy people in the broadcast industry who were kind enough to endure the questions of an eager graduate student are also owed a great debt. In addition, thanks should be expressed to Nanette Lemmerman, whose patience and diligence in producing the final typed manuscript was critical.

Finally, the sensitivity of my wife Susan, who was always ready at the right time with an encouraging word, was absolutely essential to my being able to carry through the entire project.

CONTENTS

LIST OF TABLES AND CHARTS

TABLES IN THE APPENDIXES

LIST OF CHARTS

1

THE PROBLEM
AND THE
RESEARCH
STRATEGY

INTRODUCTION

This study concerns several factors that have shaped news and public affairs programming on commercial television stations in the 50 largest population centers of the United States in the period 1966-71. The phrase "news and public affairs programming" refers to all programming involving the direct and explicit dissemination of information and opinions or the articulation of viewpoints on subjects of concern to governments. Examples of such programming were regularly scheduled news broadcasts, interviews with public figures, round-table discussions, documentaries on political topics, editorials, television "white papers," live coverage of public events or of speeches by important public officials, and the like.

The primary objective of this study was the identification and analysis of major factors that accounted for the quantity and proportion of news and public affairs programming shown on commercial television. An effort was also made to explain why certain types of programs—for example, news broadcasts—were far more frequently aired than were other types of programs—for example, documentaries. No content analysis of programming was undertaken, so that only a very limited discussion of factors influencing the content of programs was possible.

This study rests on two basic assumptions: first, that news and public affairs programming had an impact on the formation of public opinion; and, second, that the television medium was itself a part of the political system and that its news and public affairs programming therefore constituted a form of political behavior whose analysis was an appropriate project for a political scientist.

Although the extent to which television affected public opinion was frequently exaggerated, few would deny that there was any effect at all.[1] As an agent of political socialization for children and adults alike, television presumably had some impact upon the formation of the "political culture" of the United States.

As for the second assumption—that the medium was itself part of the political system, or, more precisely, an actor in the system— political scientists would readily accept such an idea. But students of journalism, broadcasters, and others outside the discipline of political science were extremely reluctant to agree. In fact, one of the major political strategies of the broadcasters as political actors was to foster the belief that journalists were outside observers of the political process, not participants in it.[2]

If "political behavior" is understood as behavior that affects the "authoritative allocation of values and resources," to use Easton's celebrated phrase, then public affairs programming is surely political behavior.[3] For such programming clearly affects what goods, services, honors, statuses, opportunities, immunities, licenses, and so forth were distributed and to whom and by whom they were distributed.

The time for this study was ripe. Research began in early 1967. Before that date very little attention had been paid to those factors that shaped the behavior of the media themselves. Political scientists and others had long been interested in the media, but their interest had largely been limited to the effects of the media's behavior upon the attitudes and behavior of others.

In 1922 Walter Lippmann examined the role played by the media in the formation of public opinion.[4] In 1944 Paul F. Lazarsfeld and his associates examined the impact of media coverage on electoral choice in Erie County, Ohio.[5] In his comprehensive study of American politics V. O. Key limited his discussion of the media to a short account of their role in political campaigns.[6] Daniel Lerner and his colleagues inquired into the role played by the media in the modern- ization of "traditional societies."[7] Bernard C. Cohen examined the impact of the press generally upon the formulation of foreign policy.[8] Only in the latter part of the 1960s have political scientists turned to a more theoretical assessment of the media in political systems generally.[9]

Even studies published while this research was being completed tended to stress the effects of television programming rather than the processes shaping programming. For example, two students of the media examined the impact of political broadcasts on the electoral results in two Yorkshire constituencies.[10] Lang and Lang wrote on the impact of television programming upon attitude formation.[11] Herbert I. Schiller examined the impact of U.S. media abroad.[12] Only Bryce Rucker, among academic students of the media, devoted con- siderable attention to factors shaping programming.[13] The Alfred I. Du Pont-Columbia University broadcast surveys, begun in 1969, also devoted considerable attention to programming processes.[14]

At the same time that the media generally and television in particular were receiving increasing academic attention, several former members of the media and one Federal Communications Commission (FCC) commissioner wrote fairly popular books about television and the press.15 Even the works of Marshall McLuhan, especially Understanding Media, became part of the popular culture during this period.16

This increasing intellectual concern with television and the media generally was no doubt partly because some of the principal controversies in American politics during the second half of the 1960s—the war in Indochina, urban disorders, and events in Chicago during the 1968 Democratic Party Convention—became intimately associated with the press and the television coverage that they received.

This convergence of popular and academic interest in the media made it inevitable that political scientists would begin to look more closely at the media. Somewhat prophetically perhaps, the Caucus for a New Political Science arranged a special panel at the September 1968 American Political Science Association meeting in Washington, D.C., entitled, "The Creation of 'News': Mass Media and Their Impact on American Politics."17 In short, this study was timely.

HOW FACTORS SHAPING PROGRAMMING WERE IDENTIFIED

In the absence of a rich literature on the processes involved in television programming, an extensive preliminary survey of available materials on broadcasting was made.18 As already noted, most of the existing research in this field had been written by journalists and teachers of broadcast journalism. Those publications that devoted considerable attention to programming were particularly helpful.19

Various government reports on the activities of broadcasters, particularly those emanating from inquiries conducted by congressional committees and the FCC, were consulted. And, finally, a series of interviews with knowledgeable students of the industry was conducted. These preliminary research activities culminated in the formulation of several hypotheses about the forces shaping public affairs programming.

It was immediately apparent that a complete, exhaustive analysis of factors shaping the quantity and character of public affairs programming was beyond reach. The study was therefore limited to four elements that appeared to play an important role in shaping the extent and types of programming shown. These were as follows:

1. The ownership structure of the television industry
2. The regulatory environment created by the policies and practices of the FCC

   3. The economics of survival and prosperity in the
      broadcast industry
   4. The policies of the national networks and their
      relations with their affiliates.

There was no way of being certain beforehand that these four "determinants" of public affairs programming were the four absolutely most
significant factors shaping this programming. It should further be
pointed out that the unit of analysis adopted in this study was that of
the firm—the network organization and the station organization. The
character of the determinants reflects that choice. Had the news
divisions of the networks and station organizations been taken as the
unit of analysis, economic pressures and the regulatory environment
might have appeared to be far less significant and the biases and
political preferences of individual broadcasters far more important.
   In any case, preliminary research suggested that these four
determinants had much to do with the quantity and types of programming
shown. Even the content of programming appeared to be somewhat
related to these determinants. Why were these particular determinants
selected?
   The decision to examine the ownership structure of the industry
was the result of an ongoing controversy within broadcasting concerning the degree to which the ownership of television stations in the
largest cities was concentrated in so few hands as to pose a threat
to the diversity of information and viewpoints available to the public.
This was a matter of growing concern to students of broadcast journalism, to an extremely vocal minority at the FCC, and to civic groups,
such as the American Civil Liberties Union.
   At the time the study was begun, negotiations toward a merger
between the American Broadcasting Company (ABC) and the International Telephone and Telegraph Company (IT&T) were at an advanced
stage. Applications for the transfer of ABC's broadcast licenses to
the merged corporation were before the FCC. Here the concentration
issue was being raised in dramatic form. Since it was widely suggested
that there was an important and possibly threatening connection between the ownership structure of the television industry and the
character and quantity of public affairs programming, it seemed
appropriate to analyze ownership structure as a possible determinant
in this study.*

_____

   *Since the behavior of the broadcasters through their news and
public affairs programming was the ultimate concern of this research,
the question of ownership would have arisen in any case. For it would

The inclusion of the regulatory environment in a political scientist's examination of public affairs programming was perhaps inevitable. Certainly the FCC had consistently claimed that it had attempted to increase the quantity and change the character of public affairs programming. This was especially true in the area of news broadcasts and editorializing. Complaints by broadcasters reflected in trade publications certainly implied that FCC policies, however well intended, were materially and significantly affecting broadcasters' programming policies. The prevailing view within the industry was that the FCC's policies were discouraging precisely the kinds of programming that they were attempting to foster.

There was another reason for including a consideration of the regulatory environment in this study. The ownership structure of the industry was largely in the "control" of the FCC, in the sense that new license grants and license transfers were within the FCC's power to withhold. Therefore, the existing ownership structure was, at the very least, the result of FCC acquiescence, if not the result of deliberate FCC policy. Therefore, the regulatory environment was of interest because of its connection with ownership structure.

Finally, it was widely suggested not only by members of the public but also by newspaper critics of television that the various shortcomings of public affairs programs on commercial television (and the deficiencies of commercial television generally) were the consequence of undue timidity on the part of the FCC. Implicit in this view was the assumption that FCC actions were at least potentially important in shaping programming. This frequently alleged relationship between programming and FCC policies—whether action or inaction—led to the inclusion of the regulatory environment as a determinant of public affairs programming.

Of the various factors affecting the character and extent of television programming, surely the economics of the industry was the one whose case was most compelling for inclusion in a study of this sort. Virtually every available analysis of programming took note of the quest for profits. That profit levels were dependent upon audience size was, of course, basic. The viewing preferences of the mass audience were universally blamed for the comparatively small amounts of nonentertainment programming. The views and tastes of the mass audience and the objectives of advertisers were also frequently used to account for the character of public affairs programming that did manage to find its way to the screen.

---

have been essential to determine precisely who the owners were in order to determine on whose behalf the stations and networks were acting.

What most observers saw as an overwhelming (though decreasing) aversion to controversy in commercial television was usually attributed to the "economic facts of life." In any case, the examination of the behavior of a commercial, profit-seeking institution would have to include economic pressures as a principal factor explaining behavior. As will be shown, this factor emerged as the single most important factor.

The inclusion of the networks' policies and their relationships with affiliates flowed naturally from the inclusion of the industry's economic pressures. The networks were so demonstrably the major organizations within the industry that their policies and relations with individual stations were bound to have important effects on almost every aspect of individual stations' behavior. Furthermore, as shall be shown, the economics were such that network activities in news and public affairs programming were particularly important. The mere fact that for most stations economic viability rested upon the affiliation contract made network policies a very significant factor.

These, then, were the major reasons leading to the selection of the four determinants of news and public affairs programming on commercial television. It will be shown that these determinants were not of equal significance in shaping the quantity of programming shown or in affecting the types of programs shown. Although it comes as no surprise, a major "finding" of the study is that the quantity of programming shown, the scheduling practices of stations, the types of programs shown, and even the content of programs are extremely dependent upon the economic pressures on the stations and the networks.

The ownership structure of the industry is shown to be much less significant, and the analysis will show that there is some doubt that it is a factor that should be treated separately at all—that is, differences in the quantity, character, and other aspects of news and public affairs programming usually attributed to differences in ownership may in many cases be merely differences due to varying economic pressures.

The regulatory environment will be shown to have considerable potential as a determinant of news and public affairs programming, as the history of regulatory behavior toward editorializing makes clear. But it will be argued that, to date, the FCC, despite some lofty rhetoric, has had a very limited impact upon the character and quantity of public affairs programming and that much of this impact was indirect and unintended. Some suggestions for changes in FCC policies will be made.

As for the character of relationships between networks and affiliates, there is considerable evidence to suggest that this factor goes far in explaining differences between individual stations in the area of news and public affairs programming. The mere fact of affiliation itself will be shown to be extremely important in affecting programming. But, again, the question of affiliation quickly becomes a question of economic pressures.

Before proceeding with an analysis of the four determinants identified and studied, however, some discussion of the methods by which the study was made, the data used, and the sources for those data is in order.

LIMITING THE POPULATION OF THE STUDY

Once what appeared to be four significant determinants had been identified, a research strategy had to be developed. But a preliminary series of practical decisions had to be made.

On January 1, 1971, there were 881 television stations operating or about to begin operations in the United States. Of these, 682 stations were operating on a commercial basis, and the remaining 199 were educational and/or instructional stations. It was clear that the forces operating on these noncommercial stations were very different, and the 199 noncommercial stations were therefore excluded from the study.

Of the remaining 682 stations, 179 were operating in the ultra high frequency (UHF) portion of the spectrum (channels 14-83). In all but a few atypical parts of the country, UHF stations were not fully competitive with very high frequency (VHF) stations at the time the research was being done. On January 1, 1967, when the original research was begun, between 33 percent and 42 percent of the homes with television sets were capable of receiving UHF signals.[20] By mid-1970 UHF penetration had reached 68 percent.[21] Nonetheless, it was necessary to exclude the UHF stations from the population to be examined in the study.

There remained, then, 503 commercial VHF stations. The criteria for the further reduction of the number of stations to be included in the population were more elusive. It was intuitively apparent that a station in Glendive, Montana, was not under the same sorts of pressures as was a station in Chicago or Los Angeles. Comparisons between such disparate stations were unlikely to yield useful results.

At the very least, the development of a research strategy to deal simultaneously with such a heterogeneous group of stations posed overwhelming methodological problems. Not only would a heterogeneous population pose difficulties, but it would also require a large number of sample stations so that the heterogeneity of the total population would be reflected. The mundane problem of devising a research project that a single researcher with severe budgetary limitations could complete in a reasonable time period was an additional consideration.

A useful way of further limiting the population was suggested by an FCC action first proposed in 1965. At that time, the FCC proposed interim rules that, for the purposes of the regulation of ownership concentration, treated stations in the 50 largest "markets" (that is, single-audience areas roughly corresponding to the Census Bureau's standard statistical metropolitan areas) as a separate class of stations.[22]

When the research was originally undertaken in 1966-67, the FCC was still operating under this interim rule. By limiting the population of the study to stations located in the 50 largest population centers the number of stations involved was substantially reduced. In 1967 there were 155 commercial VHF stations operating in these 50 largest markets, and they served 75 percent of the nation's population. On January 1, 1971, there were 158 such stations.

Again intuitively, it seemed that these commercial stations on VHF channels would be sufficiently similar in character to allow systematic comparison. Yet, these stations were diverse in many ways—in station ownership, in the degree of economic profitability, in the size of the audience served, in the number of competing stations within the market, and so forth. For a variety of reasons, then, the commercial VHF stations in the 50 largest television markets became the population of the study. (See Table 3, below, for a list of these stations and their markets.)

TECHNIQUES FOR ISOLATING THE DETERMINANTS

A research strategy involving four elements was developed to facilitate the examination of the determinants mentioned above:

1. Two sample surveys of program schedules for selected stations in the 50 largest markets, one examining programming in 1966 and the other examining programming on the same stations in 1971
2. The circularization of a questionnaire to all 155 commercial VHF stations in 1967 and a second circularization of essentially the same questionnaire to the same population of stations in 1971
3. Selective interviewing of persons in a variety of positions in and around the television industry in 1967 and again in 1971
4. Conventional library research involving the examination of available published materials of relevance to the concerns of the study.

In the construction of the station sample, one basic problem had to be resolved at the outset—whether the stations should be placed in the sample in a merely random way or whether an effort should be made systematically to reproduce in the sample population the hetero-geneity of the entire population of stations. The random method was unlikely to be appropriate in this study, since one of the factors to be examined was ownership structure, and there were far more group-owned and single-owner stations than there were, say, network-owned and -operated stations.

A random selection of sample stations would have been unlikely to result in a sample with adequate representation from all types of stations. Therefore, stations were selected for the sample with a number of criteria in mind. The objectives were to reproduce in the sample a balanced geographical distribution of stations, a diversity of ownership groups represented by the individual stations, a balance of markets of various sizes, a nearly equal distribution of stations affiliated with each of the three major networks, and an adequate representation of stations that were not affiliated with any network.

Ultimately, 36 stations were selected to represent the 155 stations, a sample of just over 23 percent of the total population; and 34 stations were used to represent the same population of stations in 1971. (Further details about the construction of the station sample can be found in Appendix A, below.) These stations are listed in Tables 1 and 2. To assemble representative program information, four typical broadcast weeks were selected. The program schedules of each of the 36 stations for those four weeks were examined.

In selecting four sample weeks a number of factors were con-sidered. The year 1966 was chosen as the year from which the pro-gram schedules would be assembled. This was chiefly because the data from which the station sample was drawn were accurate as of January 1, 1967. (See the "Introduction" to Chapter 2, below, for a discussion of the sources of these data.) It therefore seemed reason-able to conduct the study of programming as close as possible to that date. Since the project itself was undertaken in March, 1967, it was not then possible to collect 1967 data.

But 1966 was a year when elections were held in many places around the country. This fact was possibly relevant in a study of public affairs programming, since the presence of hotly contested elections in one market but not in another might skew the results of the survey. Television stations typically scheduled major-party candidates for interviews and devoted some programs to important issues raised in campaigns. It was therefore decided to exclude from the program sample the weeks from Labor Day through mid-November, 1966.

Since television program schedules were to a certain extent seasonal (the "season" ran roughly from early September through

TABLE 1

The Sample, 1966-67

Station	Market	Rank	Affiliation	Owner
Network Owned and Operated				
KGO-TV	San Francisco	7	ABC	ABC
WMAQ-TV	Chicago	3	NBC	NBC
WCAU-TV	Philadelphia	4	CBS	CBS
WKYC-TV	Cleveland	8	NBC	NBC
KMOX-TV	St. Louis	13	CBS	CBS
WXYZ-TV	Detroit	6	ABC	ABC
Single-Owner Network Affiliated				
WILX-TV	Lansing-Onondaga	48	NBC	
WLAC-TV	Nashville	44	CBS	
KCRA-TV	Sacramento-Stockton	27	NBC	
WAST	Albany-Schenectady-Troy	40	ABC	
WHDH-TV	Boston	5	CBS	
WLCY-TV	Tampa-St. Petersburg	32	ABC	
WBEN-TV	Buffalo	22	CBS	
Multiple-Owner Network Affiliated				
WSAZ-TV	Huntington-Charleston	46	NBC	Capital City
WSYR-TV	Syracuse	31	NBC	Newhouse
WKRC-TV	Cincinnati	16	ABC	Taft
WAVE-TV	Louisville	50	NBC	WAVE
WNHC-TV	Hartford-New Haven	14	ABC	Triangle
WMC-TV	Memphis	35	NBC	Scripps-Howard
KHOU-TV	Houston	25	CBS	Corinthian
WLWI	Indianapolis	18	ABC	Avco
WSB-TV	Atlanta	19	NBC	Cox
WMUR-TV	Manchester	49	ABC	Eaton
WMAR-TV	Baltimore	11	CBS	Sunpapers
KDKA-TV	Pittsburgh	9	CBS	Group-W
WSPD-TV	Toledo	37	ABC	Storer
WBTV	Charlotte	30	CBS	Jefferson Standard
Multiple-Owner Nonaffiliates				
WTCN-TV	Minneapolis-St. Paul	17		Chris-Craft
WOR-TV	New York	1		RKO-General
KTLA	Los Angeles	2		Gene Autrey
KTVY	Dallas-Fort Worth	15		WKY
WTTG	Washington, D.C.	10		Metromedia
KWGN-TV	Denver	41		WGN-Chicago Tribune
Single-Owner Nonaffiliates				
KPLR-TV	St. Louis	13		
KTNT-TV	Seattle-Tacoma	21		
KTVW	Seattle-Tacoma	21		

TABLE 2

The Sample, 1971

Station	Market	Rank	Affiliation	Owner
		Network Owned and Operated		
KGO-TV	San Francisco	7	ABC	ABC
WMAQ-TV	Chicago	3	NBC	NBC
WCAU-TV	Philadelphia	4	CBS	CBS
WKYC-TV	Cleveland	8	NBC	NBC
KMOX-TV	St. Louis	15	CBS	CBS
WXYZ-TV	Detroit	6	ABC	ABC
		Single-Owner Network Affiliated		
WLAC-TV	Nashville	37	CBS	
KCRA-TV	Sacramento-Stockton	23	NBC	
WHDH-TV	Boston	5	CBS	
WLCY-TV	Tampa-St. Petersburg	31	ABC	
WBEN-TV	Buffalo	27	CBS	
		Multiple-Owner Network Affiliated		
WAST-TV	Albany-Schenectady-Troy	45	ABC	Sonderling
WSYR-TV	Syracuse	42	NBC	Newhouse
WSAZ-TV	Huntington-Charleston	48	NBC	Lee
WKRC-TV	Cincinnati	16	ABC	Taft
WAVE	Louisville	47	NBC	Orion
WNHC-TV	Hartford-New Haven	14	ABC	Capital City
WMC-TV	Memphis	33	NBC	Scripps-Howard
KHOU-TV	Houston	22	CBS	Corinthian
WLWI	Indianapolis	20	ABC	Avco
WSB-TV	Atlanta	18	NBC	Cox
WMAR_TV	Baltimore	12	CBS	Sunpapers
KDKA-TV	Pittsburgh	10	CBS	Westinghouse
WSPD-TV	Toledo	39	NBC	Storer
WBTV-TV	Charlotte	32	CBS	Jefferson Standard
		Multiple-Owner Nonaffiliates		
WTCN-TV	Minneapolis-St. Paul	17		Chris-Craft
WOR-TV	New York	1		RKO-General
KTLA	Los Angeles	2		Golden West
KTVT	Dallas-Fort Worth	13		WKY
WTTG	Washington, D.C.	9		Metromedia
KWGN-TV	Denver	38		WGN-Chicago Tribune
		Single-Owner Nonaffiliates		
KPLR-TV	St. Louis	15		
KTNT-TV	Seattle-Tacoma	24		
KTVW	Seattle-Tacoma	24		

late May or early June), weeks were chosen from across the calendar year. Finally, because of the possibility that public affairs programming might be distributed unevenly across calendar months (many stations had a review of the month's news), weeks were selected so that days falling in all parts of the month would be included in the program sample. With these various factors in mind, the following seven-day weeks were chosen:

February 1-7, 1966	(Tuesday to Monday)
May 9-15, 1966	(Monday to Sunday)
August 17-23, 1966	(Wednesday to Tuesday)
November 24-30, 1966	(Thursday to Wednesday)

The program schedules for these dates for each of the 36 sample stations were obtained from local newspaper listings and regional editions of TV Guide. (A detailed account of the problems encountered in procuring accurate program data can be found in Appendix B, below.)

In order to discover to what extent the pattern of programming had changed between 1966-67 and 1971, an additional survey of the 1971 sample was made, using 14 randomly chosen dates (two Mondays, two Tuesdays, and so forth) across the calendar year 1971. The dates chosen were as follows:

January 2	(Saturday)
January 28	(Thursday)
February 15	(Monday)
March 12	(Friday)
March 14	(Sunday)
April 12	(Monday)
May 25	(Tuesday)
June 9	(Wednesday)
July 14	(Wednesday)
August 21	(Saturday)
September 30	(Thursday)
October 19	(Tuesday)
November 5	(Friday)
December 5	(Sunday)

Again, listings in daily newspapers and regional issues of TV Guide were used as sources of program schedules.

In addition to the use of program schedules for the sample stations, questionnaires were sent to all commercial VHF stations in the 50 largest markets, once in 1967 and again in 1971. Several objectives were sought with these questionnaires: to confirm the general validity of the findings for the stations in the sample to collect some kinds of information not available in published schedules, and to permit the comparison of the findings from the sample with the declared program practices of a population of stations far larger than the sample itself.

Of the 155 stations in 1967, 78 ultimately responded to the first questionnaire, and 58 of the 158 stations in 1971 responded. These questionnaire responses considerably broadened the data based upon which the analysis in this study was made. (See Appendix C, below, for a copy of these questionnaires and for a short discussion of the details of their circularization.)

Interviews with persons in station organizations, the networks, and a variety of other positions in and around the television industry provided a supplementary source of information. These interviews, necessarily confidential, were used largely to seek confirmation of the trends that emerged in other parts of the study. Most of the interviewing was done with people in New York-based station organizations, but some visits were made to stations in the neighboring New England and Middle Atlantic markets. Interviews were also conducted with a variety of people in news and public affairs programming in the network organizations, as well as with some senior network executives. People at the FCC and elsewhere outside the industry were also consulted.

The project involved, then, the analysis of the role of four determinants of public affairs programming on commercial television. Now that an explanation has been given of how these determinants were selected, as well as the methods of isolating them for study, substantive questions can be raised. Who actually owned the major market television stations? What role did the four determinants actually play?

2

**THE OWNERSHIP STRUCTURE
OF THE
TELEVISION INDUSTRY
AND ITS IMPACT
UPON PROGRAM CONTENT**

INTRODUCTION

It has already been noted that a mounting concern with the media was observable in the last years of the 1960s. The issue of "concentration of ownership" within the media industries preoccupied many students of the media. Those attacking concentration pointed to the possibility that the information and opinions broadcast or printed were in some way limited, controlled, or slanted as a result of ownership concentration. This was what Vice President Agnew meant when he said the following in Des Moines in November 1969:

> The purpose of my remarks tonight is to focus your
> attention on this little group of men who not only enjoy
> a right of instant rebuttal to every Presidential address,
> but more importantly, wield a free hand in selecting,
> presenting, and interpreting the great issues in our na-
> tion.[1]

Those defending the existing structure of the industry pointed to the economies of scale involved in larger broadcasting enterprises. They claimed that these economies essentially financed public affairs programming by freeing resources with which to produce programs of quality.

In order to assess these arguments, a survey of the ownership structure of the industry as it was when the research was begun was first required. Comprehensive data on American television have been assembled on a continuing basis by an organization called the American Research Bureau (ARB), not a trade association but an independent concern that published its data periodically in TV Digest and in Television Factbook. This organization's publications served primarily the constituent elements within the industry itself—the advertising agencies, the sponsors, the networks, and the stations' advertising representatives. Since all these parties required the most accurate and impartially collected information with which either to plan advertising campaigns or to attract potential advertisers, there was little reason to doubt the reliability of the most commonly used source of such data.

Similar compilations by other organizations, such as the television rating services, and by trade publications, such as Broadcasting and Television, corresponded closely, with certain very minor exceptions, to those published by the ARB. Within the industry itself this latter source was widely regarded as the most authoritative source of information about the television industry, and it has been relied upon here.[2] Reliance on a single source of course ignores problems of consistency and comparability of data, if any. The 1971-72 edition of Television Factbook contained virtually all publicly available data on American television as of January 1, 1971.

On January 1, 1971, there were 230 discreet television "markets" in the United States, ranging from New York, in which there were over 5.5 million television homes, to Muskegon, Michigan, with 200 television homes. Save three exceptions, each of the 50 largest of these markets was served by at least three commercial VHF television stations. The two largest, New York and Los Angeles, had six and seven, respectively, in this category. Within the top 50 markets as a whole there were 220 commercial stations—158 VHF and 62 UHF stations. (In 1967 there were 155 VHF and 32 UHF stations.)

The ARB ranked these markets in their "nationwide sampling sweep survey" of March 1970 according to the "net weekly circulation" in that market. Net weekly circulation referred to "the estimated number of different television homes viewing a particular station at least once per week, Monday-Sunday, 6:00 a.m.-2:00 a.m., E.S.T."[3] That is, one station per market, in each case the station with the largest audience, was taken to represent the market as a whole, and the net weekly circulation for that station was taken as the circulation for that market.

This way of ranking the markets was defended as the best available since it reflected the size of actual audiences rather than potential audiences. (This difference was important because viewing habits varied considerably from city to city.) The FCC itself accepted the ARB's rankings as authoritative.[4] The 1971 rankings are shown in Table 3.

TABLE 3

1971 ARB Television Market Ratings by
Net Weekly Circulation

Rank	Market	Rank	Market
1	New York	28	Dayton
2	Los Angeles	29	Columbus
3	Chicago	30	Portland
4	Philadelphia	31	Tampa-St. Petersburg
5	Boston	32	Charlotte
6	Detroit	33	Memphis
7	San Francisco	34	Greenville-Spartanburg-
8	Cleveland		Asheville
9	Washington, D.C.	35	Johnstown-Altoona
10	Pittsburgh	36	Birmingham
11	Miami	37	Nashville
12	Baltimore	38	Denver
13	Dallas-Fort Worth	39	Toledo
14	Hartford-New Haven	40	Harrisburg-York-Lancaster-
15	St. Louis		Lebanon
16	Cincinnati	41	Grand Rapids-Kalamazoo
17	Minneapolis-St. Paul	42	Syracuse
18	Atlanta	43	Wheeling
19	Providence	44	Greensboro-High Point-
20	Indianapolis		Winston/Salem
21	New Orleans	45	Albany-Schenectady-Troy
22	Houston	46	Flint-Saginaw-Bay City
23	Sacramento-Stockton	47	Louisville
24	Seattle-Tacoma	48	Huntington-Charleston
25	Kansas City	49	Raleigh-Durham
26	Milwaukee	50	Oklahoma City
27	Buffalo		

Note: Rankings from American Research Bureau and Television
Digest, Inc., Television Factbook, No. 41 (1971-72 ed.; 2 vols.;
Washington, D.C.), II, 56a-57a.

CONCENTRATION IN THE TELEVISION INDUSTRY

It was immediately apparent that the single most pervasive
influence in American television was the three national networks.

The American Broadcasting Company (ABC), the Columbia Broad-casting System (CBS), and the National Broadcasting Company (NBC) each owned and operated stations in the very largest of the 50 major markets. Furthermore, their affiliations with other stations in virtually all 230 markets of the country made them the single most important element in the industry.

Their success in penetrating the country's markets was clear. Of the 50 largest markets, 40 were served by separate VHF affiliates of each of the three networks. In two additional markets there were VHF stations sharing an affiliation with two networks. In all the remaining markets penetration by the networks was achieved through affiliations with UHF stations.

Each of the networks owned the maximum number of stations permitted by the FCC—five VHF stations. ABC owned such stations in New York, Los Angeles, Chicago, Detroit, and San Francisco. CBS owned stations in New York, Los Angeles, Chicago, Philadelphia, and St. Louis. NBC owned its stations in New York, Los Angeles, Chicago, Cleveland, and Washington, D.C.

Although 15 of the 158 VHF stations were owned by the three networks, the remaining 143 were owned by other parties. One of these was owned by a Canadian network.* The remaining 142 stations were owned by 83 separate parties. Of these, 29 were single-owner stations—that is, stations owned by parties with absolutely no other interests in television stations. (Concentration has increased con-siderably since 1966-67. Then the nonnetwork-owned stations were dispersed among 88 parties, and the number of single-owner stations was 37.)[5]

---

*CKLW-TV in Windsor, Ontario, was an affiliate of the Canadian Broadcasting Corporation (CBC). It was included as a major market station because it served the audience of the Detroit market. Even though this CBC station accepted some advertising, it received an annual grant for operations from the CBC and was therefore not in the same situation as were American stations. Although Detroit was the only top 50 market served by a VHF station physically located outside the United States, a comparable situation existed in many other markets. Many stations were located in smaller neighboring cities and were licensed to corporations in these smaller neighboring cities. Because they nonetheless served the audience of a major market area designated by the name of the major city around which the audience lived, the stations in this situation were considered to be in the market named by the major city that they served.

These single-station owners were not, on the whole, small, local one-business organizations. On the contrary, their holdings typically included interests in newspapers, radio stations, community antenna systems, publishing houses, film production enterprises, and other communications-related industries. Most of the 29 single owners had interests in more than one of these allied industries.

Only nine of the single-station owners appeared to have no other major business interests outside of television station ownership. The breakdown is as follows: newspaper publishers owned 12 of these stations, radio stations owned 4, insurance companies owned 2, a Catholic university owned 1, and a film-maker owned 1. The remaining 113 stations (after subtracting the 15 network-owned and -operated stations, the one owned by a Canadian network, and the 29 single-owner stations) were owned by station groups—that is, by parties with interests in more than one television station.

If concentration of ownership means that comparatively few parties owned or had interests in a large number of stations, then the degree of concentration was striking. Five organizations in addition to the three networks owned the FCC maximum of five VHF stations in the top 50 markets. These firms were Westinghouse (Group-W), Capital City, Storer, Cox Broadcasting, and Taft. Four additional parties—Metromedia, RKO-General (a subsidiary of General Tire and Rubber), Newhouse, and Avco—owned four stations each. Combining these figures (three networks, five groups owning five stations each, and four groups owning four stations each), 12 parties owned 56 major market stations, or more than one-third of such stations.

Three VHF top 50 stations each were owned by Chris-Craft, Scripps-Howard Broadcasting, Hearst Stations, the Oklahoma Publishing Company, Chicago Tribune-New York News, General Electric, Poole, Time-Life Broadcast, Corinthian Broadcasting, and the Meredith Publishing Company. This meant that 86, or over one-half, of the 158 stations in the 50 markets were owned by 22 separate parties. Seven organizations each owned two top 50 stations—Post-Newsweek, Wometco, Triangle Publications, Steinman, Fisher's Blend, King, and Sonderling. If one combines all these figures, 100 stations in the 50 largest markets were owned by 29 separate parties. This condition would well be called a considerable concentration of ownership.

But there remained (beyond those group stations referred to above) 29 stations owned by groups that had interests in stations outside the top 50 markets but only one station within the top 50. Those who would argue that there was marked concentration in the ownership of the stations in the 50 major markets would find their case seriously weakened when these 29 stations are included in the figures: the 158 VHF stations were owned by 87 separate parties.

Perhaps more interesting than the number of owners of top 50 market stations was the high number of stations owned by newspapers and magazines. In 34 of these 50 markets at least one of the commercial VHF stations was owned by a firm also publishing a newspaper in the same market. A total of 38 stations in the 50 markets were owned by newspaper interests publishing in the same market in which the stations were located. The most striking case of ties between newspapers and television stations in the same market was in Dallas-Fort Worth, where the three network affiliates were each owned either by a Dallas or a Ft. Worth newspaper; and the fourth station, a nonaffiliate, was owned by newspaper interests in neighboring Oklahoma.

In the top 50 markets taken as a single unit, 51 of the 158 stations in that unit were owned by firms publishing newspapers within that unit. Another way of stating this same fact is to say that some 30 percent of the stations serving a national audience in 50 cities were owned by papers serving that very same audience. This national audience, it will be recalled, constituted at least 75 percent of all television viewers in the country.6 Two additional top 50 stations were owned by newspapers published in cities not among the 50 largest markets. In total, then, there were, as of January 1, 1971, 53 stations in the 50 markets that were owned by newspapers. This amounted to almost exactly one-third of such stations.

There was considerable concentration of ownership among these newspaper-owned stations. Of these 53 stations, 28 were owned by only nine separate concerns. Cox Broadcasting, owner of the Atlanta Constitution, among other papers, owned five such stations; the Newhouse group owned four; and four other newspaper organizations owned three each. All in all, 34 separate newspapers or newspaper groups owned these 53 stations. Among these were some of the major newspaper organizations in the country—most notably, the Scripps-Howard papers, the Hearst organization, the Philadelphia Inquirer (Triangle Publications), the Baltimore Sun, the Washington Post, the Atlanta Constitution, the St. Louis Post-Dispatch, the New York News, and the Chicago Tribune.

Those who feared that the structure of the communications media industries allowed a few powerful persons to control the flow of information and opinion to the public would have found additional grist for their mill since many of these newspaper organizations owning television stations in major markets were also the owners and publishers of major American periodicals, notably magazines.

Cox Broadcasting owned United Technical Publishers, which published five technical electronics journals, for example. More

importantly, some of these owners published mass circulation magazines. Triangle Publications put out Seventeen and TV Guide; Newhouse's more widely circulated magazines included Vogue, Mademoiselle, House and Garden, and Glamour. The Hearst organization
published House Beautiful, Good Housekeeping, Cosmopolitan, Town
and Country, Harper's Bazaar, and Popular Mechanics. The Washington Post was owned by the publishers of Newsweek, and the Cowles
interests were responsible for Family Circle and Venture and had a
half-interest in Harper's Magazine.

In addition to newspapers with both television stations and magazine interests there were six stations in the top 50 markets owned by
major magazine publishers who, as of January 1, 1971, had no newspaper interests. Three of these stations were owned by Time-Life
Broadcast, Inc., a subsidiary of Time, Inc., publishers of Time, Life,
Fortune, and Sports Illustrated, some of the most widely read publications in the country. The Meredith Publishing Company, publishers
of Better Homes and Gardens, also owned three top 50 stations.

To combine these data, 59 of the 158 stations were owned by
parties with interests either in newspapers or magazines or in both.
It should be added that some of these same interests also had stakes
in the book publishing industry. And the tie-ins between radio and television station properties were too numerous to list. (See Appendix
D, below, for more detailed data on ownership ties between newspapers,
magazines, and book publishers.)

NETWORK AFFILIATIONS IN THE 50
MAJOR MARKETS

It has been pointed out that the networks were easily the most
pervasive influence in the television industry as a whole. ABC, CBS,
and NBC not only each owned five VHF stations in the 50 largest
markets, but in 40 of the 50 each had a primary affiliate. ABC, in
addition to its five owned-and-operated stations, had affiliates on
VHF television in 38 markets and shared an affiliation with another
network in yet another market. In total, then, ABC reached 44 of the
50 markets on VHF television. CBS had five owned-and-operated
stations, 40 primary affiliates, and two shared affiliations. It thus
reached 47 markets on VHF television. NBC reached 49 of the 50
markets on VHF frequencies through five owned-and-operated stations,
43 primary affiliates, and one shared affiliate.

Of the 158 commercial VHF stations operating in the 50 markets,
there were (including currently owned-and-operated stations) 136
primary affiliates, two shared affiliates, one affiliate of a foreign
network, and 19 stations operating commercially with no network

affiliations. A list of the 50 markets with the affiliations in each can be found in Table 4.

COMMON VIEWS ABOUT STATION OWNERSHIP
AND PUBLIC AFFAIRS PROGRAMMING

Among both students and critics of the broadcast industry it was widely believed that the character of programming on television was connected in some way with the identity and interests of those who had major interests in broadcast properties. Similar assumptions pervaded the thinking of the FCC when in seeking, or at least seeming to seek, diversity of ownership in the industry, it did so in the name of diversity of programming.

It was especially common among those on the left to argue that the television industry could be relied upon to give favorable coverage to the military-industrial complex, because the corporations dominating the broadcast industry—firms such as the Radio Corporation of America (RCA), CBS, and Westinghouse—themselves had substantial interests in defense-related projects. Such arguments involved the same assumption that there was a connection between ownership and public affairs programming.

When organizations like the American Civil Liberties Union opposed the merger between ABC and IT&T in 1965 because of the fear that the merger would constitute a threat to the autonomy and integrity of news-reporting on the network (because of IT&T's vast interests abroad), the opposition rested on the fear that ownership structure and programming were connected.

Harry J. Skornia, one of the broadcast industry's most prolific, if intemperate, critics, expressed this view well when he wrote the following:

> Perhaps never before in history have the most powerful channels to the people been so completely controlled by so small a segment of the national life. Since government itself has no equivalent channels with which to talk back, and since labor, religion, and other parts of our culture have no equivalent voices, the citizens have an image which is almost wholly dictated by sales-, advertising-, and business-oriented custodians. . . .
>
> This situation is all the more serious because magazines, films, phonograph records, and radio stations are now largely controlled by the same kinds of corporations that control TV.[7]

TABLE 4

Network Affiliations in Major Markets
as of January 1, 1971

Market	Networks with Primary VHF Affiliates*	Networks with Joint Affiliates
New York	ABC(o&o), CBS(o&o), NBC(o&o)	
Los Angeles	ABC(o&o), CBS(o&o), NBC(o&o)	
Chicago	ABC(o&o), CBS(o&o), NBC(o&o)	
Philadelphia	ABC, CBS(o&o), NBC	
Boston	ABC, CBS, NBC	
Detroit	ABC(o&o), CBS, NBC, CBC	
San Francisco	ABC(o&o), CBS, NBC	
Cleveland	ABC, CBS, NBC(o&o)	
Washington, D.C.	ABC, CBS, NBC(o&o)	
Pittsburgh	ABC, CBS, NBC	
Miami	ABC, CBS, NBC	
Baltimore	ABC, CBS, NBC	
Dallas-Fort Worth	ABC, CBS, NBC	
Hartford-New Haven	ABC, CBS	
St. Louis	ABC, CBS(o&o), NBC	
Cincinnati	ABC, CBS, NBC	
Minneapolis-St. Paul	ABC, CBS, NBC	
Atlanta	ABC, CBS, NBC	
Providence	ABC, CBS, NBC	
Indianapolis	ABC, CBS, NBC	
New Orleans	ABC, CBS, NBC	
Houston	ABC, CBS, NBC	
Sacramento-Stockton	ABC, CBS, NBC	
Seattle-Tacoma	ABC, CBS, NBC	
Kansas City	ABC, CBS, NBC	
Milwaukee	ABC, CBS, NBC	
Buffalo	ABC, CBS, NBC	
Dayton	CBS, NBC	
Columbus	ABC, CBS, NBC	
Portland	ABC, CBS, NBC	
Tampa-St. Petersburg	ABC, CBS, NBC	
Charlotte	CBS, NBC	
Memphis	ABC, CBS, NBC	
Greenville-Spartanburg-Asheville	ABC, CBS, NBC	
Johnstown-Altoona	CBS, NBC	
Birmingham	ABC, NBC	
Nashville	ABC, CBS, NBC	
Denver	ABC, CBS, NBC	
Toledo	CBS, NBC	
Harrisburg-York-Lancaster-Lebanon	NBC	
Grand Rapids-Kalamazoo	ABC, CBS, NBC	
Syracuse	ABC, CBS, NBC	
Wheeling	NBC	ABC-CBS
Greensboro-High Point-Winston/Salem	ABC, CBS, NBC	
Albany-Schenectady-Troy	ABC, CBS, NBC	
Flint-Saginaw-Bay City	ABC, NBC	
Louisville	CBS, NBC	
Huntington-Charleston	ABC, CBS, NBC	
Raleigh-Durham	ABC	CBS-NBC
Oklahoma City	ABC, CBS, NBC	

*The abbreviation "o&o" in parentheses stands for "owned and operated."

To many, assertions such as this had great intellectual and ideological appeal. Unfortunately, such global assertions do not lend themselves to systematic verification.

These widespread assumptions about public affairs programming and the ownership structure of the industry really involved two separate though related inferences: that the specific economic, ideological, and corporate interests of those owning television stations, station groups, and networks shaped the public affairs programming seen on their outlets; and that the quantity and character of public affairs programming on television depended upon the degree to which ownership of stations was dispersed among many parties or concentrated in comparatively few hands. To what extent these two assumptions were true became the concern here.

In Chapter 6, below, it will be shown that the profit quest of the stations and networks in their television operations was of critical importance in shaping the quantity and the character of news and public affairs programming; that is, because the stations and networks had necessarily to be economically profitable operations, certain limits, predilections, and restrictions were imposed upon news and public affairs programming presented on the air. No fairminded student of the medium could argue otherwise.

If by asserting that public affairs programming was shaped by the quest for profits, Skornia and others who made similar arguments meant merely that the amount of public affairs programming shown and the degree to which it was hospitable to controversial ideas and personalities was related to profitability, there could be little argument. But Skornia and others argued that the wider financial and ideological interests of those owning the television industry shaped the character—and here reference is being made largely to program content—of public affairs programming. This is a different and far more dubious point.

Did The "Owners" Shape Program Content?

There was, of course, a basic problem of identifying who the "owners" were. It hardly needs to be pointed out that virtually all the major broadcast stations and certainly each of the three networks were owned by corporations, shares of which were widely dispersed among great numbers of persons. Nonetheless, there were people within each corporation who had substantial (even if minority) control by virtue of owning significant blocks of shares—people like the Sarnoffs at NBC, the Paleys and Frank Stanton at CBS, and so forth. Top management, board chairmen, and directors typically had tremendous personal financial stakes in the profitability of the corporation, at least insofar as it was reflected in share values and dividends.

Although there is, then, some difficulty of speaking of owners, it nonetheless makes sense to look at the activities of such persons when discussing the connections, if any, between owners and programming. The issue should perhaps be rephrased. Did those with substantial personal financial stakes in broadcast properties, people who were usually at the top levels of management and on the boards of directors, have an impact upon the content and character of public affairs programming? Did their wider economic and ideological interests affect programming? The evidence suggests that this was only very rarely true.

It was virtually impossible to find in the public record or in private conversation instances of intervention by "the owners" in the content of programs because of wider economic or ideological concerns. When intervention occurred at all—and it was admittedly rare—it was always justified in the name of the well-being of the corporation, not the service of wider economic or political interests. But the virtual absence of such instances forced those who saw the interests of owners as important in shaping programming to infer owner influence in vague and general terms.

Easily the best way to discover whether this influence was present would have been to study in meticulous detail the decision-making processes surrounding a number of public affairs programs.[8] Interviewing the people involved at various levels might have uncovered the presence of such influence. Such studies were very rare, and none was undertaken in connection with this study. But it should be noted that in such studies the influence would have to be shown, not inferred.

It is likely that, if such influence was operating at all, it operated imperceptibly in the unconscious and subconscious choices made by a variety of people in the programming process. The argument is frequently made that such influences are rarely explicit, that in order to advance in the hierarchies of large organizations people have to make the interests of those at the top of that organization their own interests, and that this process takes place almost subliminally.[9] If this was in fact the case, the influence of the owners would have been extremely difficult to isolate.

But, in the absence of concrete evidence of ownership influence of this kind, episodes from which such influence might be inferred were examined. Examples of such instances follow:

In 1968 the FCC reprimanded WJIM-TV in Lansing, Michigan, for failing to notify its viewers of its own financial interest in a matter on which it editorialized. Gross Telecasting, Inc., licensee of WJIM-TV, was the owner and operator of the local airport restaurant.

This restaurant was in dispute with the airport authorities and the Michigan Aeronautics Commission. WJIM-TV editorialized in favor of itself.10

KRON-TV in San Francisco was owned by the Chronicle Publishing Company, also owner of the San Francisco Chronicle. A cameraman at KRON-TV has charged that the station knowingly and self-consciously slanted and suppressed news in its coverage of newspaper strikes and consolidations in the newspaper business in San Francisco over the last several years. On March 20, 1969, the FCC announced that it would withhold renewal of KRON-TV's licenses pending an investigation of these charges.11

The Radio Corporation of America, of which NBC was a subsidiary, owned communications relay facilities in the Philippines. The foreign minister of that country came on an official visit to the United States and received no television coverage at all, with the exception of an appearance on an NBC Washington, D.C., interview program. FCC Commissioner Nicholas Johnson suggested that the maintenance of goodwill was the objective and that this single appearance on NBC was evidence of the news operation's serving a wider corporate interest.12

During the spring of 1968 when the students at Columbia University were demonstrating and occupying buildings, the various New York City television stations covered the events. Many students were quick to point out that CBS coverage was distinctly less favorable to various student viewpoints than was that of NBC and ABC. This difference was attributed to the fact that the chairman of the board of CBS was a member of the university's board of trustees.

Mark Lane, one of the prominent critics of the Warren Commission Report on the Assassination of President Kennedy, has written that in winter 1964 David Susskind invited him and Dorothy Kilgallen to be guests on his program, which appeared on WPIX in New York, a station owned by a corporation owning the New York Daily News. Several days after the invitation was accepted by Lane, the producer telephoned to tell Lane that the appearance was being cancelled because, officially, there were too many political programs that week. Unofficially, she added, according to Lane, that the Daily News, not David Susskind,

controlled who the guests were, and his appearance was
not approved.13

Even if these five anecdotes reflect actual influence of the owners
on the public affairs programs of their outlets, this handful of incidents,
although suggesting a need for further research into the matter, does
not suggest that such practices were widespread in the industry. In
all cases the people involved in the programming decision denied the
truthfulness of the above accounts. KRON-TV in San Francisco
categorically denied the story told by the former cameraman. In the
case of the accusation of NBC in connection with the visit of the Phil-
ippine foreign minister, the person who invited him to appear denied
knowledge that RCA had a communications installation.

CBS officials not only denied that William Paley's membership
on the board of trustees of Columbia University had anything to do
with the character of news coverage; they also questioned the view
that CBS's coverage was less sympathetic to students' views than
was coverage by its competitors. In the case of Mark Lane, David
Susskind reported that Lane's account was completely inaccurate.14
Only the Michigan station was unable to cast any real doubt on the
truthfulness of the charges.

Two books by former television journalists—books that were
highly critical of the industry and that included accounts of attempts
by corporate executives to shape the operations of the news divisions—
made no reference whatever to intervention in public affairs programming decisions because of wider corporate interests or personal
political or ideological preferences.15

The cases of intervention mentioned involved efforts to protect
the networks from additional regulation or to streamline news operations to increase overall profitability. Because of the candor of
these two books (and, some would add, the bitterness of Fred W.
Friendly's book), it could be inferred from the absence of criticisms
of this kind that such criticisms were rarely if ever warranted.

Friendly did, however, mention one instance where the views
of CBS President Frank Stanton did perhaps make some difference in
the character of one public affairs program. Involved in this instance
was an early "CBS Reports" program entitled "The Teenage Smoker,"
a program strongly denounced by the tobacco industry. Even though
CBS's outside finances were heavily involved in the tobacco industry,
top management agreed that this was a worthwhile program. Friendly
attributed top management's support of this program to the personal
views of Stanton, who was strongly opposed to smoking.16

MacNeil quoted only the usual arguments made on the question
of owner intervention in program content, with no personal opinions
or argument for or against these arguments. He particularly referred

to a July 1967 <u>Variety</u> in which six corporations with broadcast interests—General Electric, Kaiser, Westinghouse, General Tire and
Rubber, RCA, and IT&T—were taken to task for offering news coverage
that did not upset their contractor, the Department of Defense.17
MacNeil himself added only the following:

> When it [the industry] has to program for the widest
> audience to stay profitable, keep one eye open for dis-
> pleasure in Washington and occasionally consider the
> larger interests of parent corporations with a vast stake
> in government and defense, it is not surprising that TV
> news is cautious.18

The Industry View

When confronted with this <u>inferential</u> evidence of interested
bias in public affairs programming, network and station executives
provided what might be called "inferential evidence to the contrary."
They pointed out that the people in the news divisions were profes-
sionals who would not tolerate intervention in what they would have
called "news judgment." They noted that, where one corporation
owned five stations, those stations frequently took editorial positions
in opposition to one another on the same issue, hardly evidence of
intervention by the "top brass."

They also indicated that licensees were responsible for what
appeared on stations and that attempts by network executives to
shape programming would be an improper violation of the licensees'
obligations. One station group president pointed out that each of his
station's editorial boards had complete autonomy, except for the
overall rule imposed by the central office that forbade editorializing
on international matters or on matters whose coverage the station
was not equipped to handle itself.

Finally, spokesmen for the industry noted that theirs were large
organizations and that it was difficult to control what happened in large
organizations. Therefore, they said, even if they tried to influence
the programming, they would have had difficulty achieving success.
Although a disinterested cynic would be right in showing that these
defenses involved several self-serving fictions, he would nonetheless
be obliged to acknowledge that the available evidence did appear to
sustain the basic claims of those defending the practices of the industry.

Several quotations from a report commissioned by the station
groups in response to the FCC's proposed top 50 market concentration of ownership ruling (mentioned above) reflected the groups' point
of view on the issue:

Programming is inherently a local competitive decision, since each station must take into account the program offerings of its local competitors. However, programming decisions may or may not be made at the local level. This fact is of some concern in the Commission, since group corporate headquarters may be in a position to impose programming decisions on the stations they own. However, the results of the mail survey and field interviews show that programming decisions in group-owned stations are almost always made on the local rather than corporate level.

Moreover, in the news and public affairs area—those in which manipulation would most logically take place—the potential propagandist is impeded by the substantial cost involved in pre-empting time which might otherwise be earning a return. The revenue loss would be particularly great in pre-emption of a prime time segment generally devoted to high-yield entertainment programming. Yet, for the purposes of manipulation, prime time is generally the most desirable period in which to reach the largest audience and thus achieve an optimum effect.

Even in those relatively few cases where group headquarters lays down very general policy lines as to the approach to news and public affairs, the general responsibility for administration of the pertinent programming remains that of the individual station. The great majority of group headquarters have no set formal policies relating to news and public affairs programming by member stations.[19]

What, then, can be said about the idea that network and station owners' wider economic and political interests affected, shaped, or had a controlling influence upon public affairs programming? In general, there was little hard evidence to support such a theory. What evidence there was provided only indirect indications of such influence. Although there was little reason to doubt that corporate executives did, from time to time, attempt to shape programming decisions in such a way that they served the networks' and stations' immediate interest in profit, attempts at other types of intervention and influence were difficult to find. It may be that those who saw such influence labored under a false analogy between the small town newspaper editor who may have shaped every word in his paper and the television corporate executive who, according to the analogy, controlled what was shown on the air.*

If the wider economic and ideological interests of the owners affected the content of public affairs programming, this influence has yet to be isolated. Although students and critics and those with a regulatory responsibility were right to be vigilant in their search for

---

*There is evidence that this kind of relationship between "the owners" or the "publisher" and the content of large newspapers was also frequently exaggerated. Referred to earlier were charges by some students at Columbia University that the coverage by CBS of building occupations and police interventions at that university during spring 1968 were noticeably less sympathetic to student viewpoints than was the coverage of ABC and NBC and that some attributed this alleged difference to the membership of William Paley, chairman of the board of CBS, on the Columbia board of trustees.

A similar charge was made against the New York Times. In this case the faulty coverage was attributed to that paper's publisher Arthur Sulzberger's also being a member of the university's board. One of the New York Times reporters assigned to cover the disturbances at Columbia during the period in question revealed in a confidential interview that, several days before the police cleared the buildings, he had discovered that Tom Hayden was inside the Mathematics Building. The reporter spoke with Hayden and discovered that Hayden and others in leadership positions among the occupiers were determined not to vacate the buildings, no matter what concessions from university authorities might be forthcoming. Their objective, according to Hayden, was to force the police onto the campus and in that way to attract far wider student and faculty support for their movement.

When the reporter sought to get this story into the New York Times, he was told that he had not been assigned to talk with students in the buildings but to cover the movements of key university officials. Hayden's presence at Columbia was not reported in the New York Times until after the police intervention. The moral drawn from this episode by the reporter involved was that, even if the New York Times had been interested in presenting a biased, antistudent view of the disturbances (and this story would, presumably, have fit that perspective very well), large organizations of that type were far too bureaucratized to permit the implementation of such policies. A similar argument could be made about the large corporations in the broadcasting industry.

instances of such intervention, there was no systematically gathered evidence to warrant any presumption that such influences were oper- ating to a significant extent. The FCC put it well in its opinion of December 21, 1966, in the IT&T-ABC merger case, when it said the following:

> we nevertheless find in our experience with numbers of other licensees who encompass, along with broadcast interests, large and diversified non-broadcast activities no indication of abuse of their public trust through the intrusion of their non-broadcast concerns upon the objec- tivity of their news reporting or commentary and no demon- strated detriment in any other programming sector.[20]

STATION OWNERSHIP TYPES,
NETWORK AFFILIATION,
AND NEWS AND PUBLIC AFFAIRS
PROGRAMMING

If there was little or no persuasive evidence that the specific economic, ideological, and corporate interests of those owning television stations, station groups, and networks shaped the news and public affairs programming seen on the owners' outlets, what evidence was there for the second assumption—that the quantity and character of news and public affairs programming depended upon the degree to which the ownership of television stations was dispersed among many parties or was concentrated in comparatively few hands?

STATION OWNERSHIP TYPES AND NEWS AND PUBLIC AFFAIRS PROGRAMMING

Four sources of information were available on this question: the sample surveys done as part of this study, the questionnaire responses, publicly available research done by others, and information derived from interviews with people in and around the broadcast industry. In general, these sources suggested that ownership structure did indeed have an impact upon the quantity of programming shown, on the types of programs shown, and on the scheduling policies of programmers. It is easiest to discern the effects upon the quantity of such programming, and the discussion therefore begins there.

The data in the sample surveys show a considerable difference in the quantity of news and public affairs programming shown among stations of different ownership types. Network-owned and -operated stations presented the most such programming. The 1966 and 1971 data are quite clear in this regard. The data for both surveys also show that single-owner stations showed more such programming than did group-owned stations.* People in the broadcast industry were agreed that the owned-and-operated stations showed the most such programming. The industry people also believed that, in general, group-owned stations tended to present more such programming than did single-owner stations. The data in this study were not consistent with this latter belief.

Tables 5 and 6 show that both in 1966 and again in 1971 the single-owner stations showed somewhat more news and public affairs programming than did the group-owned stations. But in both samples of single-owner stations the ABC affiliates were underrepresented. Since ABC affiliates presented substantially less such programming than did affiliates of CBS and NBC, there was probably a tendency for these data to imply a greater difference between single-owner stations and group-owned stations than actually prevailed. (See the discussion of the major effects of affiliation status upon the quantity of news and public affairs programming shown by various stations under "Network Affiliation and News and Public Affairs Programming," below.)

Responses to the questionnaires in 1967 certainly confirmed that the network-owned and -operated stations showed significantly more such programming than did stations of other types.** But single-owner

---

*With regard to commercial television stations of various ownership types, the discussion here is limited to network-affiliated stations. The data make clear that the lack of affiliation was a far more important determinant of the quantity of news and public affairs programming than was ownership type, although group-owned nonaffiliates showed more such programs than did single-owner nonaffiliates.

**Question 3 of the 1967 questionnaire asked "What percentage of air time in a typical broadcast week on your station would you estimate is devoted to public affairs programs? (Circle one.) (a) 5% or less (b) 5-10% (c) 10-15% (d) 15-20% (e) more than 20%." (See copy of questionnaire in Appendix C, below.)

In 1967 78 different stations replied to the questionnaire circularization, but only 67 usable answers to Question 3 were received from affiliates. Six additional replies came from group-owned nonaffiliates, and five replies came from affiliates that either did not give any answer or indicated that the terminology of the question made it difficult to make an estimate. The difficulty alluded to in these replies was that the term used in the questionnaire—"public affairs programming"—was used in the industry in a more limited sense than in the 1967 questionnaire. Within the industry this term referred to nonnews programming related to public questions. This misleading use of the term was corrected in the questionnaires sent in 1971.

TABLE 5

Amount of News and Public Affairs Programming by
Ownership Type and Network Affiliation, 1966
(during four sample weeks)

Market	Ownership Type*	Network Affiliation	Minutes of Programming
Pittsburgh	Group	CBS	3,970
Baltimore	Group	CBS	2,685
Hartford	Group	ABC	1,500
Cincinnati	Group	ABC	1,470
Indianapolis	Group	ABC	1,815
Atlanta	Group	NBC	2,950
Houston	Group	CBS	3,680
Charlotte	Group	CBS	2,485
Syracuse	Group	NBC	2,940
Memphis	Group	NBC	1,920
Toledo	Group	ABC	2,470
Huntington	Group	NBC	3,000
Manchester	Group	ABC	1,270
Louisville	Group	NBC	2,995
Total			35,150
Average			2,511
Boston	Single	CBS	3,320
Buffalo	Single	CBS	3,710
Sacramento	Single	NBC	3,785
Tampa	Single	ABC	2,940
Albany	Single	ABC	1,810
Nashville	Single	CBS	2,110
Lansing	Single	NBC	3,110
Total			20,785
Average			2,983

Market	Ownership Type*	Network Affiliation	Minutes of Programming
Chicago	o&o	NBC	4,085
Philadelphia	o&o	CBS	4,445
Detroit	o&o	ABC	2,910
San Francisco	o&o	ABC	2,000
Cleveland	o&o	NBC	3,305
St. Louis	o&o	CBS	4,495
Total			21,240
Average			3,540
New York	Group	none	1,025
Los Angeles	Group	none	1,820
Washington, D.C.	Group	none	1,310
Dallas	Group	none	925
Minneapolis	Group	none	1,470
Denver	Group	none	1,725
Total			8,275
Average			1,379
St. Louis	Single	none	855
Seattle	Single	none	575
Seattle	Single	none	1,440
Total			2,870
Average			957

*The abbreviation "o&o" stands for "owned and operated."

TABLE 6

Amount of News and Public Affairs Programming by
Ownership Type and Network Affiliation, 1971
(during two sample weeks)

Market	Ownership Type[a]	Network Affiliation	Minutes of Programming
Pittsburgh	Group	CBS	2,085
Baltimore	Group	CBS	1,955
Hartford	Group	ABC	1,690
Cincinnati	Group	ABC	1,265
Atlanta	Group	NBC	2,565
Indianapolis	Group	ABC	1,320
Houston	Group	CBS	2,420
Charlotte	Group	CBS	2,155
Memphis	Group	NBC	2,780
Toledo	Group	NBC	1,750
Syracuse	Group	NBC	1,685
Louisville	Group	NBC	2,180
Huntington	Group	NBC	2,230
Albany	Group	ABC	1,410
Total			27,590
Average[b]			3,940
Boston	Single	CBS	2,165
Sacramento	Single	NBC	2,760
Buffalo	Single	CBS	2,480
Tampa	Single	ABC	1,285
Nashville	Single	CBS	1,665
Total			10,355
Average[b]			4,144

Market	Ownership Type[a]	Network Affiliation	Minutes of Programming
Chicago	o&o	NBC	2,830
Philadelphia	o&o	CBS	2,300
Detroit	o&o	ABC	1,500
San Francisco	o&o	ABC	1,670
Cleveland	o&o	NBC	1,830
St. Louis	o&o	CBS	3,165
Total			13,295
Average[b]			4,432
New York	Group	none	990
Los Angeles	Group	none	870
Washington, D. C.	Group	none	1,050
Dallas	Group	none	710
Minneapolis	Group	none	825
Denver	Group	none	880
Total			5,325
Average[b]			1,335
St. Louis	Single	none	340
Seattle	Single	none	625
Seattle	Single	none	150
Total			1,115
Average[b]			744

[a]The abbreviation "o&o" stands for "owned and operated."
[b]The average has been multiplied by 2 to make it comparable with the data for 1966.

36

CHART 1

Station-Estimated Percentage of News and Public
Affairs Programming, by Ownership Type
and Affiliation, 1967

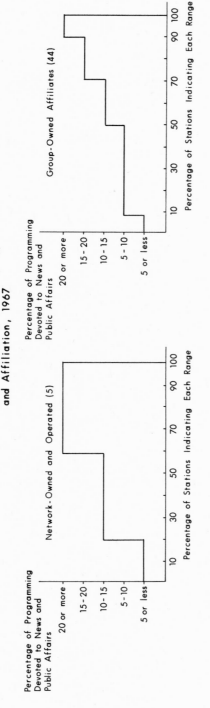

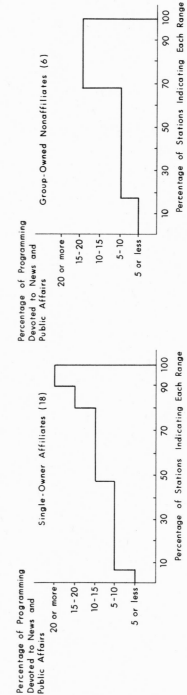

37

stations indicated that they devoted a slightly lower percentage of their broadcast time to news and public affairs programming than did group-owned stations. Again in 1971, single-owner stations indicated a slightly lower percentage of their broadcast time devoted to news and public affairs programming. (See Charts 1 and 2.)

These findings corresponded quite closely to those of other researchers who had concerned themselves with this question. The general finding is that network-affiliated VHF stations claimed that between 10 percent and 20 percent of each broadcast week was devoted to news and public affairs offerings on the average. The number of respondents among the nonaffiliates was too small to permit even this degree of generalization, although it is clear that their claims were substantially more modest.

Other research into the same question done by United Research, Inc., for the Council for Television Development (CDT) found that between 16 percent and 17 percent of the programming on American commercial television was in the news and public affairs field. Although the CTD report states unequivocally that these were the percentages for American television stations, its figures were based on questionnaire responses, as were those of this study, and should therefore properly be referred to as the stations' estimates of their own performance.[1]

Not only did the gross, overall quantity of news and public affairs programming vary among stations of different ownership types, but the character of the programs shown and the scheduling practices with regard to news and public affairs programs also differed among stations of various types. It is quite clear that the great majority of news and public affairs programs on American commercial television were regularly scheduled news programming.

But there were other types of programs—interview programs, documentaries, editorials, coverage of public events, discussions, and so forth—whose inclusion in station program schedules was not nearly as widespread as was that of news programs. Since the concern in this study was the degree to which the character of ownership structure tended to correspond with differences in the quantity and character of news and public affairs programs presented, it was important to attempt to discover whether the "mix" of news and public affairs programming varied significantly among the stations of different ownership types; that is, the percentages of nonnews presentations in the news and public affairs schedule of various stations were sought.

An examination of these figures revealed some perplexing results. Tables 7-10 make clear that in 1966 unaffiliated stations were devoting more of their news and public affairs schedule to news broadcasts than were affiliated stations. The differences among stations

CHART 2

Station-Estimated Percentage of News and Public Affairs Programming, by Ownership Type and Affiliation, 1971

Percentage of Programming
Devoted to News and
Public Affairs

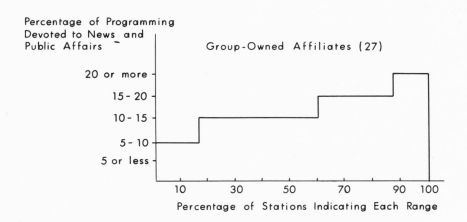

Group-Owned Affiliates (27)

20 or more
15 - 20
10 - 15
5 - 10
5 or less

10   30   50   70   90   100

Percentage of Stations Indicating Each Range

Percentage of Programming
Devoted to News and
Public Affairs

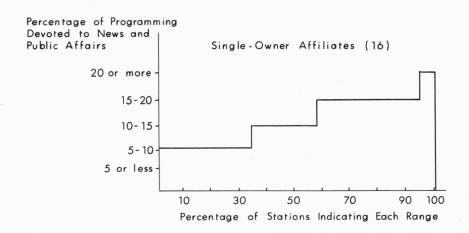

Single-Owner Affiliates (16)

20 or more
15-20
10-15
5-10
5 or less

10   30   50   70   90   100

Percentage of Stations Indicating Each Range

39

TABLE 7

News Programs as a Percentage of Total News and Public Affairs Programming, 1966
(during four sample weeks)

Group-Owned Affiliates		Single-Owner Affiliates		Owned-and-Operated Stations		Group Nonaffiliates		Single Nonaffiliates	
Market	%	Market	%	Market	%	Market	%	Market	%
Baltimore	82	Lansing	53	San Francisco	79	Minneapolis	82	St. Louis	95
Huntington	89	Nashville	82	Chicago	85	New York	37	Seattle	100
Syracuse	97	Sacramento	84	Philadelphia	81	Los Angeles	100	Seattle	80
Cincinnati	80	Albany	83	Cleveland	78	Dallas	94		
Louisville	80	Boston	80	St. Louis	85	Washington,			
Hartford	76	Tampa	94	Detroit	85	D.C.	62		
Memphis	87	Buffalo	68			Denver	91		
Houston	79								
Indianapolis	85								
Atlanta	86								
Manchester	88								
Pittsburgh	79								
Toledo	81								
Charlotte	81								
Median, news	81.5		82		83		86.5		95
Median, nonnews	18.5		18		17		13.5		5

TABLE 8

News Programs as a Percentage of Total News and Public Affairs Programming, 1971
(during two sample weeks)

Group-Owned Affiliates		Single-Owner Affiliates		Owned-and-Operated Stations		Group Nonaffiliates		Single Nonaffiliates	
Market	%	Market	%	Market	%	Market	%	Market	%
Albany	90	Boston	94	Chicago	100	New York	66	St. Louis	100
Pittsburgh	93	Sacramento	93	Philadelphia	90	Los Angeles	100	Seattle	100
Baltimore	93	Buffalo	90	Detroit	83	Washington,		Seattle	0
Hartford	80	Tampa	95	San Francisco	87	D.C.	74		
Cincinnati	88	Nashville	94	Cleveland	84	Dallas	75		
Atlanta	91			St. Louis	92	Minneapolis	86		
Indianapolis	87					Denver	79		
Houston	88								
Charlotte	91								
Memphis	89								
Toledo	91								
Syracuse	90								
Louisville	93								
Huntington	89								
Median, news	90		93		88.5		77		100
Median, nonnews	10		7		11.5		23		0

TABLE 9

Average Time per Seven-Day Week Devoted to News
and Nonnews Programs by Station Type, 1966
(minutes)

Station Type	News	Nonnews	Total
Group-owned affiliates	521	107	628
Single-owner affiliates	490	256	746
Owned-and-operated stations	731	154	885
Group-owned nonaffiliates	277	68	345
Single-owner nonaffiliates	225	14	239

TABLE 10

Average Time per Seven-Day Week Devoted to News
and Nonnews Programs by Station Type, 1971
(minutes)

Station Type	News	Nonnews	Total
Grouped-owned affiliates	884	98	982
Single-owner affiliates	968	68	1,036
Owned-and-operated stations	927	115	1,042
Group-owned nonaffiliates	303	77	380
Single-owner nonaffiliates	161	25	186

was different. Although the stations in the sample, taken together,
clearly were presenting a smaller percentage of nonnews programming,
the group-owned nonaffiliates for some reason were doing more such
nonnews programming than were any other group of stations and more
than they had done in 1966. So too, the results by affiliation status
had also changed between 1966 and 1971, with ABC affiliates presenting

a larger percentage of nonnews programs in 1971 than did the affiliates of CBS and NBC.*

But it is probable that the percentages are less important than is the absolute amount of time involved. What is immediately striking in a comparison between 1966 and 1971 is that the absolute amount of nonnews programming per seven-day week measured in minutes decreased for all the affiliated stations. The increases for the un-affiliated stations were probably not significant, given the small number of minutes involved.

Although in 1966 the single-owner affiliates presented more non-news programming in absolute terms than did stations of any other type, the 1971 data show that the owned-and-operated stations, the group-owned affiliates and the group-owned nonaffiliates all exceeded the single-owner affiliates in the amount of time devoted to nonnews programs per week. It should also be noted that, although the group-owned nonaffiliates presented the highest percentage of nonnews pro-grams (as compared to news programs) in 1971, the absolute number of minutes involved was comparatively small.

⌣ THE SCHEDULING OF NEWS AND PUBLIC AFFAIRS
PROGRAMS

The scheduling practices of stations with regard to news and public affairs programs were also of interest in this study. Did the stations tend to put such programs on in the early morning hours, when audiences were very small, or did stations put public affairs programs on during "prime time," when the potential television audience was at its peak? In general, for economic reasons stations resisted large amounts of public affairs programming during peak viewing hours. (See Chapter 6, below.)

But did the various types of stations vary in their inclination or willingness or capacity to forego some profit for the sake of showing news and public affairs presentations during the peak period? This peak period, usually referred to as "prime time," was from 7:30 p.m.

---

*In 1966 the affiliates of ABC, NBC, and CBS devoted the follow-ing percentages of their news and public affairs schedules to nonnews presentations: 16.4 percent, 17.8 percent, and 20.4 percent, respec-tively. The unaffiliated stations devoted 17.6 percent of their sched-ules to nonnews. In 1971 the ABC, NBC, and CBS affiliates devoted 13 percent, 9 percent, and 8 percent, respectively.

until 11:00 p.m.* Typically, these hours were reserved on commercial television for the most popular programs, which attracted the largest possible audiences and therefore returned to the stations and networks the largest possible advertising revenues. But most stations allocated a small proportion of this most lucrative period for news and public affairs programs. An effort was made to discover whether this practice was more prevalent among stations of one ownership type than among stations of other types.

In general, there was little evidence to suggest that ownership type had much to do with the shaping of station policies in regard to prime time news and public affairs scheduling. The median percentages for affiliated stations of various ownership types were quite close, whereas the actual percentages, station by station, varied widely. Tables 11 and 12 make this fact clear. Thus, although the policies of the stations with regard to prime time news and public affairs programming varied widely, it would appear that ownership structure had little, if anything, to do with these policy decisions.

What does emerge clearly from the figures on prime time news and public affairs programming is that affiliation itself had a great deal to do with the individual stations' policies in the area of scheduling. Between 35 percent and 45 percent of the news and public affairs programming of the group-owned nonaffiliates was presented during prime time. Of the single-owner affiliates, only three in number, little, if anything, can be said.

That the unaffiliated stations tended to broadcast a far greater percentage of their news and public affairs programs during prime time than did the affiliates came as no surprise. Since the nonaffiliates found it difficult to compete for audiences with network affiliates, they tended to engage in what is generally called "counterprogramming." This means that, when the network affiliates presented soap operas, the nonaffiliates presented films or "talk shows"; when the affiliates presented entertainment programming, the nonaffiliates offered cultural and news and public affairs programming, or other programs with an appeal to a minority audience; when the affiliates covered public events,

---

*Definitions of prime time vary, although the most frequent use of the term involves the 7:30-11:00 period. Rating services sometimes distinguished between segments of this period, with 7:30 p.m. to 10:00 p.m. being the absolute peak period. Therefore, some cynics observe, networks and stations tended to present the bulk of their prime time cultural and news and public affairs programs in the 10:00-11:00 period. Questions of "audience flow" (defined in Chapter 6, below) are aslo involved.

TABLE 11

Prime Time News and Public Affairs Programming as a Percentage of Total
Such Programming, 1966
(during four sample weeks)

Grouped-Owned Affiliates		Single-Owner Affiliates		Owned-and-Operated Stations		Group Nonaffiliates		Single Nonaffiliates	
Market	%	Market	%	Market	%	Market	%	Market	%
Baltimore	6.7	Lansing	2.90	San Francisco	0.05	Minneapolis	28	St. Louis	7
Huntington	0	Nashville	32.00	Chicago	22.00	New York	9	Seattle	40
Syracuse	2.8	Sacramento	1.60	Philadelphia	6.70	Los Angeles	66	Seattle	44
Cincinnati	0	Albany	0.06	Cleveland	1.80	Dallas	32		
Louisville	2.0	Boston	6.30	St. Louis	20.00	Washington,			
Hartford	2.0	Tampa	0	Detroit	0	D.C.	38		
Memphis	29.0	Buffalo	8.00			Denver	38		
Houston	22.0								
Indianapolis	0								
Atlanta	2.0								
Manchester	0								
Pittsburgh	7.9								
Toledo	0								
Charlotte	10.0								
Median	2.4		2.90		4.25		35		40
Average per week (minutes)	41		48		92		132		66

TABLE 12

Prime Time News and Public Affairs Programming as a Percentage of Total
Such Programming, 1971
(during two sample weeks)

Group-Owned Affiliates		Single-Owner Affiliates		Owned-and-Operated Stations		Group Nonaffiliates		Single Nonaffiliates	
Market	%	Market	%	Market	%	Market	%	Market	%
Albany	0	Boston	1.3	Chicago	14.9	New York	30.3	St. Louis	4.4
Pittsburgh	2.8	Sacramento	3.2	Philadelphia	2.6	Los Angeles	51.7	Seattle	48.0
Baltimore	3.0	Buffalo	2.4	Detroit	4.0	Washington,		Seattle	0
Hartford	5.3	Tampa	2.7	San Francisco	0	D.C.	62.9		
Cincinnati	9.5	Nashville	28.0	Cleveland	0	Dallas	19.0		
Atlanta	0			St. Louis	16.3	Minneapolis	40.0		
Indianapolis	9.1					Denver	79.1		
Houston	19.2								
Charlotte	2.8								
Memphis	14.0								
Toledo	1.7								
Syracuse	0								
Louisville	0								
Huntington	4.1								
Median	2.9		2.7		3.3		45.8		4.4
Average per week (minutes)	55		68		88		213		52

44

such as national nominating conventions or presidential speeches, the nonaffiliates presented entertainment programs.

This being the case, the nonaffiliates, particularly the group-owned nonaffiliates, presented more news and public affairs programs during prime time than did their affiliated competitors. This was true not only in percentage terms, but also in terms of the absolute number of minutes of prime time news and public affairs programming per week. Those who believe that more news and public affairs programming should be presented during the peak viewing hours may commend the nonaffiliates, but they would be commending these stations for seeking their own economic well-being, not for their comparative publicmindedness, or for any other lofty virtue.

It appears, then, that the ownership structure of the individual station did make some difference in the quantity and character of programming shown. But it should be stressed that the data show no causal relationships whatever. Nonetheless, there were some findings where a causal relationship could reasonably be inferred. For example, that the network owned-and-operated station should have presented more such programming than did other types of stations is consistent with the general argument to be made in Chapter 6—namely, that news and public affairs programming was costly for stations and that the most prosperous stations were therefore likely to present more of such programs.

The same point can be made about the owned-and-operated stations also presenting more prime time news and public affairs programs than did affiliated stations of other types. It is not clear why single-owner affiliates presented more news and public affairs programming than did group-owned affiliates. That some differences were not readily explicable made it necessary to examine these differences in programming policies from another viewpoint—that is, from the perspective of affiliations with networks.

NETWORK AFFILIATION AND NEWS AND PUBLIC AFFAIRS PROGRAMMING

Both in 1966 and again in 1971 ABC affiliates showed markedly less news and public affairs programming than did affiliates of the two other networks. In 1966 CBS affiliates presented somewhat more than did NBC affiliates; but by 1971 the amounts for the two groups were far closer, with NBC affiliates slightly ahead. The amount of news and public affairs programming (in minutes) for a four-week period in 1966 and 1971, by network affiliation, is as follows:

	ABC Affiliates	CBS Affiliates	NBC Affiliates	Non-Affiliates
1966	2,091	4,344	3,122	1,236
1971	2,972	4,532	4,582	1,421

In the matter of prime time scheduling practices, the question of network affiliation became especially important. Since the prime time schedule of individual affiliates was for all intents and purposes the prime time schedule of the network with which the station was affiliated, the question arose about whether these differences that appeared between stations of various ownership structures could not in part be explained by reference to the affiliations of particular stations.*

For example, in 1966 the only regularly scheduled prime time news and public affairs program was on the CBS network, a Tuesday evening program called "CBS Reports." It was therefore likely that CBS affiliates as a group would tend to show more prime time programming in the news and public affairs field than would the affiliates of the other networks. In fact, the differences among the stations affiliated to different networks were so striking in this regard that it would appear that ownership structure was possibly not an operative variable in this area at all. (See Tables 13 and 14.)

An effort was made with the 1966 data to discover whether the much larger amount of CBS affiliate programming during prime time was attributable to the "CBS Reports" program. When the amount of straight news programming presented between 7:30 p.m. and 11:00 p.m. on the affiliates of the three networks was examined, the CBS affiliates' total was still the greatest. The CBS stations presented an average of 226 minutes of prime time news programming during the four-week period in 1966. The NBC stations showed an average of 157 such minutes, and the ABC stations showed virtually none, with only one of the nine stations in the sample showing a single ten-minute news broadcast during that period. (The 30 minutes shown for ABC in Table 13 represented a public affairs program.) Not surprisingly, the nonaffiliates (presumably as a result of counterprogramming)

----

*Beginning in the new 1971-72 season the FCC required that one-half hour of prime time programming (between 7:30 p.m. and 11:00 p.m.) be programming in which the three networks had no interest. Therefore, this statement is somewhat less true today than it is for the bulk of the period under examination in this study.

TABLE 13

Amount of Prime Time News and Public Affairs Programming
by Network Affiliation, 1966
(during four-week period)

CBS Affiliates		NBC Affiliates		ABC Affiliates	
Market	Minutes	Market	Minutes	Market	Minutes
Baltimore	180	Huntington	0	Cincinnati	0
Houston	810	Syracuse	60	Hartford	30
Pittsburgh	300	Louisville	60	Indianapolis	0
Charlotte	240	Memphis	550	Manchester	0
Nashville	675	Atlanta	60	Toledo	0
Boston	210	Lansing	90	Albany	10
Buffalo	300	Sacramento	60	Tampa	0
Philadelphia	300	Chicago	900	San Francisco	10
St. Louis	910	Cleveland	60	Detroit	0
Total	3,925		1,840		50

TABLE 14

Amount of Prime Time News and Public Affairs Programming
by Network Affiliation, 1971
(during two-week period)

CBS Affiliates		NBC Affiliates		ABC Affiliates	
Market	Minutes	Market	Minutes	Market	Minutes
Pittsburgh	120	Atlanta	0	Albany	0
Baltimore	120	Memphis	780	Hartford	180
Houston	930	Toledo	60	Cincinnati	240
Charlotte	120	Syracuse	0	Indianapolis	360
Boston	60	Louisville	0	Tampa	60
Buffalo	120	Huntington	180	Detroit	120
Nashville	930	Sacramento	90	San Francisco	0
Philadelphia	120	Chicago	840		
St. Louis	1,040	Cleveland	0		
Total	3,560		1,950		960

47

presented more prime time news broadcasts than did any other group of stations.

These prime time figures do not reflect the total picture insofar as news broadcasts are concerned. The prime time schedules suggest that the performance of the unaffilated stations and of the CBS affiliates was markedly better than was that of the affiliates of NBC or ABC in 1966. If the number of minutes of news programming presented during the period from 6:00 p. m. until 11:00 p. m. are examined—that is, including the early evening news programs that were locally originated, as well as the half-hour network news programs in which nationally known reporters such as Brinkley, Cronkite, Smith, Reasoner, Reynolds, and others appeared—the results are somewhat different.

NBC affiliates tended to present more locally originated early evening news broadcasts in 1966 than did any other group of stations, presenting an average of 1, 384 minutes of such programming per week. The CBS affiliates were close behind the NBC stations, presenting 1, 272 minutes. The ABC affiliates and the nonaffiliates presented significantly less news programming during this period, offering 549 minutes and 433 minutes, respectively. By 1971 the number of minutes of news programming on the affiliates of all three networks had increased substantially.

It was pointed out, above, that the prime time schedule of network affiliates was largely the network schedule formulated in New York by the three networks. Although this was generally the case, there were circumstances where the network schedule for prime time was abandoned by some affiliates. This practice must also be analyzed in a discussion of network affiliation and programming policies.

The role of the networks in shaping the program schedules of the affiliates has probably been underestimated in this study so far. Much of the programming around the country was done in the New York network headquarters. Certain periods of the daytime schedule, some weekend periods, and the period from 7:30 p.m. until 11:00 p.m. each evening were programmed almost exclusively by the networks. The individual affiliates served as mere relay points for these network programs. By focusing on the programming policies of individual stations—affiliates and nonaffiliates—this basic fact has tended to be obscured.

In the area of news and public affairs programming the role of the network schedules was particularly crucial. It was rare even for the station groups, to say nothing of individual stations, to have sufficient financial and human resources to develop, for example, newsgathering organizations capable of coverage on a national or international level. News and public affairs presentations dealing with national or international topics were the virtual monopoly of the networks, with the syndicators playing a minor role. Regional and local affairs, however, were frequently covered by programs originated by individual stations.

Despite the overwhelming significance of the network programmers, it would be an oversimplification to see the schedules of the individual stations as the mere creatures of the networks. There were several circumstances where the schedule from the network was abandoned by some of the affiliates in favor of other programming. (This practice is mentioned below and in Chapter 6.) This practice of "rejecting" the network program was especially important in relation to network news and public affairs programming. In fact, this occasional failure of network affiliates to accept network programming constituted an important consideration for those at the network level with the responsibility for programming.

Although the FCC had no direct regulatory control over the networks per se, it had long prohibited individual stations from entering agreements or contracts where the stations were not totally free to accept or reject individual programs obtained from sources outside the station; that is, the FCC insisted that responsibility for programming, whatever its source, was with the station whose signals carried the program. (See Chapter 4.) This long-standing position of the FCC meant that affiliation contracts between networks and individual stations always contained stipulations such as the following:

> With respect to programs offered or already contracted
> for pursuant to this affiliation contract, nothing herein
> contained shall prevent, or hinder:
>   (a) The Station from:
>   (i) rejecting or refusing network programs which
>   the Station reasonably believes to be unsatis-
>   factory or unsuitable or contrary to the public
>   interest, or
>   (ii) substituting a program which, in the Stations'
>   opinion, is of greater national importance . . .2

It is important to stress this right of affiliates to reject network programming because the stations tended to exercise this right most often when the network was sending out news or public affairs programs; that is, from the point of view of encouraging more such offerings, the FCC insistence on the right to reject was counterproductive. Although there was no way of establishing the precise extent of such rejections, there was no question that stations tended from time to time to reject some network news and public affairs programs and to replace them either with local public affairs programs or with programs that brought in larger audiences, such as feature films. A

discussion of this phenomenon is included here because a major factor
affecting an individual station's tendency to do this was its ownership
structure, as will be shown. *

    That affiliate rejection of network public affairs programs was
a real problem at the network level is easily demonstrated. Walter
Cronkite of CBS pointed out in a New York speech in late 1966 that
between 70 and 80 of the CBS affiliates in the country were not carrying
the CBS weekend news program.[3] An independent producer who frequently worked under contract to ABC estimated that, when ABC attempted to put a public affairs "special" into the prime time network
schedule, as many as 25-30 percent of the affiliates could be expected
to reject the program and to replace it with something with a larger
audience appeal. Back in 1958 "CBS News" carried an interview with
Nikita Khrushchev; 20 percent of the CBS stations refused to carry
it.[4]

    This failure, on occasion, of affiliates to "clear" for network
public affairs programs was still a problem during the period of
research for this study. When, for example, on Tuesday, November
29, 1966, the "CBS Reports" program featured an interview with
Senator Edward Brooke of Massachusetts, just over 21 percent of the
CBS affiliates in the United States refused to accept the program. **
Public affairs programs offered during prime hours were especially
likely to be rejected. The chances were greater also if the public
affairs program did not carry with it advertising (and therefore revenue).

----

*The practice of affiliates' rejecting or "failing to clear for"
network public affairs programs meant that networks in shaping public
affairs programs tended to be somewhat mindful of the program's
likely acceptability to its affiliates and their audiences. It also meant
that the networks, when criticized for failing to produce this or that
type of public affairs programming in sufficient quantity, could always
point out that their affiliates would not accept it and that they (the networks) had no way of forcing it upon them.

**According to clearance figures for this program provided by
CBS on a station-by-station basis, 41 stations refused to carry the pro-
program. Of these, 24 were located in the South. It was pointed
out by several people in the industry that stations in the South are particularly "lucky," in the sense that they can reject the comparatively
unprofitable public affairs programs that might "offend" their audience
more frequently because of their "built-in excuse," whereas stations
elsewhere cannot so easily mask their primary concern with profits.

Regularly scheduled programs, such as news broadcasts involving nationally known reporters, were far more popular, therefore more lucrative for individual stations, and therefore less likely to be rejected. (Network news broadcasts on weekends, which Walter Cronkite spoke of in 1966, were a different matter.) The "CBS Evening News" with Walter Cronkite on August 17, 1966, a Wednesday, was carried by all but nine of CBS's 194 affiliates. [5]

NBC's "Huntley-Brinkley Report" on November 29, 1966, was cleared by 99 percent of NBC's affiliates. When on May 11, 1966, the then Secretary of Defense, Robert McNamara, testified before the Senate Foreign Relations Committee on the Administration's policies in Vietnam, 91 percent of NBC's affiliates carried the NBC coverage from 10:00 a.m. to 1:30 p.m. When on Sunday, February 6, 1966, NBC carried a sponsored special entitled "Voice of the Dragon," a documentary on recent developments in China, 161 stations, or 93 percent of its affiliates, carried the program. [6] These figures suggest that, although it is easy to exaggerate the importance and the extent of the phenomenon of rejection, it was nonetheless a practice sufficiently widespread among network affiliates to warrant examination.

The question that this study was concerned with was whether or not any particular group of stations was more likely to reject network public affairs programs than were other groups and, if so, which ones and why. Jack Gould, then television critic of the New York Times, writing in 1958 about the Khrushchev program referred to above, said the following:

Ironically, stations in smaller cities often will carry out public service attractions whereas large-city outlets, with a better chance to substitute local commercial programming, will pass them up. [7]

Some firsthand information about rejection practices was derived from the questionnaires sent in 1967 and again in 1971 to all commercial stations in the top 50 markets. (See Questions 5 and 6 in both questionnaires in Appendix C, below.) Although the results were not as clear-cut as Gould's comment might have led one to expect, they generally did suggest that stations in larger markets tended to reject programs somewhat more often than did stations in smaller markets. The general results are shown in Table 15.

Some general observations about these results are in order. Out of the 118 affiliated stations from which usable responses were received, just under two-thirds (77) reported that they did from time to time reject network news and public affairs programs. If the results are examined according to station ownership type, it is clear (although from a tiny population) that the owned-and-operated stations

TABLE 15

Responses on Network Rejection Practices for News
and Public Affairs Programs by Affiliates, 1967 and 1971

Affiliation	Single-Owner Affiliates	Group-Owned Affiliates	Owned-and-Operated Stations	Total
Occasionally rejected				
ABC	5	15	0	20
CBS	4	22	1	27
NBC	7	16	0	23
Joint	2	5	0	7
Total	18	58	1	77
Never rejected				
ABC	4	7	3	14
CBS	3	5	0	8
NBC	10	8	1	19
Joint	0	0	0	0
Total	17	20	4	41

Note: The results have been combined from the two circularizations because the results from each were almost identical, except
where noted in the text; 78 responses to the 1967 circularization and
51 responses from stations not replying to the 1967 questionnaire were
received. Eleven respondents did not answer questions 5 and 6.

as a group stated with the highest frequency that they did not reject
such programs. Single-owner stations were evenly split between those
that said they did reject such programs and those that denied such
rejections. Almost 75 percent of the group-owned stations (58 out of
78) stated that they had, in fact, rejected such programming from the
network from time to time.

These results seemed consistent with what was known about
television stations with various structures. The owned-and-operated
stations, despite their juridical and institutional "independence" from
the network headquarters were obviously most reluctant to resist the
efforts of the networks that owned them to put on news and public

affairs programs. The single-owner stations, heavily dependent upon their network affiliations as a source of popular and lucrative programming, were also comparatively reluctant to resist the will of the networks. This reluctance was also a reflection of economies of scale from procuring programs from other outside sources or from producing one's own programs being less readily available to single-owner stations than to group-owned stations.

When the results of the questionnaire circularizations are examined by affiliation, one fact is immediately apparent—at least from the 1967 responses—namely, that 87 percent (all but two) of the responses from CBS affiliates indicated that those stations did reject news and public affairs programs, whereas the other affiliates were more or less evenly divided between those replying affirmatively and negatively.

This disparity disappeared in the 1971 responses. By 1971 NBC also had a prime time news and public affairs program, whereas in 1967 CBS was the only network with such a program. It is therefore likely that CBS stations in 1967 were rejecting that particular program from time to time, whereas affiliates of the other two networks were not asked on a regular basis to devote some of their most lucrative broadcast time to programs with little prospect of truly massive audiences (and therefore revenue).

When stations indicated the reasons for their occasional rejections, they basically cited one of two reasons. Most frequently they said that they rejected a network news or public affairs program so that they could put on a local news or public affairs show. They also referred to "prior program commitments" as a reason. Surprisingly, only two of the 118 respondents mentioned what appear to be more important and plausible reasons—the impact on revenue, and therefore profit, or the fear of controversy. In the words of one ABC affiliate,

> We quit carrying the ABC Evening News when it went from
> 15 to 30 minutes in length. (We use the ABC Def's [sic]
> and produce a daily 15 minutes "world news" locally. . . .
> But, as of this moment, don't carry the ABC Evening
> News)—We don't think the extra time is needed for the
> news . . . (And, too, we make more money with "Lucy"
> reruns in place of the ABC News.)

The one station manager citing concern with program content as a reason for occasional rejection referred to the vagaries of the "Fairness Doctrine" and his determination to avoid "abusive, foul language."*

---

*The reluctance of stations to speak of their concern for profits generally was a striking characteristic of both the questionnaire

The rationales offered by representatives of the stations concerning their occasional rejection of network news and public affairs programming (for example, in order to show local presentations of the same type) were high-minded. Despite this fact, there can be little doubt that the fundamental impetus for such behavior was the quest for larger audiences and their concommitant high advertising revenues. It might also be pointed out that, had the stations been asked whether they occasionally delayed carrying network news and public affairs programs (that is, put such a program into some less preferred part of the schedule so that the economic costs of carrying it would be minimized), the results would have been all the more striking.

It is clear that the stations were able to exercise their legal right to reject news and public affairs programs to varying degrees. The decision whether to reject such programs or not was for each station a fundamentally political judgment. It was political in the sense that it accurately reflected the station's assessment of its power position vis-à-vis the network. When station managers felt that they could reject these programs without serious risk to their affiliation contract, the incentives to do so were high; but in some cases the risk to the contract was a real fear.

For most television stations the affiliation contract was, with the single exception of the FCC license, the most valuable asset of the station. Stations located in markets where there were four or more commercial VHF stations authorized or on the air knew that, if the network president found the affiliate unduly difficult, he might begin to shop around (or at least threaten to do so) among the other stations in hopes of finding a more pliable and reliable affiliate. It should be clear that a station manager eager to protect the station's profitability could not face the prospect of the possible loss of affiliation with equanimity.

Although there is no reason to doubt that many station managers were delighted to carry network news and public affairs programs because they were eager to perform "a public service" or because of a desire to cultivate an image within the market, there were also many who did so because they felt they could not afford to refuse a powerful network organization—and the bargaining position of the affiliate with the network depended in part upon the situation in the

---

responses and of many interviews. Since the research led to the conclusion that the quest for profit was the single most important determinant of news and public affairs programming, one can only infer a reluctance on the part of managers of stations and networks to speak frankly about their raison d'être.

market. As UHF development proceeds, there is every reason to believe that most affiliates in the top 50 markets will ultimately have to confront the situation where the network could find another station in the market to serve as its affiliate. There was therefore every reason to anticipate that network influence over affiliates would grow.

No study has been made here of the market as a variable shaping the quantity and character of news and public affairs programming. It was just noted that affiliates in three-station markets were in a better bargaining position vis-a-vis the network than were stations in four-station or five-station markets. Many observers of broadcasting had the impression that, in general, stations in markets with large audiences—such as Chicago, St. Louis, New York, and the like—presented more news and public affairs programs than did stations in smaller markets. This study does not at all confirm that widespread impression.

It was probably true that the aggregate number of news and public affairs programs available to audiences in larger markets was considerably greater than it was in smaller markets, but this was the result of the greater number of stations in larger markets and the consequently keener competition for audiences. In a market such as New York it made sense for a station to attempt to draw the 6 percent or 8 percent of the audience interested in a news or public affairs program during the evening. There were, after all, seven VHF stations serving that audience. In a market such as Toledo this was not so much the case.

This study suggests that ownership structure, affiliation or nonaffiliation, and the identity of the network with which affiliation was maintained were far more important variables in shaping programming policies. These factors were in part the result of varying situations from market to market.

CONCLUSIONS

It seemed clear, then, that CBS and NBC affiliates presented more news and public affairs programming than did ABC affiliates. It also appeared that NBC and CBS affiliates presented substantially more prime time programming of this type. CBS affiliates had in 1966 presented more such programming than had NBC affiliates, but by 1971 the two group of affiliates were presenting similar amounts of such programming, although CBS affiliates were still presenting more during prime time.

Scheduling practices of the nonaffiliates were strikingly different from those of affiliates, with the nonaffiliates presenting a far greater percentage of their news and public affairs offerings during prime time.

For reasons that were not apparent, single-owner stations seemed to devote a larger proportion of their broadcast time to news and public affairs programs than did group-owned stations, although the differences were not large.

There were also apparent differences among affiliates of the three networks with regard to their rejection practices. The degree to which the network prime time schedule constituted the individual affiliates' schedule varied considerably among stations of different ownership structures. The group-owned stations indicated that they rejected network programming more frequently than did either the single-owner stations or the owned-and-operated stations.

In short, network affiliation and the ownership structure of the stations have both been shown to have effects upon the quantity, character, and scheduling of news and public affairs programming shown.

4

THE REGULATORY ENVIRONMENT
AND NEWS AND PUBLIC AFFAIRS
PROGRAMMING

⌐The primary responsibility for the public regulation of the television industry lies with the FCC. Its original mission was to act as a "traffic policeman" of the airwaves through the issuing of licenses for their use. The direct successor to the Federal Radio Commission (FRC), the FCC has been concerned, virtually since its creation, with the character of what is broadcast on the air. The task of issuing and renewing licenses put the FCC in a position to define and establish standards and rules by which television stations would operate.

Although the first amendment to the U.S. Constitution severely limited the extent to which the FCC might become involved in the regulation of programming on television, the FCC was nonetheless aware from the beginning of its activities in 1934 that its actions would have the effect of forbidding or encouraging certain types of programming. Within limits, the FCC even sought a role in shaping programming generally. It therefore seemed appropriate here to examine the extent to which the FCC sought to, and actually did, affect the sector of programming under study.

THE GENERAL REGULATORY ROLE OF THE FCC

Perhaps the best statement of the general role of the FCC in the regulation of television (and radio as well) was made by the FCC itself in its annual report for 1970:

> Broadcasting is the use of radio communications most
> familiar to the public because it brings information, enter-
> tainment, news and educational programs into the homes
> via the air waves. The broadcast services are AM radio,
> FM radio and television.

Unlike many other countries, the United States has no government-controlled service broadcasting to the public. Most programing is commercially supported by advertisers. Broadcast stations are not common carriers and are not obligated to sell time to all who seek to buy. They set their own commercial rates. At license renewal time, however, the Commission considers whether the number of commercials broadcast by the station is in the public interest.

The Commission allocates spectrum space for AM and FM radio and TV stations, assigns frequencies and call letters to the stations, sets power and operating time, licenses stations and operators and inspects equipment. Licenses are ordinarily issued for a three-year period; station service is reviewed by the Commission periodically, usually at renewal time or if there have been substantial complaints.

License applicants must be U.S. citizens who can demonstrate legal, technical and financial qualifications and the intention to operate in the public interest.

Licensees must operate in accordance with the Communications Act of 1934, Commission rules and policies, and the terms of their licenses. Penalties for violations may include fines up to $10,000 and revocation or nonrenewal of license. The public may challenge license renewals.

Programing is the broadcaster's responsibility, but he is required to meet the needs and interests of his community. He must log programs and commercials, as well as technical information.

Under the Commission's Fairness Doctrine, the licensee must broadcast both sides of controversial public issues. Section 315 of the Communications Act requires him to give equal opportunity to all legally qualified political candidates for use of the station's broadcasting facilities, and the Commission's rules require that he record requests for political time.

The Commission may not censor programing.

Networks are not licensed (except for stations they own), but there are FCC rules designed to further competition in network broadcasting. For example, no network may operate dual networks simultaneously or in overlapping territory, and certain terms of network affiliation contracts are regulated.

One individual or company is permitted to own no more than seven AM, seven FM and seven TV stations and

may not own two commercial stations in the same service
covering the same area. No more than five of the seven
TV stations may be VHF.[1] [Emphasis added.]

✓ One question here concerns the tools, if any, that the FCC has
at its disposal with which it might influence the news and public affairs
programming of individual stations and of the networks. Like all the
"independent" regulatory agencies, the FCC has a variety of devices
by which it could seek to affect, change, control, limit, or otherwise
influence the behavior of those whom it exists to regulate.

The primary mechanism is, obviously, the issuing or withholding
of licenses to use the airwaves. By defining the qualifications for
holding a television license, by establishing the standards of performance required for the renewal of such licenses, and by insisting on
certain procedures for challenging its licensing policies, the FCC has
tools that could, at least in theory, be used to shape programming.

The FCC also has in its arsenal some of the other weapons
common to American regulatory bodies: the right to issue cease-and-
desist orders to individual broadcasters who are in violation of the
law or FCC rules, the right to formulate general rules for broadcasters in the form of rule-making procedures, and the right to levy
fines for failure to comply with these rules and orders.[2]

In addition to using these quasi-judicial tools, the FCC can attempt
to persuade broadcasters to behave in certain ways. It can issue general reports incorporating enunciations of general principles; and it
can, within the confines of its budget, commission studies of areas
where it believes further evidence might warrant action on its part.
(Here, the mere undertaking of a study might itself induce broadcasters to change their behavior.)

The FCC can also send out letters or engage in other forms of
direct communication with individual broadcasters, requesting information, seeking explanations of broadcasters' policies, and the like;
it can seek, through the general or specialized media of communication,
to mobilize others within the political system to press for changes in
broadcasters' behavior; and individual commissioners, especially the
chairman of the FCC, can make speeches or publish views and criticisms of television programming policies.[3]

Finally, the FCC can ally itself with other actors in the political system. From time to time other actors have developed an interest
in some segment of television programming or in some aspect of the
industry that has indirect effects upon programming. Such actors
could include interest groups, the Antitrust Division of the U.S. Department of Justice, the Federal Trade Commission, committees or
subcommittees of Congress and their staffs, and, occasionally, other
agencies and bureaus within the executive branch. On such occasions

the FCC can cooperate by supplying information or other types of support.

In short, although limited by the Constitution and by its legislative mandate, the FCC nonetheless has a seemingly impressive array of potential resources that it can combine in a variety of strategies to influence and shape programming on commercial television. How it actually uses these resources to shape public affairs programming and how the industry responds become, then, the questions at issue.

The FCC's General Program Regulation Objectives

The FCC claims that it has consistently encouraged each television licensee to fulfill its "public trust" by offering a reasonable amount of news and public affairs programming. In fact, statements by the FCC imply that there is an insistence upon such programming. Generally typical of positions that the FCC has taken in this respect is a statement made by its chairman in 1963, E. William Henry, in testimony before a House subcommittee:

> One of the most important services is to contribute
> to the development of an informed public opinion through
> the public dissemination of news and ideas concerning the
> vital public issues of the day. Because of this, the Com-
> mission, under the public interest standard, has long rec-
> ognized the necessity for licensees to devote a reasonable
> percentage of their broadcast time to the presentation of
> news and programs devoted to the consideration and dis-
> cussion of public issues of interest in the community
> served by the particular station.[4]

Chairman Henry's claim that the FCC imposed upon each licensee a certain responsibility to present a reasonable amount of public affairs programming grew out of a more general objective in program regulation—the fostering of what the FCC called "balanced programming." This concept was given its earliest and most authoritative formulation by the FRC in a 1929 case involving the Great Lakes Broadcasting Company:

> The entire listening public within the service area of a
> station is entitled to service from that station. . . . [This
> means] that the tastes, needs, and desires of all substantial
> groups among the listening public should be met, in some
> fair proportion, by a well-rounded program, in which enter-
> tainment, . . . religion, education, . . . public events,

discussion of public questions, weather, market reports,
. . . news, and matters of interest to all members of the
family find a place.[5]

Other elements also came to be included in the concept of a well-
rounded program. In the same FCC report in which the 1929 formulation was quoted there appeared a listing of these additional elements:
(a) local self-expression must be encouraged, (b) the development of
local talent must be fostered, (c) children's programs must be presented, (d) there must be educational programs, (e) editorials by
broadcasters are a part of a well-rounded program schedule, (f) agricultural programs should be presented, (g) sports should be covered,
and (h) the station should offer services of interest to minority groups.[6]

This quest for balanced programming was reflected in the forms
that applicants for new television licenses and applicants for the renewal of existing licenses were required to fill out. These forms
sought specific information not only about the past performance of
the station but also about the programs plans of the station during the
up-coming three-year license period. In connection with these applications, the FCC designated what it called a "composite week," a
seven-day period for which the program logs of each license renewal
applicant had to be filed with the FCC at the time of the renewal application. These composite-week logs constituted a major source of
data about programming for the FCC.

But, in addition to these raw data, the renewal applicants were
asked to include a "Statement of Television Program Service." This
part of the form asked the applicant to state the number of hours and
minutes during the composite week devoted to news, public affairs,
and all other programs exclusive of entertainment and sports. Applicants were also required to indicate the percentage of total air time
during the composite week devoted to these three categories of programming.[7]

The FCC, through its licensing function and rule-making procedures, rarely sought to affect programming directly; that is, the
First Amendment and a reluctance to become entrapped in the complexities of regulating program content made it hesitant even to develop general principles to guide programming decisions by broadcasters. Except where questions of obscenity or the Fairness Doctrine, to be discussed below, were involved, the FCC did not consider
the merits of individual programs or series of programs.

On those occasions when individual members of the FCC sought
to persuade their fellow commissioners to engage in direct, explicit
program regulation, they were virtually never successful. By direct,
explicit program regulation is meant the imposition, or even the threat
of imposition, of sanctions because of inadequacies in a renewal

applicant's past programming record or in the station's proposed programming for the up-coming license period.

For example, when in 1967 the FCC renewed the license of WHBQ-TV in Memphis, that station in its renewal application had promised to devote 3.8 percent of its broadcast time to news programming. Commissioners Kenneth Cox and Nicholas Johnson argued that renewal should have been denied because this percentage was too meager, but they failed to persuade their five colleagues.[8]

Conversely, in January 1969 the FCC rejected a renewal application from WHDH-TV in Boston and granted the license to a competing applicant; and some thought that this action was taken on the basis of the programming record, among other factors.[9] But this latter case was truly exceptional in a number of respects and was by no means representative of the general flow of FCC policy.

In 1968 Commissioners Cox and Johnson made a far more ambitious attempt to move the FCC more directly into programming concerns. In a mammoth study of broadcast practices among radio and television stations in Oklahoma they showed that only one of the 10 commercial television stations seeking renewal had devoted as much as two hours per week to local news and public affairs programs and that three television stations seeking renewal had carried less than eight hours of news per week. They also noted that there was not one regularly scheduled prime time program in the entire state devoted to public affairs.

These points were made in a 308-page report that was written in an effort to persuade the remaining five commissioners to oppose automatic renewal in such cases and to authorize the secretary of the FCC to send letters to stations with very low percentages of news and public affairs programming asking why such a small portion of the broadcast week was being devoted to such programming. Again, they failed.[10]

In short, although the FCC's rhetoric suggested that it was a consistent advocate of news and public affairs programming and that it was prepared to use its regulatory powers to require a reasonable amount of such programming by licensees, the bald truth was that up to 1968 it had never refused a renewal (or even delayed a renewal) because of a failure to meet its balanced-programming standard.

On February 19, 1971, the FCC changed its policies somewhat in this regard, announcing a potentially revolutionary decision (proposed rule-making) to require stations in the 50 largest markets to devote at least 15 percent of their programming to locally originated materials and at least 15 percent to news and public affairs programs. By a vote of five to two the FCC for the first time displayed a willingness to regulate programming in a fairly direct way.[11] It remained to be seen whether this effort would prove successful.

The FCC's Quest for Other Regulatory Objectives

Discovering the difficulties of persuading their colleagues to engage in direct, explicit regulatory actions to increase the amount of news and public affairs offerings, some at the FCC sought to forward their objective through the regulation of the pattern of ownership of broadcast properties, through the pursuit of increased competition in the industry generally, and through an insistence on individual licensee responsibility for program content. But these general regulatory objectives, it will be argued, were basically incompatible with the aim of encouraging more news and public affairs programming.

The findings of this study in regard to the other determinants of news and public affairs programming—the ownership structure of the industry, the economics of the industry, the role of network affiliation, and so forth-suggest that the FCC in its pursuit of increased competition, ownership diversification, and licensee responsibility for program content probably discouraged rather than encouraged increased amounts of news and public affairs programming. Admittedly, this view was somewhat at odds with the view of those on the FCC who were most interested in program regulation.

A review of some of the major conclusions from other chapters of this study will make this argument clearer. Owned-and-operated stations were found to present substantially more such programming than did stations of other ownership types. (See the discussion under "Station Ownership Types and News and Public Affairs Programming," in Chapter 3, above.) But the FCC has never shown any inclination to allow the networks to own more than five VHF stations.

The differences in the quantity of news and public affairs programming as between group-owned affiliates and single-owned affiliates were negligible. (See the discussion in Chapter 3, above, just referred to.) Presumably, the FCC's efforts to diversify ownership and increase competition ultimately meant encouraging the wider distribution of station properties, a step that would entail reducing the number of stations owned by groups and increasing the number owned by single-owners. If the data in Chapter 3, above, are correct, this step would have had little or no effect upon the quantity of news and public affairs programming presented.

That unaffiliated stations presented markedly less news and public affairs programming than did affiliated stations was very clear. (See Tables 5, and 6, above.) Yet the FCC has never declared as an objective the reduction of the number of unaffiliated stations. If anything, it has been worried about the increasing power of the networks. The economics of the industry are such that the FCC can do little either to encourage or to discourage these few nonaffiliates; their continued existence, except in the very large markets, is very much in doubt. (See Chapter 6, below, for a discussion of economic factors and affiliation.)

The more general finding that stations with high profits were more likely to present more such programming, including broadcast editorials, suggests that, to the extent the FCC actually succeeded in diversifying the ownership of broadcast properties, the resulting re- ductions in profitability might have led to a reduction in the quantity of news and public affairs programming.

Presumably, diversification and the increase of competition by necessity involved the reduction of profits for individual stations since the markets for station services became more competitive. With in- creased competition stations would have sought to protect and to in- crease their profits through more mass audience programming—that is, by reducing the amount of nonentertainment programming, of which public affairs and news were an important component. (See Chapter 6 for an extended discussion of the economic pressures operating on stations and Chapter 5 for a discussion of profitability in relation specifically to editorializing.)

If, as suggested a moment ago, the FCC's attempts to encourage diversification resulted in more single-owner stations and fewer group- owned stations, the effect on the total amount of public affairs pro- gramming would have been negligible. But the tendency for single- owner stations to devote a larger percentage of their news and public affairs schedule to nonnews programs would, presumably, have been reflected in the changed pattern of ownership. (See Tables 7 and 8, above.)

One of the major objectives of those at the FCC who championed diversification and decreased concentration in the industry was the elimination of the fear that powerful vested interests in society would use their broadcast properties' news and public affairs programs for the furthering of their interests. Although few would deny the possible abuses that could occur with the major media in the hands of a few, there was little hard evidence to confirm suspicions that such abuses were in fact prevalent. If such abuses were few and far between, then the FCC's attempts to champion diversification would have little or no effect save the elimination of possible conflicts of interest.

In only one area—that of stations' rejections of network public affairs programs, especially during prime time—might the FCC's attempts to diversify ownership have paid dividends in increased amounts of news and public affairs programs on the air. For it was found that group-owned affiliates rejected such programs with a con- siderably higher frequency than did single-owner stations. (See the latter part of the discussion under "Network Affiliation and News and Public Affairs Programming," in Chapter 3, above.)

Thus, if the number of group-owned affiliates was reduced and the number of single-owner affiliates correspondingly increased as a result of FCC actions, the number of stations carrying network public affairs programs, especially during prime time, would, presumably, also have increased.* This result would make it easier for the networks to present such public affairs programs.

In short, those critics of the industry and their allies on the FCC who were anxious to prevent further concentration of ownership in the television industry were, by and large, the same people who hoped to encourage more news and public affairs (and cultural) programming. To increase competition through diversification, however, meant reducing the amount of news and public affairs programming.

The FCC's Pursuit of Diversification and Increased Competition

Despite its rhetoric, the FCC rarely showed a commitment to ownership diversification or increased competition as general regulatory goals. In the words of one student of the FCC, Bernard Schwartz, the following was the case:

Some sixty television cases involving completing applications have been decided by the FCC. During November and December, 1957 I analyzed in detail all of these FCC decisions. This involved a minute study of the Commission opinions themselves, as well as the FCC records in different cases. My analysis indicated a disturbing inconsistency on the part of the Commission in its decisions.

Just as significant, from the legal point of view, was a tendency in the FCC's decisions to favor concentration of ownership and control in the field of broadcasting.[12]

Another student of the FCC's actions in this field, Harry J. Levin, has suggested that diversification of ownership was but one of many objectives that guided the FCC in its licensing policies and that this objective was frequently neglected because of its incompatibility with some of the FCC's other objectives. Levin has pointed out that, even

----

*Even this small "dividend" would only have prevailed if those group-owned stations rejecting network public affairs programs were replacing them with nonpublic affairs, entertainment programs. This was not clear from the available data.

where there were two or more equally qualified candidates for a license, other criteria—such as the encouragement of local ownership,
the integration of ownership and management, the participation of the
licensee in local civic activities, and the past performance and broadcast experience of the applicant—led the FCC to decisions inconsistent
with its general ownership diversification objective.[13]

Even if the factors mentioned by Levin did make it difficult for
the FCC to pursue its policy of diversification, the IT&T-ABC merger
case presented it with an opportunity to show its determination on the
diversification question. In the original decision affirming the transfer of ABC's licenses to the merged corporation, the FCC expressed
its lack of such determination quite unequivocally:

> While there may be imperfections in the structure of the
> American broadcasting industry, it has, on the whole,
> served the American public well, and we are not convinced
> that any substantially different structure would perform
> better or serve the public better.[14]

That the merger did not ultimately come to fruition had less to
do with the actions of the FCC than with the intervention of the Antitrust Division of the Department of Justice and with the growing im-
patience of IT&T to bring the long process to a conclusion one way or
another.[15]

An even more protracted series of actions and inactions on the
part of the FCC further evidenced this basic lack of concern with concentration, at least when confronted with concrete cases in which
concentration could be reduced only at the expense of specific licensees. On June 21, 1965, the FCC formulated an interim rule pending a formal rule-making procedure that committed it to withhold
more than three VHF and two UHF licenses to one licensee if the
properties were located in the 50 largest markets. This was the result of an inquiry dating back to 1964.[16]

The rule-making did not contemplate the divesting of existing
holdings by licensees but only the prohibition of any further acquisitions
in violation of the interim rule. In fact, the FCC never withheld approval of a license transfer because of the violation of the rule that
they claimed to be operating under. Rather, in each subsequent case
coming before it where the rule ought to have been invoked, the FCC
found a specific reason why the rule could not in that specific case
be applied. The initial approval of the FCC of the aforementioned
merger between ABC and IT&T was itself a waiver of the interim
rule.

Without a rehash of the tortuous reasoning used by the FCC in
granting each of its exceptions to the rule, by August 1967 the logic

with which Television magazine assailed the ludicrous situation into
which the FCC had put itself was compelling:

> Since the commission issued its notice of proposed rule-
> making and interim policy, its majority obviously lost con-
> fidence in the miracle it had set out to perform. So far
> nobody who tried has failed to get a waiver of the interim
> policy.
>   (The transfer of ABC's licenses to the ABC-IT&T·
> conglomerate would be the biggest waiver of all.) The best
> intelligence is that the commission is looking for a grace-
> ful way to forget it ever made the proposal.[17]

When in September 1967 the FCC granted the fifth successive waiver
to the rule, allowing the Kaiser Broadcasting Corporation to purchase
50 percent of WAFT-TV in Cleveland, Broadcasting pointed out that
the rule was a dead letter.[18]

Finally, in February 1968 the FCC found the device for its grace-
ful self-reversal. It decided not to limit formally the number of television stations under a single ownership in the nation's 50 largest
markets. Giving its reasons, the FCC pointed out that the proposed
rule was drawn up in 1965 and that UHF development since that time
had reduced the concentration in the 50 markets. It further vowed to
continue the policy of "careful scrutiny" of each application for new
stations and transfers in the 50 markets.[19]

In only one respect were the diversification efforts of the FCC
at all successful. The FCC had for at least two decades sought to reduce the number of television stations in the hands of newspaper interests. Whereas 45 percent of the stations in 1952 were in the hands
of newspapers, only 29.4 percent were owned by papers in 1966.[20]
In short, in the period from the origin of the FCC through the beginning of 1968 the FCC's seeming commitment to ownership diversification and increasing competition within the television industry was
largely rhetorical. Each occasion on which the FCC was faced with
actually refusing a license on the basis of diversification criteria,
it balked.

In March 1970 the FCC adopted new rules, which had first been
proposed in early 1968, with regard to ownership concentration in
broadcast properties. It prohibited common ownership of stations
in different broadcast services in the same city or area (AM-FM-TV)
but, typically, did not require the divestiture of existing combinations
of this type.[21] The new rules applied then to applications for new
stations and, more importantly, to applications for license transfers.

On March 25, 1970, the same day that the rules referred to
above were formally adopted, the FCC proposed a new rule-making

procedure to amend the multiple ownership rules to include newspaper-broadcasting combinations. The proposed rules, still in process by mid-1971, requires divestiture within five years, so that no party in a given city or audience area would own more than (a) one or more daily newspapers, (b) one television station, or (c) one AM-FM combination.

As the data in Chapter 2, above, and Appendix D, below, suggest, this rule would seriously modify the structure of media ownership in many cities around the United States.22 The past record of the FCC in adopting and then implementing such rules has been so poor, however, that one can not but be sceptical about the chances of this rule's really being applied. Even if the FCC succeeds in this effort, it would not begin to modify national concentration of ownership but only regional concentrations.

The argument thus far should be reviewed. The FCC pretended that it used its regulatory powers to elicit "balanced programming" from licensees, and news and public affairs programming constituted a part of such balanced programming. But, it was shown, this was largely verbal posturing. The commissioners were extremely reluctant to engage in direct, explicit program regulation. Therefore, some commissioners hoped to affect programming (for example, to increase the amount of public affairs programming) indirectly through the pursuit of general regulatory objectives.

Among these objectives were the diversification of ownership in the industry and a concommitant increase in competition. In fact, these objectives were incompatible with the objective of increasing the amount of news and public affairs programming. But, the FCC's record in the pursuit of these objectives, again, showed little more than talk. It was difficult to underestimate the zeal with which the FCC sought diversification and increased competition within the industry, although there were signs between 1968 and 1971 that some changes in FCC policy were at hand. The reasons for this posturing and largely rhetorical regulation became a matter of interest therefore. Why did the FCC claim to do one thing but in fact do the opposite?

SOME REASONS FOR THE FCC'S
RELUCTANCE TO REGULATE AT ALL

Anthony Lewis of the New York Times has written that the "FCC has not finally refused a renewal because of inadequate programming since the present statute [the Federal Communications Act of 1934] was passed in 1934."23 These words were almost as true in 1971 as when they were written in 1959. Lewis went on to explain, at least in part, why this had been the case:

What could be the key power of the commission is its control over renewals. But here again the power has not much
been used. The commission has six employees who check
renewal applications, and five of them do that job only part-
time. They spend, on the average, five and one-half hours
reviewing the record of each station for the last three years.
    This check at renewal time is chiefly statistical. The
station supplies a time log of the types of programs it has
broadcast—so much network, local, religious, agricultural,
and so forth. The checker compares a typical week with
what the broadcaster promised when he got his license.
    There is no examination of the actual content of the
programs as a general rule, because the F.F.C. [sic] does
not monitor anyone's programs. Its checkers do not go
beneath the designation of the type of program. But they
do consider any complaints that may have come in from
the public about the station.[24]

The point that Lewis' analysis makes clear is that, whatever
the wishes of the commissioners, the FCC lacked the resources to
use the programming records of renewal applicants as a basis for
denying or granting a license. For fiscal 1970, for example, the FCC's
appropriation was $24.5 million, and its total staff included 1,510 em-
ployees, of which approximately 250 were in the FCC's Broadcast
Bureau, the subdivision responsible for radio and television regulation.[25]
    With 691 commercial TV stations on the air, and one-third of
these coming up for license renewal each year, the FCC has a very
heavy workload indeed. It should be added that the FCC's workload
includes regulation not only of television but also of 4,370 commercial
AM radio stations and 2,260 commercial FM stations. Satellite communications, telephonic communications, and a variety of special
services also come under the FCC's regulation. The skeletal moni-
toring staff at the FCC is responsible only for verifying that technical
specifications of various types of licenses are being met—for example,
that a land-mobile radio system is within the limits of power authorized
in its license.
    This inadequacy of the FCC's resources was but a reflection of
a more basic fact—that the FCC was nearly impotent. Broadcasters
and their political allies had succeeded in preventing it from being
able to carry out its task effectively. That the FCC was something
of a paper tiger was evident in the comments of several prominent
broadcast executives:

The FCC is seven people who are terribly understaffed and
who spend most of their time fighting with one another.

> The FCC doesn't amount to much.

> At best, the FCC can set a mood.

> The FCC is a tower of jello.

> The FCC is a, . . . just a thing. We get letters from them
> asking why we did this or didn't do that. We get letters
> from all sorts of groups—the American Cancer Society,
> the American Legion, and so forth. . . .   This is not for
> attribution.

Although there were doubtless a few broadcast executives who saw
the FCC as a powerful, and occasionally tyrannical, regulator, they
were certainly a minority.* The last remark by an executive among
those just cited included the phrase "this is not for attribution."
This phrase points up the situation of broadcasters. They have to
pretend that the regulators are frighteningly powerful while recog-
nizing that they are little or no threat, except in the most extreme
circumstances.

The desire to maintain the appearance of a fear or at least some
respect for the regulatory activities of the FCC was reflected in responses to the questionnaires. (See Question 11 in the 1967 questionnaire and Question 12 in the 1971 questionnaire in Appendix C, below.)
When asked whether the FCC had an impact upon the station's decisions with regard to news and public affairs programming, 57 percent
of those replying in 1967 said that it did indeed affect their decisions.

In 1971 a larger majority—75 percent—indicated such an effect.
But most were hard put to explain in what way the FCC had an impact. Many explained its effect with such phrases as "they remind
us of our obligation to the public," hardly evidence of strenuous regulation.**It should also be remembered that in the two circularizations

---

*One prominent student of the broadcast industry suggested that
those few network executives and station-group presidents who held
such a view of the FCC did so only because they had too little to do.
In his words, "they have too few tasks to occupy their minds, so they
begin to fret and worry unrealistically. We've all experienced that
kind of thing ourselves."

**Of the 78 questionnaires returned in 1967, 77 had usable re-
plies to this question; 33 said no and 44 said yes. In 1971 there were
47 usable replies to this question, with 12 saying no and 35 saying yes.

between 25 percent and 42 percent of the responding stations said
flatly that the FCC had no effect whatever.

Perhaps this is to belabor an obvious point. Students of the independent regulatory agencies had realized that this was the situation
with the FCC for a long time. In his report on the regulatory agencies
to President-elect John F. Kennedy, James M. Landis singled out the
FCC for particular criticism:

> The FCC presents a somewhat extraordinary spectacle.
> Despite considerable technical excellence on the part of its
> staff, the Commission has drifted, vacillated and stalled in
> almost every major area. . . . The available evidence indi-
> cates that it, more than any other agency, has been suscep-
> tible to ex parte presentations, and that it has been subser-
> vient, far too subservient, to the subcommittees on com-
> munications of the Congress and their members. A strong
> suspicion also exists that far too great an influence is ex-
> ercised over the Commission by the networks.[26]

Landis went on to explain this phenomenon as follows:

> This tendency toward industry orientation is subtle and dif-
> ficult to deal with. It arises primarily from the fact that of
> necessity contacts with the industry are frequent and pro-
> ductive of intelligent ideas. Contacts with the public, how-
> ever, are rare and generally unproductive of anyting ex-
> cept complaint. . . .
> Irrespective of the absence of social contacts and the
> acceptance of undue hospitality, it is the daily machine-
> gun like impact on both agency and staff of industry repre-
> sentation that makes for industry orientation on the part of
> many honest and capable agency members as well as
> agency staffs.[27]

Newton N. Minow, President Kennedy's choice as chairman of
the FCC, saw the ability of the broadcast industry to dominate the
FCC as the result of the invisibility of the FCC's activities.[28] Both
David Truman and V. O. Key had long ago pointed out that the

It is interesting that in 1971, when there were signs of a somewhat
tougher regulatory stance at the FCC, the percentage of stations denying its influence was down considerably. But the small numbers
involved should make inferences from these data very cautious.

independent regulatory agencies were more likely to protect interests than to regulate them.

But Marver Bernstein's classic study of the independent regulatory agencies perhaps made clearest the situation in which the FCC found itself.[29] Bernstein developed what he called a "life cycle" of the regulatory commissions. In the period of "gestation" there is usually a public clamor and demand for a solution to given problems. This results in the creation of a commission. (The FRC, predecessor to the FCC, was unique in that the radio interests themselves demanded a commission, Bernstein pointed out.)[30]

In its early years, which Bernstein calls the stage of "youth," the commission is characterized by vigor, idealism, and courage. As time passes, however, the regulated industry gradually saps the energy and vitality of the agency and makes it part of its own industrial structure. This is the period of "maturity." Thereafter, the commission becomes "senile" and declines. Bernstein suggests that in the case of the FCC it was already in 1955 in the close of its period of maturity.

The FCC was what might be called in Bernstein's terms a "freak," because it nearly omitted the stage of "youth" altogether.[31] Bernstein's description of the period of maturity certainly reflected the situation of the FCC up to the end of the 1960s:

> The close of the period of maturity is marked by the commission's surrender to the regulated. Politically isolated, lacking a firm basis of public support, lethargic in attitude and approach, bowed down by precedent and backlogs, unsupported in its demands for more staff and money, the commission finally becomes a captive of the regulated groups.[32]

It should be clear then that, whatever the theoretical resources available to the FCC were, the reality was that the FCC's political situation made it very difficult indeed to use the tools at its disposal. The resources available to the broadcast industry were enormous. The industry in 1969 had earned revenues of $2.8 billion.[33] The industry's interest group, the National Association of Broadcasters (NAB), was headquartered in lavish new quarters in Washington, D.C., in 1969. In 1967, for example, when the FCC's appropriation was just over $17 million, the NAB budget was $2.3 million.[34]

Obviously, in case of need the resources of the entire industry could be mobilized to fight the FCC. This impoverished situation was even noted in the broadcast industry's own trade press. Leonard Zeidenberg wrote the following in the pages of Television magazine:

In the 32 years of its existence the Federal Communications Commission has at times been characterized by those
it regulates as an omnipotent bureaucracy with the capacity
and desire to impose its will on the actions of its every licensee. If the characterization ever had validity, it is now
sadly out of date.[35]

Most observers seemed agreed that a major reason for the im-
potence of the FCC was the long-standing alliance between broadcasters and Congress. The FCC was the creation of Congress, and
its annual appropriation was a matter for Congress to decide. Many
have noted the close cooperation between the industry and Congress,
as can be seen from the following observations.

In 1965 Nan Robertson of the New York Times estimated that
360 of the 435 congressmen and 60 of the 100 senators had regular
"public service" programs for their constituents. The air time for
these programs was donated by local stations.[36] Dave Berkman estimated in the Columbia Journalism Review in 1965 that approximately
two-thirds of the members of Congress availed themselves of free
time on local outlets. In Berkman's words, "the NAB frequently re-
minds station owners that they should not feel abashed about reminding
their congressmen of this benefit at opportune moments."[37]

Lawrence Laurent, television columnist for the Washington
Post and Newton Minow's editor, wrote the following in an editor's
note in Minow's book:

Major broadcasters have been reviled by some of their
critics for their obeisance to larger advertisers and for
their willingness to bow to small pressure groups on such
things as blacklisting of performers suspected of connections with disloyal factions. There has rarely been any
fear, however, of the federal regulators. This lack of
fear comes from the broad political power that goes with
a radio or television station. A broadcaster gets a re-
spectful hearing when he talks with a congressman.[38]

In 1960 Broadcasting did a survey that revealed that 13 senators and
17 congressmen had holdings in 36 AM stations, 12 FM stations, and
27 television stations.[39] In 1965 the Columbia Journalism Review
noted the following in an editorial:

We also find ourselves troubled by the fact that at least
nine Senators and fourteen Representatives have either

direct or a family-related interest in broadcasting stations.
(There may be others whose interests have not been clearly
established.)[40]

John Gardiner wrote in 1967 that only five members of Congress
had personal or family financial stakes in broadcast stations, noting
a decline in this phenomenon in recent years. He added, however, that
a far more pervasive influence of broadcast interests upon Congress
resulted from a substantial number of senators and congressmen
having law firms that had recently represented or were still representing broadcast interests.[41] Opotowsky in 1961 estimated that more
than 30 members of Congress owned all or substantial portions of the
stock of television stations.[42]

The reasons for this alliance were perhaps best put by Drew
Pearson in a 1968 column, where he noted that there were three reasons for "the television industry's hold over Congress":

(1)   Congressmen like to see themselves on TV and TV
      stations offer a lot of free time.

(2)   The radio-TV industry has more influence on Capitol
      Hill than any other lobby, except possibly the highway
      lobby. The National Association of Broadcasters has
      lined up station owners in every state who can be called
      upon to apply pressure upon their Congressmen. When
      the occasion demands, the NAB can back this up with
      letters from its 3,600 member stations. . . .

(3)   Many Congressmen have a pocketbook interest in
      broadcasting through personal and family holdings in
      radio-TV stations. Equally significant, Congressmen's
      law firms have radio-TV clients.[43]

One student of the television industry has suggested that the "alliance" between broadcasters and congressmen was not quite as automatic as Pearson had suggested. Berkman has noted that the alliance
was weak between broadcasters and congressmen representing densely
populated urban areas. In such places there were too many congressmen for stations to be able to afford to offer free time.[44] In support
of this argument Berkman pointed out that, when FCC Chairman E.
William Henry attempted to persuade Congress to enact a statute that
would have limited the amount of time stations could devote to commercial messages, only 43 of the 360 members voting supported the
bill, and these 43 votes came largely from such urban constituencies.

In addition to the institutional and political reasons for the FCC's weakness, several people in the broadcast industry indicated confidentially that the abilities of most of the commissioners and their staffs were meager, suggesting that this was a factor explaining the inability of the FCC to be an effective regulator. This view was also expressed by an academic observer in 1959 as follows:

> When men of the caliber of William O. Douglas, Joseph
> Kennedy, James M. Landis, and Jerome Frank sat on the
> commissions, the country took notice of what they said and
> did. The same is decidedly not true today. A recent ap-
> pointee to the FCC has been quoted as saying, "I may not
> be smart, but I'm awful clean." Nobody is interested in
> third-raters—honest or not.[45]

This idea that the abilities and resources of the commissioners themselves were important in understanding the FCC's effectiveness as a regulatory body was to some extent confirmed by a study of Newton N. Minow's term as chairman from 1961 to 1963.[46] Charles Doyle found that the FCC was able to change programming policies of broadcasters to some extent under Minow's leadership. The amount of children's programming increased as a result of FCC encourage- ment, Doyle claims, as did the number of stations editorializing.[47] (See Chapter 5, below, for a more detailed account of the FCC's im- pact on station editorializing practices.) Doyle pointed out a particular role played by the FCC under Minow in encouraging public affairs programming:

> Possibly the most important indicator of Minow's influence
> on public affairs programming was the extraordinary pro-
> gram change announced by the networks after Minow's im-
> pending resignation became widely known. With the end of
> the current season [1962-63], the following regularly sched-
> uled new/public affairs programs were dropped: "David
> Brinkley's Journal," "Chet Huntley Reporting," Howard K.
> Smith's "ABC Commentaries," and the Bell and Howell
> sponsored "ABC Closeups." . . .
>   Although the data is [sic] insufficient to establish
> anything more than a time relationship between notice of
> Minow's resignation plans and the networks' program
> changes, it does seem a rather fantastic "coincidence"
> that programs which "just happened" to appear at the
> time of the Wasteland speech "just happened" to disappear
> when he did. The sequence, in any event, illustrates a

fatal weakness in Minow's techniques, for—even if it were
definitely established that Minow was the cause of improved
programming—it, like the public affairs shows, could be
withdrawn on his departure.[48]

Even an FCC under the direction of a highly capable chairman,
however, was limited in its capacity to affect programming policies
of television stations. Doyle points out that Minow appears to have
been moderately, if temporarily, successful in encouraging programming public affairs, childrens' presentations, and local live shows,
as well as in persuading stations to editorialize. These program objectives had been sought verbally by the FCC for years, and virtually
all commissioners were in agreement on these objectives.

In other areas of programming, where the FCC had not previously
taken positions or where there was known to be disagreement among
the various commissioners about appropriate tactics toward particular
objectives—the increase in the quality of entertainment programs, the
offering of free time to political candidates, and the offering of news
broadcasts during prime time—Minow's efforts were to no avail.[49]

Television magazine confirmed Doyle's claim that the increase
in the amount of local live programs was the direct result of Minow's
efforts. Beginning in 1961 the Broadcast Bureau of the FCC had sent
out letters requesting justification of what it saw as the meagerness
of local live plans for some renewal applicants. When in July 1965
the FCC decided to cease sending out such letters, Television stated
the following in an editorial:

> Applicants soon discovered that they could expedite re-
> newals by adjusting their program promises to include as
> much local live programs as they guessed would satisfy
> the FCC. . . .
> Short of a complete reading of the FCC's massive
> files, there is no way to know how much local program-
> ming has been sprayed into the air for the primary pur-
> pose of filling enough local time to please the FCC. It is
> a fact, however, that every television station license in the
> nation came up for renewal once during the four years of
> FCC letter writing.[50]

In short, the FCC was severely limited in its capacity to take effective
regulatory actions.

WAS THE FCC A DETERMINANT
OF PUBLIC AFFAIRS PROGRAMMING?

There was one other area of regulation where the FCC appeared to have a significant impact upon public affairs programming. This area involved the Fairness Doctrine, according to which licensees were required to give an opportunity to spokesmen for a variety of views, especially if they were controversial. The questionnaire responses implied that this doctrine was perhaps the single most important area of the FCC's direct impact upon public affairs programming.

One question asked whether the FCC had had an impact upon station policies with regard to public affairs programming. Those who replied in the affirmative were asked in what way the FCC affected their decisions. (See Question 11 in the 1967 questionnaire and Question 12 in the 1971 questionnaire in Appendix C, below.) One-third of the respondents who did indicate in what way the FCC affected their decisions referred to the Fairness Doctrine and the constraints it placed on individual stations.*

This doctrine, first adopted in 1949, was made part of a 1959 amendment to the Federal Communications Act of 1934. The language of the doctrine required broadcast licensees "to afford reasonable opportunity for the discussion of conflicting views on issues of public importance."[51] Both the questionnaire responses and interviews with individual broadcasters made it clear that this doctrine was seen as a factor inhibiting television stations in the field of public affairs broadcasting by exposing broadcasters to the possibility of a violation of law. In June 1967 the Federal Appeals Court in Washington, D.C., upheld the constitutionality of the doctrine as a result of an action brought by individual broadcasters and the NAB.[52]

The doctrine can best be seen as part of the FCC's effort to impose responsibility for program content on the individual licensee, even though he may not himself determine the content of his programs. If the broadcasters' expressed opinion of the doctrine is accepted, then the result of the policy was to make individual stations hesitant to involve themselves in the legal tangles associated with the application of the doctrine.

---

*In addition, several referred to the "Equal Time" requirement in regard to candidates' appearances, and several to various aspects of renewal forms that inquired into program balance and the extent to which surveys of the community's needs had been made.

Not only did the broadcasters resist such court actions; they also were reluctant to provide time—their most precious resource—for exponents of views opposing those originally expressed on the air. The extension of the principle to cigarette advertising as a result of the actions of John Banzhaf and his organization Smoking and Health made the doctrine especially distasteful to broadcasters generally.

That broadcasters disliked the doctrine was clear. How much it actually discouraged public affairs programming involving controversial ideas could not be gauged, at least not precisely. But there could be no doubt that its effect was, if anything, to discourage programming involving controversy, although it did, presumably, give exponents of unpopular views previously unknown access to the television screen.

CONCLUSIONS

The FCC had a limited influence upon the quantity and character of news and public affairs programming, except in special circumstances. By the FCC's giving verbal support to such notations as "balanced programming," it appeared that such programming was encouraged. But, it has been shown, this was little more than a pose. By committing itself to "diversification" and "increased competition," the FCC appeared to be risking decreasing the quantity of such programming.

In addition, by pursuing licensee responsibility for program content through the Fairness Doctrine, the FCC was probably making broadcasters slightly more reluctant to touch controversial questions. Nonetheless, since the FCC has been shown to have had little commitment to these regulatory goals, with the exception of the Fairness Doctrine, the net effects on public affairs programming were, presumably, negligible.

The FCC, by not doing what it said it was doing, probably allowed situations encouraging more public affairs programming to arise. By allowing a concentration of ownership to develop and by doing nothing to decrease the economies of scale enjoyed by some station groups and the networks, the FCC was probably unwittingly "encouraging" news and public affairs programming.

In its informal activities, through general enunciations of principles and through the efforts of individual commissioners to persuade broadcasters to adopt different programming policies, the FCC on occasion had an impact. It is, of course, important to realize that broadcasters would in any case be reluctant to concede that regulation—that is, the limitation of their freedom to act in certain ways—had salutary effects upon the character of their programming. Also, although broadcasters no doubt exaggerated the degree to which the FCC's actions restrained and inhibited them, their complaints were not without basis.

At least insofar as the economic giants of the industry—the networks, their owned-and-operated stations, and the major station groups, such as Westinghouse, Metromedia, and others—in fact presented more news and public affairs programming than did their less prosperous colleagues, the FCC's occasional temptations to limit further domination of the industry by these giants ran the risk of reducing the amount of public affairs programming on the air.

It seems clear that those who seek to use the FCC's regulatory role to shape news and public affairs programming would be best advised to attempt direct, explicit program regulation. There was by the end of the 1960s a widespread fear among broadcasters that the FCC was about to embark upon a more activist phase of regulation, particularly in the programming area. But the constraints of the First Amendment and broadcasters' quick cries of "censorship" make it unlikely that program regulation could be pursued very extensively.

5

**EDITORIALIZING
ON
TELEVISION**

By the second half of the 1960s the broadcasting of editorials had become fairly widespread among commercial television stations. This type of public affairs programming requires separate consideration. The forces shaping editorials were somewhat different from those operating in shaping news programs, documentaries, interviews, and other types of public affairs programming.

EDITORIALIZING DEFINED

Editorials differed from other public affairs programs in several ways. They were never commercially sponsored. With a few rare exceptions, editorializing was a station function and not a network product. Unlike some other types of public affairs programming, editorials were almost exclusively locally produced. Also, the regulatory environment with regard to editorializing was somewhat different in character from that affecting public affairs programming generally. Therefore, it seemed appropriate to analyze editorialization separately.

There have been various attempts to define what a broadcast editorial is. The FCC in its 1949 decision granting permission for editorializing by broadcasters defined it as "the use of radio facilities by the licensee thereof for the expression of the opinions and ideas of the licensee on the various controversial and significant issues of interest to the members of the general public afforded radio [or television] serviced by the particular station."[1] The NAB defined an editorial more tersely: "A broadcast editorial is an on-the-air expression of the opinion of the station licensee, clearly identified as such, on a subject of public interest."[2]

More important than the particular verbal formulation by which editorials are defined is the distinction between points of view clearly identified as those of the station's management and biases or opinions that emerge from news broadcasts or from statements by individual reporters. For example, in 1959 NBC broadcast a 55-minute documentary entitled "The Second Agony of Atlanta." At the conclusion of this presentation NBC's Chet Huntley proposed that the National Association for the Advancement of Colored People and "the militant Negro leadership" withdraw from the struggle against segregation because they had become rallying points for dangerous tensions in the South.3

So too in June 1966 CBS permitted its senior reporter, Eric Sevareid, to use 30 minutes of air time to present his personal views on the war in Vietnam. In this broadcast he doubted the accuracy of the published figures on U.S. war casualties and criticized Pentagon officials.4 Both of these were cases not of broadcast editorials but of "personal commentaries." Still, both were explicitly labeled as opinions.

Personal commentaries were not the only way in which the opinions and viewpoints of reporters could be made known. There were other, more subtle methods. For example, the placement of news items on a news broadcast, the selection of only certain extracts from speeches or demonstrations, the exclusion of certain facts from a news item, the transmission of unattractive likenesses of public figures— these were some ways in which broadcasters could imply an opinion of viewpoints, and all but the last involved inescapable choices. Such practices are not included within the term "editorialization," however.

THE EXTENT OF EDITORIALIZATION
ON TELEVISION

Since program schedules as they appeared in local newspapers and regional editions of TV Guide seldom listed editorials separately, it was necessary to rely upon the questionnaires exclusively to discover how extensive editorializing was. Of the stations replying in 1967 to the questions concerning editorials, 52 percent reported that they were editorializing during the four sample weeks of 1966. In 1971, it is clear, the extent of editorializing had increased dramatically. Of an admittedly smaller absolute number of respondents (50 usable replies out of a total of 158 in the population of top 50 market VHF stations circularized), 78 percent indicated that they were editorializing. (See Tables 16 and 17 for a breakdown of these stations by ownership type and affiliation status.)

TABLE 16

Extent of Editorialization Among Top 50 Market Stations by
Station Type, 1966

Ownership Type	ABC Affiliates	CBS Affiliates	NBC Affiliates	Joint Affiliates	Nonaffiliates	Tot
Editorialized						
Owned-and-operated	3	1	0	0	0	4
Group-owned	7	11	7	1	1	27
Single-owner	1	3	4	1	0	9
Total	11	15	11	2	1	40
Did not editorialize						
Owned-and-operated	0	0	1	0	0	1
Group-owned	5	5	9	1	6	26
Single-owner	3	2	4	1	1	11
Total	8	7	14	2	7	38

Note: Based on responses to questionnaires sent in 1967.

TABLE 17

Extent of Editorialization Among Top 50 Market Stations by
Station Type, 1971

Ownership Type	ABC Affiliates	CBS Affiliates	NBC Affiliates	Joint Affiliates	Nonaffiliates	Tot
Editorialized						
Owned-and-operated	0	0	0	0	0	0
Group-owned	9	9	8	1	2	29
Single-owner	4	2	4	0	0	10
Total	13	11	12	1	2	39
Did not editorialize						
Owned-and-operated	0	0	0	0	0	0
Group-owned	1	1	2	0	1	5
Single-owner	2	0	3	0	1	6
Total	3	1	5	0	2	11

Note: Based on responses to questionnaires sent in 1971.

Tables 16 and 17 appear to show a variety of contradictory trends. The 1966 data should be examined first, if for no other reason than that the rate of response to the questionnaire was considerably higher than was that for 1971. (Of 152 stations circularized in 1966-67, 78 sent responses. Of 158 stations circularized in precisely the same way in 1971, 58 sent responses. This means that the result for the 1971 survey must be regarded with greater scepticism than are those for 1966. [See Appendix C, below, for a discussion of this problem.])

Even the comparatively rich 1966 data appear to show little relationship between ownership structure (that is, whether a station was group-owned, network owned-and-operated, or single-owner and editorialization policies. The likelihood that the owned-and-operated stations were editorializing during 1966 appears to have been greater than was that for any other group of stations, but the figures involved here were obviously too small for a confident inference. (The owned-and-operated stations were found to be the most active of all types in news and public affairs programming generally, and this finding was therefore consistent with that fact. [See Tables 5 and 6, above.])

What does emerge clearly from the 1966 results is the connection between network affiliation, on the one hand, and policies with regard to editorializing, on the other. The Percentages of Stations Responding to the questionnaires with a positive answer—that is, stating that they did editorialize—follow:

	1966	1971
CBS Affilliates	68.2	93.5
NBC Affilliates	44.0	70.0
ABC Affilliates	55.0	81.0
Nonaffilliates	12.5	50.0

The percentages for stations that editorialized from among each of the three networks' affiliates varied widely. CBS stations were editorializing more during 1966 than were those stations affiliated with NBC and ABC, and NBC affiliates were editorializing less than were ABC affiliates. (It should be noted that, although the percentages for 1971 were remarkably higher, the same generalization could be made.)

The identity of the network with which a station was affiliated appears to have had some connection with its editorializing policies. But the mere fact of network affiliation appears to have been far more important. Of the eight nonaffiliates, seven reported that they did not editorialize during 1966. This was a striking proportion, despite the small absolute number of stations involved.

Other surveys on editorializing suggested good reasons why this finding was probably an accurate reflection of reality. (See the discussion of the NAB study, below, near the end of this section.) These surveys showed that the resources of an individual station were the single most important factor in explaining whether a station editorialized or not. The largest and most profitable stations were consistently the network-affiliated stations. The nonaffiliates were not nearly as profitable as were their affiliated competitors. (See Chapter 6, below.) Therefore, they seldom had the resources that made it possible for a station to editorialize. (It was not, of course, possible to compute the "cost" of an editorial.)

If the lack of network affiliation, with its consequent lower profitability, was significant in explaining why the nonaffiliates editorialized little, if at all, then the data on ownership structure should be reexamined in the light of that fact. It should be noted that seven of the eight nonaffiliates responding to the 1967 questionnaire were group-owned stations. Two of the group-owned stations responding were joint affiliates, as were two of the single-owner stations.

If the eight nonaffiliates and the four joint affiliates are excluded and, thus, only the primary group-owned and single-owner affiliates are considered, the results are quite different. Of the group-owned primary affiliates, 25 were editorializing during 1966, and 19 were not. Of the single-owner primary affiliates, eight were editorializing in 1966, and nine were not.

Although the figures are obviously too small to permit confident inference, there is some reason to think that the higher percentage of group-owned primary affiliates editorializing reflected reality. Of the eight single-owner primary affiliates that reported they were editorializing, four indicated that they did so only sporadically and irregularly; that is, of the 17 responding single-owner primary affiliates, only four editorialized on a regularly scheduled basis. Conversely, of the 44 group-owned primary affiliates, 22 (or exactly one-half) editorialized on a regular basis.

Similar results were achieved in 1971. Of the 30 group-owned primary affiliates responding, 26 indicated that they editorialized, and 21 of those said that they did so on a regular basis. Of the 15 single-owner primary affiliates responding in 1971, 10 indicated that they editorialized, but four of those said that did not do so regularly; that is, only six of the 15 single-owner primary affiliates responding editorialized regularly.

To summarize the factors that appear to have characterized stations that editorialized, network affiliation appears to have been the most important single factor. Clearly, nonaffiliates editorialized far less than did affiliated stations. Among affiliates CBS stations editorialized most often; ABC affiliates did so less often than did CBS stations but more than did those affiliated with NBC.

Although this survey gathered no data on owned-and-operated stations in 1971, the 1966 results and the consistency of those results with the finding that owned-and-operated stations were generally more active in the whole field of news and public affairs programming (and were the most prosperous) suggest that owned-and-operated stations editorialized as a group more than did any other type of station. Although there was some indication that group-owned stations tended to editorialize somewhat more than did single-owner stations, there could be no absolute assurance that this was in fact true. But the irregularity with which many single-owner editorializing stations engaged in the practice was striking when compared with group-owned affiliates.

Despite the smallness of the numbers responding to the questionnaire, the conclusions that emerged from the 1966 responses were generally consistent with those of other studies on editorializing. One such study made by Television magazine resulted in the following findings:

Network Affiliation	% Stations Editorializing
ABC-TV	53.5
CBS-TV	63.0
NBC-TV	60.0
Independents	21.4

Darlington's figures reflected a questionnaire sent to all commercial stations in the United States in early 1967.[5] The conclusions broadly correspond to the findings of this study in the sense that nonaffiliates (independents) were far less likely to engage in editorializing and that CBS affiliates did so most often. But Darlington found that a substantially higher percentage of NBC affiliates were editorializing in 1966 than were found in this study. Overall, the 1966-67 study found that 52 percent of the stations editorialized. Darlington's Television study found that 53 percent did.

Another less ambitious study done in 1966 by the NAB had similar results. The NAB found that 56 percent of the television stations were broadcasting editorials.[6] Unfortunately, neither Darlington's study nor the NAB study inquired into the relationship between ownership structure and editorializing policies, and there were therefore no data with which to compare the findings of this study.

Perhaps the most striking aspect of the results of the two circularizations of questionnaires was that the incidence of editorializing had increased so markedly between 1966 and 1971. For reasons not immediately clear, the respondents to the 1971 questionnaire were obviously drawn disproportionately from stations that editorialized.

Although the possibility that 78 percent of the television stations were editorializing in 1971 cannot be foreclosed, this seems somewhat doubtful.

Stations in 1971 were asked whether they had been editorializing in 1966, and 62 percent indicated that they had. From three separate sources (the 1966 survey done as part of this study, the Darlington study, and the NAB study) there is evidence to suggest that the percentage was between 52 percent and 56 percent, however, and certainly not as high as 62 percent. Given somewhat of a tendency to over-represent the extent of editorializing in 1966, there is some reason to believe that these stations implied a greater degree of editorializing in 1971 than actually prevailed.

If the differences involved were comparable, then 68 percent of stations overall that editorialized was probably closer to the mark than was the indicated 78 percent. In any case, although there is no way of being certain, there is good reason to suspect the "findings" of the 1971 questionnaire in this regard. The comparatively small response obviously made such difficulties likely.

The NAB study referred to above did suggest one reason for the tendency found both in 1966 and 1971 for group-owned affiliates to editorialize more than did single-owner affiliates. That study showed that the level of resources available to the individual station was the single most important factor that distinguished stations that editorialized from stations that did not:

> What characteristics of the editorializing station dis-
> tinguish it from the non-editorializer? From all the
> descriptive information which stations provided about
> themselves, only one factor—size—appears to bear any
> significant relationship to whether or not a station
> editorializes. More specifically, radio stations whose
> gross revenues exceed $500,000 are far more likely to
> editorialize than stations grossing less than $250,000
> (73% versus 54%). The same is true for television:
> stations which gross one million dollars or more yearly
> have a higher incidence of editorializing (59%) than those
> with revenues below this level (48%). One other dimension
> of size is whether a station's owner has investment in
> other media. Among stations whose owners have a con-
> trolling interest in both radio and television outlets,
> editorializing is more prevalent (63%) than where the
> station is the only media property owned (54%).[7]

If the NAB study was correct in pointing to the significance of the level of resources, then it also becomes clearer why the tendency for group-owned affiliates to editorialize more than single-owner affiliates did not become apparent until the group-owned nonaffiliates (stations with, presumably, smaller resource levels) were eliminated.

Although the NAB finding with regard to resources explained some matters, it raised other problems. For example, since ABC affiliates were generally less profitable stations than were the other two affiliates within a given market, why was it that ABC stations with less resources tended to editorialize more than did the richer NBC affiliates? It should be clear that the level of resources available to the individual station was not the only important factor determining whether or not a station editorialized.

Another factor, not surprisingly, was the attitude of management toward editorializing, especially at the network level. Interviews with network officials at NBC, as compared with those with their CBS and ABC counterparts, made it clear that NBC people doubted the general desirability of television stations' editorializing, whereas the CBS and ABC executives were clearly more enthusiastic about editorializing. Although it is obvious that these network executives had no part in the decisions of independently owned affiliates with regard to editorializing, their attitudes appear to have been a factor shaping those independent decisions.

The network owned-and-operated stations, however, could be fairly expected to reflect accurately the attitudes of their corporations' top management. Although only a single reply from an NBC owned-and-operated station was received, it was the only owned-and-operated station responding that reported that it did not editorialize. It is quite likely that discussions at periodic affiliates' meetings affected the decisions of individual station managers with regard to editorializing. The behavior of the networks' own stations might also have had an influence. It was difficult to know which of these might have been more important in swaying individual stations.

Although this all suggests how one might make predictions as to which stations were likely to editorialize, it has not yet been established why the management of stations actually decided to editorialize. There was no apparent connection between editorializing and the quest for profit, the raison d'être of the station organizations. The NAB survey and the Darlington study made no headway on this question. In the NAB survey stations not editorializing were asked why they did not do so. The major reason advanced by stations was that they lacked the personnel and/or the time required for a competent job. But, assuming resources to be available, what induced practical businessmen to editorialize at all? The answer, in large part, was the encouragement of editorializing by the FCC.

The FCC and Editorializing on
Television

In 1949 the FCC rescinded an earlier ruling forbidding broadcast editorializing.[8] This earlier ruling certainly had not encouraged those broadcasters who thought that they should be allowed to editorialize. Indeed, it brought constant complaints from broadcasters until in 1947 the FCC ordered hearings held on the question of broadcast editorializing.

These hearings culminated in the publication of an FCC report on editorializing on June 1, 1949, that reversed the Mayflower decision and permitted, but did not encourage, broadcasters to editorialize, with the proviso that they be fair to all parties in any dispute. With this ruling, the FCC developed what came to be called the Fairness Doctrine, to which reference has been made elsewhere. (See Chapter 4, above, for further discussion.)

The earliest editorials were broadcast not by individual stations but by the CBS television network. The first such editorial was presented on August 26, 1954, when CBS made a 15-minute editorial plea in prime evening time for permission to cover the Army-McCarthy hearings then scheduled to begin the following week.[9] CBS presented several more editorials in the course of the years, but the network editorial soon gave way to the individual station editorial.

Among the topics on which CBS editorialized were American complacency despite recent Soviet technological advances (1958); proposed systems of colored television (1958); the right of television to gain access to congressional hearings (1958); proposed amendment of Section 315 of the Communications Act, which requires "equal time" for political candidates (1962); and postal rate increases (1962).[10]

CBS's activities led one critic to write as follows in 1965:

> Most of the editorials CBS had broadcast since 1949,
> when the rule was revised, seem to have been only dis-
> guised efforts to serve its own rather than the public
> interest, viz., they were against pay television and equal
> time requirements for political broadcasts, and in favor
> of other issues in which CBS itself has very heavy fi-
> nancial stakes.[11]

WTVJ in Miami, Florida, claims to have been the first television station to broadcast editorials, beginning in 1957. But the practice did not really take hold until the early 1960s.[12] Despite the claims of the broadcasters to the contrary, the available evidence suggests that the activities of the FCC, particularly those of President Kennedy's new chairman, Newton Minow, had much to do with the increased number of stations broadcasting editorials in the first years of the 1960s.

To establish the degree to which the FCC's policies influenced the decision of individual stations, two approaches were possible. First, managers of stations could be asked whether, in fact, the FCC's policies and recommendations had any influence upon their decisions with regard to editorializing, and, second, the actual policies of stations could be examined over time to see whether changes in FCC positions were reflected in the practices of individual stations. With the second approach, there was, of course, the possibility that, despite an increase in the number of stations editorializing coincident with increased FCC encouragement of the practice, there was no influence or causation involved. Both approaches were used.

It will be recalled that 78 stations responded to the questionnaire in 1967. One question in that questionnaire was whether the FCC's recommendations with respect to broadcast editorializing had any impact upon a station's policies. (See Question 12 in the 1967 questionnaire and Question 13 in the 1971 questionnaire in Appendix C, below.) To this question only 21 stations replied "yes." The remaining 56, with one exception, categorically denied that the FCC had had any influence upon them in this respect. (One station failed to reply to the question.) That is, less than 28 percent of the stations acknowledged any FCC influence. In 1971 the comparable figure was 26 percent.

Of the 21 stations reporting such an influence, 14 were actually editorializing during the 1966 sample weeks; seven were not. Conversely, of the 56 stations denying any FCC influence, 26 were editorializing; 30 were not. The 1971 results were fully comparable. If the FCC's policies were influential, the great majority of the stations were either incapable of perceiving the influence or they were not willing to admit that such an influence existed.

On what basis, then, can one claim that the policies of the FCC were important in shaping the decisions of individual stations? In the country at large, among broadcasters and especially among members of the FCC, sentiment in favor of broadcast editorializing grew at the end of the 1950s. In April 1958 FCC Commissioner John C. Doerfer spoke before the NAB at its annual convention in Los Angeles. In his speech, the commissioner argued that broadcasters could surely no longer be shocked by the change in FCC policies on editorializing (the change had come nine years earlier) and that it was high time that broadcasters began to show some initiative in editorializing.[13]

At the NAB meeting a year later in Chicago, its president, Harold E. Fellows, delivered a speech with virtually the same message.[14] He urged members to begin editorializing if they had not already done so, and he pointed out that those few stations that were broadcasting editorials were confining themselves largely to bland, noncontroversial matters. Fellows further announced the intention of the NAB to publish a guide for stations interested in dealing with some of the complexities of the FCC's Fairness Doctrine. At the same time, the American Civil Liberties Union reversed its ten-year standing policy and announced that it favored broadcast editorializing.[15]

If sentiment in favor of editorializing was "in the air" by the end of the 1950s, the FCC took formal notice of it when in July 1960 it released its report on programming.[16] In this report the FCC set out 14 elements of broadcast service that had been found "necessary or desirable to serve the broadcast needs and interests of many communities." These were described as follows:

> The major elements usually necessary to meet the public interest, needs and desires of the community in which the station is located as developed by the industry, and recognized by the Commission, have included: (1) Opportunity for Local Self-Expression, (2) The Development and Use of Local Talent, (3) Programs for Children, (4) Religious Programs, (5) Educational Programs, (6) Public Affairs Programs, (7) Editorialization by Licensees, (8) Political Broadcasts, (9) Agricultural Programs, (10) News Programs, (11) Weather and Market Reports, (12) Sports Programs, (13) Service to Minority Groups, (14) Entertainment Programming.[17] [Emphasis added.]

When Newton Minow assumed the chairmanship of the FCC, he used his office to try to reshape programming on television. One of his recurrent themes was the desirability of broadcast editorials. In one of his many speeches to broadcasters, Commissioner Minow not only encouraged editorialization by radio and television stations but also saw a particularly heavy responsibility to offer such programming on the part of stations in markets where there were no competing newspapers.[18] In a first-rate study of Minow's term as chairman of the FCC Charles E. Doyle asserts the following:

> On the basis of the scanty documentation available, editorializing by broadcasters seems to have increased significantly during Minow's chairmanship. Although editorialization had been on the increase prior to Minow's arrival, it seems very likely that at least part of the increase resulted from the vigorous, widely-publicized endorsement by Minow, and his defense of several

TABLE 18

Percentage of Stations Airing Editorials
by Frequency, 1961-63

Frequency	1961	1962	1963
Stations editorializing	44	48.1	55.0
Daily		27.8	25.4
Weekly		11.6	21.8
Occasionally		60.4	52.7

Note: Data taken from annual surveys of local programming done by Television magazine. See George W. Darlington, "The Many Worlds of Local TV," Television, XX, 8 (August 1963), 96, and "The Many Worlds of Local TV," Television, XIX, 8 (August 1962), 107. The 1961 figures were not available in Television, but the general figure of 44 percent was referred to in the surveys of later years—for example, the August 1964 survey, XXI, p. 84.

TABLE 19

Percentage of Stations Airing Editorials
by Frequency, 1964-67

Frequency	1964	1965	1966	1967
Stations editorializing	57.0	56.0	54.1	53.0
Daily	41.0	26.1	31.4	33.3
Weekly	12.7	22.3	15.2	13.0
Occasionally	46.2	41.5	53.3	53.7

Note: Data from George W. Darlington, "The Many Worlds of Local TV," Television, XXIV, 8, (August 1967), 41.

editorializing broadcasters who afterwards received
pressure to stop from various groups and individuals.[19]

This same assertion has been made by Laurence Laurent, television
critic for the Washington Post and editor of Newton Minow's book,
Equal Time.[20]

But more impressive than these mere assertions of knowledgeable students is hard statistical evidence corroborating these assertions. The publicly available statistical data show that the percentage
of stations editorializing, as well as the frequency with which the
stations presented editorials, increased steadily during Minow's term
at the FCC (which ended in 1963, although his successor, E. William
Henry, was just as energetic in encouraging editorials until his departure in 1964), that these percentages reached their zenith during
1963-64, and that thereafter they decreased fairly steadily until the
late 1960s. (See Tables 18 and 19.)

Other Factors Inducing Stations to
Editorialize

In addition to the apparent influence of FCC policies, several
other factors appear to have shaped the decision of individual broadcasters. The 1966 NAB study mentioned above is most suggestive in
this regard.[21] The broadcast executives were asked to select those
reasons that seemed most important from a number of possible reasons
for editorializing. The most frequently selected reason was "to help
fulfill the broadcaster's obligations as a responsible member of the
community," a reason chosen by 87 percent of those replying to the
NAB questionnaire; 60 percent indicated that their reason was to provide additional editorial viewpoints for people to think about; and 57
percent felt that editorializing was a desirable practice because it
increased the station's "prestige."*

---

*This last reason, the impact on the station's prestige, was an
interesting one. It was suggested confidentially by one very prominent
broadcaster that public affairs programming generally, and editorializing in particular, were extremely useful in creating an image of
community responsibility and reliability for the station. In his view,
in each market there tended to be one station to which most people
habitually tuned when they felt inclined to watch television but were
not tuning in to a particular program.
The policies of this executive's station group were purposely

There were then several factors that contributed to the decision of each station's management. Particularly important were the resources available to the station. The NAB survey documented some interesting facts in this regard. Station managers were asked whether the possible loss of advertising revenue was a factor that shaped their editorial practices. Of the stations replying, 29 percent indicated they had had at least one experience in which an advertiser had either threatened or actually taken action as the direct result of an editorial that they had presented.22 Nonetheless, only one of the factors listed was identified by over half of the respondents as having no influence on the selection of issues for editorials—whether the expression of the station's opinion could affect revenue.

The NAB further attempted to discover what the character of sponsors' reprisals to editorials had been. In a majority of the reported cases of advertiser intervention it appears that the advertiser merely let his views be known. In only 16 percent of the cases was advertising canceled as a result of an editorial; in 8 percent the sponsor actively sought to change the station's editorial position; and in 4 percent of the cases the advertiser retaliated by increasing his spending in competing media.

Even though the great majority of television stations had not encountered advertisers' responses to editorials (in radio the trend was slightly more pronounced than in television), the possibility of advertiser intervention made station management particularly conscious of the need for ample station resources before editorializing could be undertaken—that is, a relatively prosperous station was, presumably, better able to risk the loss of a few idiosyncratic accounts than was a station whose profitability was marginal.

----

developed with an eye to becoming that station in each market where they were located. The most important element in this commercial strategy was an aggressive and well-publicized series of public affairs programs. Courageous and interesting editorials, he felt, were an important element in this strategy.

This idea that the commercial success of a station or of a group of stations would be materially increased by the use of public affairs programming, including editorials, was clearly a minority viewpoint in the industry. But the NAB poll suggests that many broadcasters (more than half of those replying to the questionnaire) did think at least in part along the same lines.

THE CONTENT OF EDITORIALS

Of even greater interest than the factors influencing the decision about whether or not to editorialize were the factors shaping the content of the editorials themselves. What were television editorials typically about? How did stations decide which issues to consider?

The questionnaire sent out as part of this study elicited responses that showed that editorializing was primarily oriented toward local and regional issues rather than toward national or international matters. Respondents were asked whether their editorials were (a) more on local and regional issues than on national issues, (b) more on national issues than on local and regional issues, or (c) evenly divided between local/regional issues and national issues. (See Question 10 in the 1967 questionnaire and Question 11 in the 1971 questionnaire in Appendix C, below.)

Of the 40 stations that were editorializing during the 1966 sample weeks, 34, or 85 percent, reported that their editorials were more frequently concerned with local and regional issues than with national topics. In 1971 89 percent of the editorializing stations indicated such content. The remaining stations said that their editorials were evenly divided between local/regional issues and national ones. Only one station broadcasting editorials (in 1971) reported that its editorials were more often concerned with national issues than with local and regional issues.

Again, these findings were basically consistent with those of the 1966 NAB survey.[23] Of the NAB respondents, 69 percent stated that they had discussed only local issues in their most recent editorial. (In the NAB survey questions were phrased to refer to the most recent editorial rather than to editorial policies generally.) Just under 25 percent of their replies indicated that the most recent editorial had been on a topic of either statewide, national, or international interest. In short, it is clear that television editorials were overwhelmingly local in orientation. If anything, this was more true in 1971 than in 1966-67.

According to the NAB study, only 2-3 percent of the stations had broadcast their most recent editorial on a topic that the NAB called "nonissues"—such matters as driving safety or Smokey the Bear and the danger of forest fires. If the NAB figures were accurate, they reflected what must have been a precipitous decline in concern for such nonissues as compared with the early days of editorializing.[24]

Even though a very small minority of stations were still discussing nonissues in 1966, there was nonetheless some question about how controversial and contentious editorials tended to be. Were broadcasters eager, indifferent, or reluctant to deal with matters of controversy? According to the NAB survey, 55 percent of the television stations reported that at least five of their last 10 editorial topics had been "significantly controversial ones."25

The questionnaire sent in connection with this study did not specifically ask how controversial editorial topics were. But a sense of broadcasters' conceptions of controversy was derived from the responses. In one question respondents were asked whether the station was willing to allow politically controversial ideas or person- alities to appear. Where the answer was "yes," stations were asked to cite a few examples. (See Question 13 in the 1967 questionnaire and Question 14 in the 1971 questionnaire in Appendix C, below.)

Not surprisingly, all but three of the stations replying to this question in 1967 (73) claimed that they were hospitable to controversy. In 1971 all replying to the question answered affirmatively, save one, which said "it depends." Three honest executives said flatly in 1967 that they were not willing to allow controversy in their public affairs programs. The information in Tables 20 and 21 suggests the broad- casters' conceptions of controversy. Although the questionnaire re- sults show that virtually all broadcasters considered their news and public affairs programming as hospitable to controversy, the NAB survey on editorializing gave a different impression.

When asked about five of the 10 most recent editorial topics, broadcasters were far less able to claim that "significant controversy" had been involved in at least five. Consistent with its other findings, the NAB poll also discovered a relationship between the size of a television station's operation and the propensity of the station to describe its 10 last editorial topics as "significantly controversial."

> It's been shown that the larger broadcast operations
> are likely to editorialize . . . and to do it more actively.
> The size factor is also related to the number of contro-
> versial issues about which stations editorialize. Consider
> gross revenue: 81% of the radio stations grossing $500,000
> or more rate at least five of their last ten editorials
> "significantly controversial." In contrast, 42% of the
> stations which gross less than $250,000 feel that this
> many of their editorials were controversial. Without
> going into the actual figures, the same relationship was
> found to hold for television.26

It need hardly be pointed out that the controversy that the NAB study spoke of was controversy as defined by the broadcasters them- selves. The relevance of the list of controversial ideas and person- alities collected in the questionnaires for this study is obvious. In- cluded in the lists in Tables 20 and 21 was every legible entry found on the questionnaires.

TABLE 20

Controversy in News and Public Affairs Programming, 1966-67

Item	Number of Mentions	Item	Number of Mentions

Controversial Topics

Item	Number of Mentions	Item	Number of Mentions
Prostitution	1	Prejudice	1
Vietnamese war	2	Atheism	1
Poverty program	1	Sunday store closing laws	1
Human rights	1	Sex education	3
Strip mining	1	Prison reform	1
Race relations	2	Drug addiction	2
Open housing	2	Capital punishment	1
Urban renewal	1	Uterine cancer	1
Racial disorders	1	Legalization of parimutual betting	1
Welfare programs	1	Intermarriage	1
City sales tax	1	Constitutional Convention	1
Unidentified flying objects	1	Liquor control enforcement	1
Black power	1	Housing code enforcement	1
Drug distribution	2	Juvenile delinquency	1
Abortion	5	Negro activism	1
Fluoridation	1	Homosexuality	1
Teachers' strike	2	Warren Commission Report critics	1
Police problems	1	Viet Cong policies	1
Birth control	1	Bond issues	2
Income tax	1	Civil rights	1
Daylight saving time	1	Legalization of liquor-by-the-drink	1

Controversial Public Personalities

Item	Number of Mentions	Item	Number of Mentions
Robert Welch	1	Jim Garrison	1
Adam Clayton Powell	1	Rap Brown	1
Wayne Morse	1	Martin Luther King, Jr.	6
Cassius Clay	1	General Edwin Walker	1
George Wallace	12	Billy James Hargis	1
Benjamin Spock	1	Ronald Reagan	1
Stokely Carmichael	1	Max Rafferty	1
George Lincoln Rockwell	3	Cesar Chavez	1
Father Groppi	3	Lyndon B. Johnson	3
William Buckley	1	Joan Baez	1
Robert F. Kennedy	1	Jesse Unruh	1
Jacob Javits	1	Eugene McCarthy	1
Harrison Williams	1	J. William Fulbright	1
Gus Hall	1	Dean Rusk	1
Clifford Case	1	Lincoln Lynch	1
Helen Gurley Brown	1	Pat Brown	1
Timothy Leary	3	Richard Flower	1
Malcolm X	1	Joseph Weinburger	1
Dick Gregory	3		

Representatives of Controversial Groups

Item	Number of Mentions	Item	Number of Mentions
Janus Society	1	Organized labor	1
American Nazi Party White Citizens Council	3	Management organizations	1
		Black nationalist groups	4
Socialist Party	2	John Birich Society	3
Sexual Freedom League	1	Mattachine Society	2
Antiwar groups	6	Ku Klux Klan	2
Draft protest organizations	2		

TABLE 21

Controversy in News and Public Affairs Programming, 1971

Item	Number of Mentions	Item	Number of Mentions
Controversial Topics			
Legalization of betting	1	High cost of funerals	1
Atheism	2	Air pollution	1
Communism	1	Water pollution	1
Marijuana	2	Prison reform	3
Long hair	1	Student activism	2
Conscientious objection	3	Black militancy	5
Bussing	4	Black Panthers	4
Gun control	3	Muslims	1
Parochial school aid	1	Womens' liberation	4
Black lung disease	1	POWs	1
Sex education	3	Bias on television	1
No-fault insurance	1	Rock music	1
Nuclear power	1	Drug abuse	2
United Mine Workers' revolt	1	Abortion reform	7
Controversial Public Personalities			
William Kunstler	3	Ku Klux Klan Grand Dragon	2
Leslie Bacon	1	William Buckley	3
James Fair	1	Ralph Nader	3
Cesar Chavez	2	Abbie Hoffman	1
Bobby Seale	1	Daniel Ellsburg	2
Jerry Rubin	1	Huey Newton	1
Madelyn Murray O'Hare	2	Angela Davis	1
Jane Fonda	1	Gloria Steinem	1
Russell Kirk	1	George Wallace	1
John Lindsay	1		
Representatives of Controversial Groups			
"Seattle Seven"	1	Ku Klux Klan	2
United Farm Workers	1	SDS	1
Ministers' Association	1	John Birch Society	1
Black Panther Party	2	Progressive Labor Party	1
Black Muslims	1	Socialist Worker Party	1
Radical Feminists	1	Vietnam Veterans Against the War	2

Obviously, concepts of controversy varied among broadcasters, and also among broadcasters from different regions of the country. For example, the legalization of liquor sales by the drink was seen as controversial in Nashville in 1967, as was daylight saving time in Fort Worth and uterine cancer in Tampa. Long hair was perceived as controversial in 1971 in Indiana, as were funeral costs in California.

One type of controversial editorial was comparatively rare in 1966—only 4 percent of the stations editorialized in favor of particular candidates for public office. In fact, only 9 percent of the television stations responding to the NAB poll reported that they had even once in their entire history endorsed or opposed a candidate.

Among the handful of stations that had in fact made such endorsements or had opposed particular candidates, no particular preference for local elections over statewide or national elections was evident. Somewhat surprisingly, there was no relationship discernible between the profitability or gross revenues of television stations and the likelihood that they would have undertaken this type of editorialization.

CONCLUSIONS

Three major conclusions based on the examination of editorial practices should be stressed because of their wider possible significance in public affairs programming. First, stations with higher gross revenues and profits were more likely to editorialize than were their poorer colleagues. Every indication was that this principle held generally for public affairs programming.

Second, the FCC was able, given the will and the energy, to change the programming policies of broadcasters by encouraging editorializing. There was little indication that the FCC was truly interested in affecting other kinds of programming in the same way, but the possibility that the FCC might at some future point become interested in this always remained.

Third, Broadcasters' conceptions of controversy varied tremendously; and, although virtually all wished to describe their programming as hospitable to controversy it was doubtful that controversy properly understood was all that prevalent in news and public affairs programming, including editorials, in 1966 or 1971.

6

ECONOMIC DETERMINANTS
OF NEWS AND PUBLIC AFFAIRS
PROGRAMMING

Economic pressures materially affect the behavior of people in any profit-making or profit-seeking organization. The broadcast industry was no exception. In fact, there can be little doubt that the economic factors taken together constituted the single most important determinant of news and public affairs programming. The television stations, the networks, the program producers, the advertisers, the advertising agencies—in fact, everybody associated with the broadcast industry—operated within limits imposed by the quest for profit. This truism will surprise no one. But the precise ways in which economic pressures shaped the quantity and character of the programming have to be explained in some detail.

THE ECONOMICS OF COMMERCIAL
TELEVISION: THE ROLE OF ADVERTISING

The conventional view of the economics of the television industry was as follows. The programs were seen as the products of the industry. These programs were "manufactured" by the networks, independent producers, and individual stations and station groups. They were paid for by the advertisers in return for the opportunity to broadcast messages to the audiences of these programs. The viewers were the consumers of the product—that is, the programs.

Commissioner Nicholas Johnson of the FCC has perceptively pointed out how ill conceived this perspective is. He takes a hard-boiled view, as follows:

The television network market is confusing because we usually think of the viewer as the consumer and the program as the product. That is certainly the perspective

99

of the regulator whose duty it is to see that the interest of
the public—i.e., the viewer—is served. But in an economic
sense this is at best a shadow analysis. The medium may
be the message, as McLuhan tells us, but the true consumer
is the advertiser, and the true product is the viewer. The
advertiser pays for the viewers which the network can
deliver. The program is but the vehicle for delivering
viewers—potential purchasers of the advertiser's wares.[1]

Although the logic of Johnson's argument is convincing, there have
nonetheless been somewhat romantic students of broadcasting who
have seen the situation quite differently. For example, one such
student wrote the following:

In American broadcasting, where the Federal government
formulates public policy, stations and networks do the
programming, and advertising provides the financial
backing, the listeners are the raison d'être of the entire
enterprise.[2]

Still another view of the economics of the broadcast industry
was developed in 1961 by the National Labor Relations Board. The
board held that the services of a broadcast station were not only a
product in themselves but also a factor in the production processes
of other products. In the words of the board, "the station by adding
its labor in the form of capital, enterprise and service to the automobiles which it advertises . . . becomes one of the producers of
automobiles."[3]

Although Commissioner Johnson's view was perhaps the most
persuasive, adoption of this view risks turning the broadcasters into
mere robots, with no independent interests and with little or no freedom
of action. It is important to point out that to place great emphasis
on the role of economic pressures in shaping their behavior is not
to say that they were the mere agents of these pressures.

But there could be little doubt that the advertising function was
the fundamental element in the economics of television. The advertisers, in essence, contracted out the task of delivering customers
to purchase their products (or, in some cases, to "buy" their corporate
image). The contract went to an advertising agency, which then sub-
contracted the task to television.

The advertiser's costs included the air time used for the commercial message, the costs of producing the commercial message
itself, the costs of the program surrounding the message (if the ad
was in fact associated with a program rather than being a "spot"),
and costs based on the circulation of the advertiser's message

achieved by the network. The advertiser found the whole practice
profitable because it increased his sales. The advertisers would add,
of course, that the process benefited consumers as well, since the
resulting larger market enabled the producer to reduce his per unit
costs and so to keep his sales prices lower. Some doubted this claim.
One student noted the following:

> Some of the most interesting case histories (Johnson's
> Car Wax, Revlon, Hazel Bishop, and Alberto Culver, for
> example) illustrate the ability of advertising to ENABLE
> THE PRODUCER TO CHARGE HIGHER PRICES. In
> fact, prices have been doubled or tripled as a part of
> many successful television advertising campaigns.[4]

The television networks and the individual stations found themselves best off when they delivered the largest possible audiences at
the lowest costs. There was, then, no essential difference of interest
between the advertiser and the broadcaster, except of course in the
amount to be charged the advertiser for the broadcaster's service.
The advertiser measured his success in his "cost per 1,000"—that
is, his total costs divided by the number of thousands of viewers who
saw his commercial message (and, incidentally, the program surrounding it). Obviously, the larger the audience, the lower the cost
per 1,000, since all but his circulation costs were fixed.

Broadcasters were successful in extracting payments for
circulation because advertisers were in competition with one another
for a scarce resource—the opportunity to convert the maximum
number of television viewers into customers for their product. In
short, these purchasers were the end product of the whole process,
and all parties to the process shared an interest in maximum pro-
ductivity. This basic fact had important implications for the programming used, implications that will be discussed shortly.

Before explaining the impact of these facts upon news and public
affairs programming, some discussion of the various types of advertising and the objectives of the advertisers is in order. There are
basically three types of advertising on television: network advertising,
national spot advertising, and local advertising.

In network advertising an advertiser purchases from the time
sales division of one of the network organizations "time" in which to
display his commercial message, time associated with a specific
program or program series. The program and the network commercials are sent out via coaxial cable or microwave relay to a
"line-up" of network-affiliated stations. (These stations are said
to be "interconnected.") The advertiser pays for the cost of the time,
the cost of producing the commercial, and the program costs (or his

share of the program costs where, as usually happens, two or more advertisers are sharing a program).

National spot advertising is national, nonnetwork advertising— that is, there is no "interconnection" of stations. Typically, films of commercials are distributed by mail to each station on which the message is to appear.* The advertisement may or may not be associated with a specific program, and this program may be either a network program or a syndicated or locally produced program.

Thus, in national spot advertising the broadcast of the commercial is initiated from the individual stations and is not usually seen simultaneously all over the country. This type of advertising is typically arranged through "national spot representatives," who arrange for the placement of commercial spot announcements (ranging from a few seconds to a minute in length) in the schedules of individual stations. National spot advertising is frequently used where an advertising campaign is focused on a particular region of the nation.

In local advertising the arrangements are almost identical to those in national spot advertising except that the advertisers are local and the commercials are placed directly on a local station through the station's time sales department, rather than through a national spot representative. These "local spots" are usually inserted during "station breaks" in the network schedule, although they may also be associated with locally produced programs or with syndicated shows. It is not unusual for a single program—for example, a network program—to be accompanied by commercials of all three types.[5]

According to FCC statistics, during 1963 48 percent of the total amount spent on television advertising was spent on network advertising, 35 percent on national spot advertising, and 17 percent on local advertising. During the 1960s national spot advertising has gradually increased at the expense of network advertising. During 1959 the corresponding percentages were 51 percent for network ads, 32 percent for national spot, and 17 percent for local.[6]

In even this highly simplified account of advertising arrangements on commercial television, several complicating factors must be mentioned. The networks use a combination of three criteria by which

―――――――――――

*The language associated with broadcasting is confusing. The noncommercial, educational "network," the NET, is really not a network in the proper sense. NET's programs are distributed in much the same way as are national spot ads—that is, by mail in "cans," rather than over cable or through the air, from one point to all the affiliates.

to price "time" on the network. The time of the broadcast day in
which the commercial would appear is one such factor, the program
with which the ad would be associated is a second, and the number of
markets ordered and cleared is the third.

This last criterion is somewhat complicated. Advertisers can
not be obliged by the networks to buy time on all the network affiliates
carrying a specific program. Therefore, advertisers within certain
limits can choose which markets they wish to carry their advertising.
The network is not always in a position, however, to assure the advertiser that all the markets in which he is interested will "clear" for
the program (and therefore for the associated network commercials).

Under long-established FCC rules, stations affiliated with networks always have the right to refuse to carry (to clear) network
programming, and stations sometimes exercise that right. The result
for the network is that it can not make good its promise to deliver
all the markets in which the advertiser seeks to broadcast his commercial. Thus, the success of the network in gaining clearance is
reflected in the rates paid by the advertisers.[7] CBS and NBC can
frequently cover 98 percent of American television homes with a
live broadcast, whereas ABC's live coverage extends usually to
approximately 92 percent of these homes. These differences in
stations ordered and cleared are reflected in the advertising revenues
of the networks.[8]

Given all these facts, what kinds of objectives does the advertiser have? In what kinds of programs are advertisers typically
interested? It should be said at once that no single objective or set
of objectives in programming is shared by all advertisers. Nonetheless, certain generalizations can be made. A spokesman for Proctor
and Gamble articulated his firm's programming concerns most candidly before the FCC when he tried to describe the kind of programing in which Proctor and Gamble was not interested:

> There will be no material that may give offense either
> directly, or by inference, to any organized minority group,
> lodge, or other organizations, institutions, residents of
> any state or section of the country, or a commercial
> organization of any sort. This will be taken to include
> political organizations, fraternal organizations, college
> and school groups, labor groups, industrial, business
> and professional organizations, religious orders, civic
> clubs, memorial and patriotic societies, philanthropic
> and reform societies (Anti-Tobacco League, for example),
> athletic organizations, womens' groups, etc., which are
> in good standing.[9]

Although few advertisers would state their aversion to controversy so candidly, it can be said that most advertisers shared the aversion. This was especially so where the advertiser produced a mass consumption item—such as soap or toothpaste or aspirin—that is, low-cost items that are purchased frequently. In such cases advertisers tended to see the program merely as an "environment" in which to present their commercials. The best environment was naturally one that was totally inoffensive.[10] At least, that is what the advertisers believed to be the case. But one of the major television advertising agencies, Young and Rubicam, did a study that showed little or no relationship between program content and commercial recall.[11]

A somewhat different perspective on advertising objectives emerges from a first-rate study done at the Columbia School of Journalism. The author of this study rightly pointed out that "for today's advertisers—and almost everyone in the business agrees on this—it is less important how many people overall watch a show. The composition of the audience is the crucial point."[12] That is, different advertisers had different needs. They sought an audience appropriate to their product and to the kind of appeal that they wished to make

Petersmann studied one such advertiser—General Telephone and Electronics (GT&E)—in some detail. In the case of GT&E the promotion of its products for sale to the public was only one objective of its advertising campaigns, according to George Norton, Vice President, Advertising. Petersmann quoted Norton as follows:

> Like every other company, GT&E is dependent on intelligent young people willing to work for the company so that its growth in the future is secured. But the name of General Telephone and Electronics is a bad name as far as young people are concerned. I don't think it carries with it the excitement they are hoping to find in the world of business.
>
> The word telephone sounds "untility" [sic], it sounds slow. You take a very bright young man, and he says "you go into the utility business and you climb the seniority ladder and then one fellow falls off the top through death or retirement and you move up another notch. . . .
>
> One of the things I wanted to do is to give the impression that this is a fast moving, alert, marketing-oriented company where young people can display their talent. I felt that television was one way we could show this.[13]

In order to achieve this objective GT&E sponsored "CBS Playhouse," on which original dramas were shown. It sensitively placed its ads only at the beginning and the conclusion of each drama. The corporation also sponsored CBS's weekly Tuesday evening public affairs program "CBS Reports." Of course, equal amounts were spent on spots for items like electronic components and Sylvania television sets.

Differences of objectives in advertising, then, depended on the nature of the product or the service of the various firms and on differences of policy and approach to advertising itself. Those companies that spent the largest amounts on television advertising—firms such as Proctor and Gamble, Bristol-Myers, General Foods, Colgate-Palmolive, and Lever Brothers—had little interest in placing their commercials on public affairs programs. They were seeking the mass audience that typically did not watch such programs. (See below for a discussion of audience viewing habits and news and public affairs programming.)

A comparison of the major advertisers of network news and public affairs programming, on the one hand, and the major television advertisers in general, on the other hand, is revealing on precisely this point. Although most of the firms advertising on television included a token amount of public affairs programming in their advertising budgets, truly minuscule percentages of some of the largest advertising budgets were devoted to public affairs programming. It was not clear whether those firms that invested tiny percentages of their budgets in public affairs did so in order to develop good relations with the networks or if they sponsored this type of programming out of a sense of community responsibility or other such notion.

In some cases the percentage of the advertising budget devoted to news and public affairs (at the network level) was incalculably tiny. For example, Proctor and Gamble, the largest advertiser year after year, spent a total of $179.1 million on television advertising in 1966. During 1965 it spent only $269,100 on network public affairs advertising. The American Tobacco Company, the tenth largest advertiser in 1966, sponsored absolutely no news or public affairs programming during 1965, even though its total budget only one year later was $40.8 million.

Although these two advertisers were more nearly typical of their colleagues than were those spending larger percentages on public affairs, there were notable exceptions. Of interest here are not the absolute amounts involved but the relative size of the total television advertising budget and that spent on news and public affairs programming. American Home Products, the sixth largest advertiser

in 1966, spent $14.4 million on news and public affairs network program-
ming during 1965. This amount compared with a total budget of $57.1
million in 1966.*

The Economics of Advertising and the
Quantity of Public Affairs Programming

The low levels of expenditure on the part of advertisers for
news and public affairs programming were indicative. There were
good commercial reasons for their evident lack of enthusiasm for
this kind of advertising. One prominent broadcaster explained it very
baldly when he said the following:

> If your income depends on getting Right Guard into
> as many armpits as possible, then why sponsor Huntley-
> Brinkley? The CBS Reports audience cannot possibly
> be convinced that an important part of his future
> depends on his mouth odor or armpit. He isn't that
> gullible, and the advertiser seeks out gullibility above
> all.

A more basic reason for the general lack of advertiser interest
in public affairs sponsorship was at work. The fact was that the
range of audience sizes available for public affairs programs was
somewhat smaller than was that for other types of programming.
Generally speaking, advertisers wished to reach the mass audience.
Public affairs programs, especially if regularly scheduled news
programs are excluded, reach very small audiences, comparatively
speaking.
For example, CBS for many years allocated one hour of prime
time on Tuesday evenings for a public affairs program that was called,

––––––––––––––––––

*See the charts in Appendix E, below, for detailed figures for
most advertisers. It should be noted that the above comparisons
were between 1966 total budget figures and 1965 network public affairs
figures. This was necessary because of the unavailability of a breakdown for 1966 figures as far as public affairs program sponsorship
was concerned. More recent data on total advertising were available,
but there was no breakdown of news and public affairs advertising
with which the total figures could be compared. The sources for
these data can be found in Appendix E.

first, "CBS Reports"; then, "the CBS News Hour"; and, most recently, "Sixty Minutes." This program consistently had the very lowest prime time ratings. On one Tuesday night in September 1966 the program reached 16 percent of the total viewing audience between 10:00 p.m. and 10:30 p.m. and 15 percent between 10:30 p.m. and 11:00 p.m. NBC's Tuesday movie, running at the same time, reached 39 percent and 40 percent in the two time periods; and ABC's "The Fugitive" reached 36 percent and 38 percent, respectively.14

This basic fact about audience viewing habits was an old story. During 1961 the FCC conducted an investigation of network program practices. James T. Aubrey, Jr., then president of the CBS television network, testified that his network had lost $5 million on news and public affairs programs during 1961. He cited many individual programs and their poor audience ratings to explain why this was so. Among them was included another "CBS Reports" program—one in October 1961 that featured President Eisenhower in a discussion of the presidency. The program reached only 11 percent of the largest audience that the network achieved during 1961. It had run against NBC's "Sing Along with Mitch" and ABC's "The Untouchables."15

This difficulty of reaching large audiences with public affairs programming was sometimes overcome, however. In September 1967 ABC ran a four-hour documentary entitled "Africa." This was the longest scheduled documentary in television history and was extensively promoted beforehand. According to the Trendex overnight report, the program reached 31 percent of the television audience, a very respectable audience share for any program.16 But this experience of ABC's was hardly typical.

Because of the difficulty of attracting large audiences with public affairs programs, another problem—that of gaining affiliates' clearance—frequently developed. It was pointed out earlier that affiliates had the right to determine what they put on the air. They could and sometimes did reject network public affairs programming. They then replaced the network program with a feature film, a syndicated program, or a locally produced show. They tended to exercise this right to reject more frequently with network public affairs programs than with popular entertainment programs. The latter programs generally brought the large audiences upon which their revenues depended. Broadcasting gave the following figures on station clearances for September 1968 (numbers indicate the number of stations that cleared for each program):17

ABC		CBS	
NCAA Football	224	NFL Football	206
Lawrence Welk	213	Lucy Show	205
Don Rickles Show	123	CBS Evening News	199

ABC Five O'Clock News	124	Sixty Minutes	166
		Blondie	157

NBC

Bonanza	222
All-Star Baseball	208
Huntley-Brinkley	201
NBC White Paper	171
Jerry Lewis	177
Phyllis Diller	177

It would at first appear that the above figures fail to confirm what has been argued. But the entertainment programs that reached smaller numbers of stations—ABC's "Don Rickles Show," CBS's "Blondie," and NBC's "Jerry Lewis" and "Phyllis Diller" shows—were new shows in the first month of the season. They were all quickly taken off the air because of their unpopularity. The failure of stations to clear for these programs was but a reflection of the smaller audiences that they attracted. It should also be noted that the regularly scheduled news programs—particularly "Huntley-Brinkley" and the "CBS Evening News" (with Walter Cronkite)—secured clearances by considerably more stations than did the other news and public affairs programs.

Failing to clear for a network show was one defense that the stations had against programs attracting smaller audiences, and the public affairs programs typically attracted only smaller audiences. The stations therefore tended to reject public affairs programs much more frequently than entertainment or sports programs, and networks had to reckon with this adverse factor. (See the latter part of the discussion under "Network Affiliation and News and Public Affairs Programming," in Chapter 3, above, for a more extensive discussion of this problem, for additional data on its dimensions, and for an analysis of some of the consequences that it had for news and public affairs programming.)

One of the students of broadcasting who held a more conspiratorial view tended to think that the low rating achieved by public affairs programs sent out by the networks was largely a reflection of this clearance problem rather than vice versa. In fact, he implied that this fact was conveniently ignored by all those who sought to defend commercial television's record.

When CBS and NBC put on "White Paper," Meet the Press," or "The Nation's Future," hundreds of affiliated stations do not carry them. The people of those areas are not allowed to vote for these programs by the only ballot available: the ratings. In most cases

they receive old movies instead. They receive the films
because the local station makes more money on them.
Ratings then prove that the people want old movies.18

The figures published by Broadcasting suggested that Skornia greatly
exaggerated the dimensions of the problem by speaking of "hundreds"
of affiliates rejecting such programs. There were only 223 markets
in the continental United States. He was of course right in saying
that they did so far more frequently with this type of programming
than with other types. He was also right in pointing out that the
stations made more money on their own old movies than they did on
programs like "NBC White Paper."
   This difference in revenues was merely a question of audience
size, and that is what was behind Skornia's point. Although the contracts between stations and networks were notoriously complicated,
they did result in the seemingly anomalous situation in which network
programming that attracted medium-sized or smaller audiences was
less profitable for the affiliates than were locally produced or syndicated programs initiated locally with audiences of the same size or
even with slightly smaller audiences.
   This odd situation prevailed because the contracts were arranged
in such a way that stations received 100 percent of a smaller pie rather
than approximately 30 percent of a larger one. If the station put on an
old James Cagney film for which it had to pay, it then procured local
advertising or national spot advertising to insert with the film. Whatever revenues resulted were all for the station. Conversely, affiliates
received approximately 30 percent of the advertising revenues from
network programs. (To be more precise, they received 30 percent
of the advertising revenue paid to the network by the advertiser that
was attributable to that station's carrying the program. These attri-
butions were computed by an extremely complicated method that is
not of interest here.)
   In short, where programming attracted comparatively small
network audiences, revenues were correspondingly smaller. There
came a point where the affiliates were better off not to carry the
network program at all and to substitute something else. This point
was most often reached with network public affairs programming.
With most entertainment programming, the mammoth audiences
attracted made this situation rare. With feature films, however, it
was sometimes possible for individual stations or station groups to
secure popular old films that would attract approximately equally
large audiences to the films sent out by networks. Therefore, rejections of network films were also fairly common.
   An additional attraction of the highly popular network programs
was the presence of station breaks, into which local spots could be

inserted. These were called "adjacencies" and were a precious commodity to the individual station. Local and spot advertisers were very anxious to air their commercials inside, say, the "Ed Sullivan Show," and the stations found these adjacencies extremely lucrative. "CBS Reports," without such large audiences, did not carry with it such an advantage.

Ultimately, the whole process depended on audience size. The ratings measured the audience, and they showed that news and public affairs programming—with the exception of the evening news programs (those on CBS and NBC stations particularly) and the increasingly popular locally produced late evening news—were the least watched type of television programs.

The 1966-67 season's ratings were a case in point: "Bonanza" had the highest rating, with over 31 percent of the audience; ABC's "Stage '67" was rated 81, with 13 percent of the audience; the "Bell Telephone Hour" (specials) was 91 (last), with just over 8 percent; and the "CBS News Hour" was just above that, with just under 10 percent of the audience.[19] The same pattern prevails year in and year out.

There were, then, good commercial reasons why advertisers tended to shy away from news and public affairs programming. There were, however, also good reasons for some advertisers to seek opportunities in public affairs, and there was even some indication that it was becoming an increasingly attractive way to advertise. These reasons were well summarized by one official of one of the major television advertising agencies when he wrote the following:

> Now, with broadcast costs soaring, a budget of $1.5 million to $2 million for an ambitious corporate campaign purchases little continuity, frequency, and meaningful environment—if you are looking at entertainment series or specials, movies, or sports. You turn to network news department (you might use independents if they can work through these departments).
>
> Here are affordable documentary specials (about $150,000 to $350,000 per hour). Inherent in the form itself are lower production costs; and because of public service commitments, networks often sell at less than the full amount of these costs. Also, talent works less. Low-cost repeats in prime or fringe time further reduce unit costs. . . .
>
> Documentaries DO increase awareness of corporate names, associate diverse products and divisions with those names, and establish reputations for new and exciting product development, especially

among younger, better educated, higher income males.
This, then, may indeed be for some the best of all
advertising worlds.20

Irish was right in pointing out that there were sometimes
"bargain basement" values to be found in the sponsorship of public
affairs programs. For example, the ABC documentary "Africa,"
mentioned earlier, was sponsored in its entirety by the Minnesota
Mining Company. The cost for that privilege was $650,000. As it
turned out, the program reached over 31 percent of the audience.
The program cost ABC far more, and the New York Times
estimated that the losses to ABC would be over $2 million for this
program alone.21 Of course, such bargains were rarely available.
(George Gent attributed these heavy losses not only to unusually high
production costs but also to a compensation to stations and losses of
revenue from the cancellation of regularly scheduled programs.)
But advertisers seemed increasingly aware of these opportunities.
In the view of one of the networks' senior executives, there certainly
was a market for news and public affairs programming, at least in
prime time. He attributed this to the advertisers' having virtually
no program costs for this type of programming and consequently
incurring a very low cost per 1,000. He added that these public affairs
advertisers "were some of the biggest chiselers in the business."
One sponsor, Gulf Oil Corporation, found the sponsorship of
news and public affairs worthwhile. It had an arrangement with NBC
that was unique. It sponsored what were called "instant specials,"
fast-breaking stories that demanded immediate coverage. The Gulf
advertising staff required only a two-hour notice of NBC's intent to
cover some story, such as an earthquake in Alaska or the fall of the
Soviet leadership or any other unpredictable news event. The production costs were met by the NBC news division, and the result was
that these arrangements tended to yield Gulf a very efficient buy
in terms of the cost per 1,000 viewers. This open-ended sponsorship
arrangement for public affairs programs was the only one of its type
at the time of writing.22
It was easier to find enterprising sponsors for news programs
than for scheduled documentaries or other "specials." In addition to
audiences being smaller for this type of program, the costs were
very much higher. The networks rarely recouped more than 40 percent of their costs in these programs according to one network official. The news programs, however, probably did yield direct profits
to the networks, because of their comparatively larger audiences and
therefore their greater advertising revenues.
But it was actually difficult to assess whether such programs
as the "NBC Evening News" and "CBS Evening News" were really

profitable. The real costs were incalculable. Should the fixed costs of maintaining a worldwide staff for all news shows and special coverage be included in the costs of these specific programs, and, if so, what percentage of those costs? The network executives seemed convinced that, if such a computation were possible, it would have shown the network news programs, especially the evening news, to be moderately profitable.

This distinction between news, on the one hand, and other public affairs programs—such as documentaries, coverage of special events, interviews, and so forth—on the other hand, was reflected in the experiences of individual stations and station groups. They too found it far less difficult to find sponsors and audiences for local news than for other types of local public affairs programs. They too found local news programming moderately profitable. One knowledgeable observer of broadcasting even characterized sponsors' attitudes toward news sponsorship as a "rush."[23] Few broadcasters, however, would have gone that far.

There was absolutely no doubt that news and public affairs programming was basically less lucrative than was that for almost any other type of show. Richard Salant, president of CBS News, stated this fundamental truth in a provocative way when he said that, if CBS substituted entertainment shows for all of its news and public affairs programs, its before-tax profits would have increased by approximately 65 percent.[24]

Salant's point raised an interesting question. Was it correct to measure the profits of public affairs programs merely by the advertising revenues that they generated themselves? There were some in broadcasting who claimed that public affairs programming policies, especially with regard to news, had important effects on the market positions of individual stations generally; that is, some believed that the station that was seen as the most authoritative news station in a given market was more often than not the most popular station in that market in terms of overall audience size.

This argument means that news and public affairs programming was equivalent to supermarkets' "loss-leaders"—that is, items whose price was below cost, but whose availability yielded more than counterbalancing gains in overall sales.[25] (See the beginning of the discussion under "Other Factors Inducing Stations to Editorialize," in Chapter 5, above, for additional comments on this subject.)

THE IMPACT OF ECONOMIC
PRESSURES ON SCHEDULING

The economic forces in broadcasting have been examined thus far largely from the perspective of the advertiser and his objectives.

This perspective went far toward explaining the quantity of public affairs programming shown. But economic pressures also had much to do with the scheduling policies applied to these programs.

A quick examination of broadcast schedules revealed that extremely little public affairs programming was to be found during the evening, especially on network affiliates, although this was more true in 1966-67 than in 1971. This fact was but a corollary of audiences tending to be smallest for this type of programming. Therefore, it made little commercial sense for the networks or for the stations to insert shows with little audience appeal during time periods when the potential audience was largest.

This problem was most acute during prime time, which was variously defined as 7:00-11:30 p.m., 7:30-11:00 p.m., or 7:30-10:30 p.m. Public affairs programming was much more easily found in the schedules for Sunday daytime programming, when potential audiences were very small. The same was also true of other types of programming with little appeal, particularly "cultural programming," which did not appeal to mass tastes.

The reasons for severly limiting news and public affairs programming during prime time were all intimately associated with the large size of audiences at that period. But it was not simply a question of foregoing larger audiences for, say, a 30-minute segment of prime time for one evening. Audience research suggested that people tended to watch one station for long periods, irrespective of the program being shown.

What was involved here was the phenomenon known in the industry as "audience flow." This term took into account that people frequently tuned in purposely to a particular program, typically a very successful entertainment show, and then stayed with the programming of that station for the remainder of their viewing evening. The FCC's Office of Network Study noted the following:

> The networks spend much time and effort, including
> a large amount of research, in determining the compo-
> sitions of their schedules so as to attract and retain
> "audience" during a given evening. Experience shows
> that viewers tend to stay on the same channel unless
> they are displeased with a particular program so that
> a continuous flow of "popular" programs is desirable
> in order to maintain "circulation." Indeed, one of the
> factors which is considered by advertisers is the "lead
> in" which a particular time slot provides. This concept
> is called "audience flow" and it is the endeavor of the
> network to so arrange its programs so as to attract
> an audience of satisfactory size at the outset of a given
> period—usually in evening "prime time" and, if possible

to retain or increase that audience from program to
program.26

The impact of this phenomenon was obviously greatest in the earlier
part of the prime time period. The maximum audiences were available
between 7:30 p.m. and 9:30 p.m. Thereafter, the audience-flow problem
was somewhat less acute.27

It was the scheduling practices resulting from the phenomenon
of audience-flow, not the absence of advertisers willing to pay for
prime time to sponsor programming of interest to "specialized audiences," that accounted for the virtual absence of anything besides
mass entertainment fare in prime time television. The former head
of the FCC's Office of Network Study, Roscoe L. Barrow, explained
why:

> The influence of the advertising function has been to
> bring about a serious imbalance in television program-
> ming. Gresham's Law operates in television to drive
> out programs of interest to substantial minority audi-
> ences, and to bring in those attracting the maximum
> number of viewers. But the institutional advertisers
> and advertisers of products used only by a part of the
> viewing public are potential sponsors of programs with
> limited appeal. In addition, advertisers who wish to
> reach viewers repelled by mass appeal advertising
> and advertisers who are attracted to the market as a
> whole are other possible sources of sponsorship of
> this type of entertainment. These advertisers direct
> their message to a "target" audience which may desire
> high quality cultural programs. However, advertisers
> attempting to reach selected audiences have very
> limited access to network television, particularly in
> the prime evening hours. One reason for this limited
> access is the importance to the network of maintaining
> audience flow. Inclusion in the network schedule,
> particularly in early evening, of a program designed
> for a limited audience results in a loss of viewers
> to networks counter-programming shows with mass
> audience appeal. Although the network may seek to
> recapture the lost audience by exhibiting a mass appeal
> program in the succeeding time period, a portion of the
> lost audience will continue to watch the other network
> schedule because of audience "inertia."28

Barrow's analysis was confirmed by the schedules. Where
such programming did manage to penetrate the prime time network

schedules, it almost invariably was found in the period after 10:00 p.m., when the size of the audience lost would be smaller and when there was no first-class, mass appeal, revenue-earning program that would lose audience thereafter. With the FCC-required one-half hour of nonnetwork programming in prime time beginning in fall 1971, many stations were pushing the late evening news back to 10:30 p.m. and thus conforming to the regulation. (See Chapter 4, above.)

The hearings that the FCC's Office of Network Study held in connection with its research suggested that sponsors with an interest in programs aimed at selected audiences were in fact available, but that the networks were rarely disposed to accommodate such advertisers during prime time.[29] Not only were scheduling practices in the various time periods of the broadcast day affected by economic pressures, but it was sometimes suggested that scheduling across the broadcast month also involved some complicated calculations.

In an ultimate sense, advertising revenue to the networks and stations was determined by the ratings. The most authoritative rating service was that run by A. C. Nielsen. The Nielsen ratings were not taken continuously. Its ratings were based on data for two weeks out of each month. Something under 1,200 families had an audimeter attached to their television receivers. This instrument recorded what was seen on that set.

Each two weeks the families sent into the Nielsen company the record of their viewing habits.[30] Some expert and cynical observers of the broadcast world believed that public affairs programming and other low-audience presentations were least likely to turn up in the schedules of the networks for the Nielsen rating weeks. One student even suggested that NBC was more adept than was its two competitors in playing this game.

It should be clear, then, that the quantity of news and public affairs programming on commercial television was severely circumscribed by the complicated economics of broadcasting. It should further be clear that, when such programming did reach the television screen, the timing of its appearance significantly affected the profit quest of the networks and the stations. What should also be examined are the ways in which the advertisers and their needs shaped the content and character of public affairs programming that did reach the television screen.

ECONOMIC PRESSURES
AND PROGRAM CONTENT

As soon as the question of content is raised, a distinction must be made; for to raise a question about the relationship between the advertisers and program content is to raise two distinct questions:

first, how did the sponsorship of programs itself shape the character
of the program, if at all; and, second, to what extent and in what ways,
if any, did the sponsors themselves intervene in the creation or
editing of programs that they sponsored? These questions will be
examined in turn.

In 1948 Paul F. Lazarsfeld and Robert K. Merton identified the
function of the media as the affirmation and supporting of existing
social and economic structures. They attributed this function largely
to the existence of commercial sponsorship of the media in the United
States.

> Since the mass media are supported by great busi-
> ness concerns geared into the current social and
> economic system, the media contribute to the main-
> tenance of the system. This contribution is not found
> merely in the effective advertisement of the sponsor's
> product. It arises, rather, from the typical presence in
> magazine stories, radio programs, and newspaper
> columns of some element of confirmation, some element
> of approval of the present structure of society. . . .
> Hence by leading toward conformism and by
> providing little basis for a critical appraisal of society,
> the commercially sponsored mass media indirectly
> but effectively restrain the cogent development of a
> genuinely critical outlook. . . .
> Since our commercially sponsored mass media
> promote a largely unthinking allegiance to our social
> structure, they cannot be relied upon to work for changes,
> even minor changes, in that structure.[31]

To the extent that the advertisers wished to avoid controversy
in the programs that they sponsored and to the extent that they
succeeded in imposing their wishes on the people responsible for
programming, Lazarsfeld and Merton were certainly correct. For
to eschew controversy is either to raise no substantial issues at all
or to affirm what is. That this viewpoint was prevalent among the
majority of advertisers is beyond doubt. This was made clear in
the following testimony before the FCC's Office of Network Study:

> Another witness, a representative of one of the most
> active and largest of the agencies in television testified
> that "generally speaking" the object of national broadcast
> advertising is to "create as pleasant and favorable [an]
> impression on the part of as large an audience as possible,"
> for the company or product sponsoring the program. . . .

Question: Would it be true that a program which
might raise issues which would be displeasing to some
part of the audience would not normally be chosen by
you as a vehicle for national television advertising?
Answer: Yes.
Question: In other words, there is a limit to the
subject matter, a subject matter limitation.
Answer: Correct.32

Although the overall validity of these generalizations is probably
beyond doubt, there have been a sufficient number of exceptions,
especially in recent years, to require some qualification. Public
affairs programs have been sponsored that have directly or indirectly
raised the most serious and controversial issues about society. An
example of such a program was CBS's "Hunger in America," broadcast on May 21, 1968, which led directly to the creation of Senator
George McGovern's Select Committee on Nutrition and Human Needs
in October 1968 and the proposed legislation emanating from that
committee's work in 1969.33

Some people have argued that the aversion to controversy was
really the work of the advertising agencies rather than the advertisers
themselves; that the agencies, anxious to retain all their accounts,
were neurotic in their attempt to keep their clients out of difficulty;
and that the easiest way to achieve this objective was to veto the
slightest reference to controversial matters on the programs whose
sponsorship they arranged. This point of view was put forth by producer Mark Goodson in a court case emanating from the "blacklisting"
of radio personality John Henry Faulk:

[Mark] Goodson: A sponsor is in business to sell his
goods. He has no interest in being involved in causes. He
does not want controversy.
[Louis] Nizer: He does not want what?
Goodson: Controversy. The favorite slogan along
Madison Avenue is "Why buy yourself a headache?"
The advertising agency's job is to see to it that the
products are sold but that the sponsor keeps out of
trouble, and an advertising agency can lose a great
deal, it can lose the account. The sponsor can lose a
little bit of business, but he still can recoup it. The
agency can lose the account and I would say that a
great portion of an agency's job is concerned with the
pleasing and taking care and serving a client.

> So I think in many instances, the clients were perhaps
> even less aware of all this than the advertising agency,
> which considered one of its principal jobs keeping out of
> trouble, just keep out of trouble. I don't think that they
> took a political position, I think it was apolitical. It was
> just anti-controversial.[34]

There were liberal-minded persons who believed that the "corporate establishment" systemafically prevented "antiestablishment" views from gaining access to the American people via television. Some saw this phenomenon as a vicious threat against the people's right to know. Although the evidence available does not support this view, there were, nonetheless, informed and intelligent critics of broadcasting who persisted in it.

FCC Commissioner Nicholas Johnson was one such person. Appearing before the President's Commission on the Causes and Prevention of Violence, the commissioner said that "economic, corporate power over free speech is today, in my opinion, an even greater limitation than those feared by the drafters of the Bill of Rights."[35] Johnson cited as evidence for his view that the tobacco industry and broadcasters for years succeeded in keeping off the airwaves "any mention of cigarette smoking and cancer and heart disease"; that the auto industry and broadcasters were partners in a conspiracy of silence on the question of automobile safety; and that "black lung disease" was a topic blacked out in coal-mining states.[36]

Although many fair-minded people would agree with the basic point of Johnson's indictment of broadcasters and their corporate clients, there was a tendency to exaggerate its validity. In 1955 Edward R. Murrow's "See it Now" did a provocative and even-handed treatment of the question of smoking and health, when two one-half hour programs were devoted to the topic.[37]

One can accept generally the liberal indictment of television for failing to raise and to treat the most important problems confronting society without at the same time attributing this failure merely to the self-serving behavior of the "corporate establishment." That such news and public affairs programming was comparatively scarce and that viewers were rarely able to see such programs at times when they were actually inclined to watch television are beyond dispute.

The advertisers' policies and objectives had much to do with this; but it is not fair to put all the blame for broadcasting's failings on the backs of the advertisers. Edward R. Murrow made an excellent overall assessment of television's record in this regard in a speech before the Radio and Television News Directors Association in 1958:

Our history will be what we make it. And if there
are any historians about fifty or a hundred years from
now, and there should be preserved the kinescopes for
one week of all three networks, they will there find recorded in black-and-white, or color, evidence of
decadence, escapism, and insulation from the realities
of the world in which we live. I invite your attention
to the television schedules between the hours of eight
and eleven p.m., Eastern Time. Here you will find
only fleeting and spasmodic reference to the fact that
this nation is in mortal danger. There are, it is true,
occasional informative programs presented in that
intellectual ghetto on Sunday afternoons. But during
the daily peak viewing periods, television in the main
insulates us from the realities of the world in which
we live.38

There may well have been some change in the extent to which
Murrow's words held true in the period since that speech was made.
The networks and the stations were scheduling far more news and
engaging in editorializing, something that only a handful of stations
had done in 1958; and even in the prime time period there was some
increase in the quantity of public affairs programs.* Even in the
period of this study the amounts of news programming and editorializing increased substantially—that is, from 1966-67 to 1971.

One could even argue that the widespread criticism of the
television news departments, which reached a fever pitch after the
Democratic Party Convention in Chicago in 1968, came about in large
part because, in one sense, television was doing its job better. That
advertisers were to be found who could not succeed in persuading the
networks to sell prime time for public affairs "specials" may leave
the networks open to criticism, but it certainly shows that the shortcomings of television's record were not purely a function of the advertisers and their aims.

Many who continued to blame the advertisers for inadequacies
in public affairs programming or programming in general were
influenced in their thinking by well-publicized incidents in which a
particular advertiser sought to change or to eliminate programming
with which his corporate name was to be associated. Certainly, any

------

*In the 1968-69 season NBC joined CBS in sponsoring a prime
time evening public affairs program, "First Tuesday," once a month.

discussion of the economic determinants of public affairs programming would be incomplete without considering cases.

Were the economic forces such that advertisers did actually intervene in programming decisions, and, if so, was their power such that their interventions tended to succeed? There was no way of going about answering these questions in any systematic way. In theory, of course, there was no relationship whatever between advertisers and program content, especially with respect to public affairs programs. Yet incidents of attempts to shape programming were too numerous to be dismissed out of hand.*

How could some impression about the relationship among advertisers, their agencies, and those who determine program content be gained? Interviewing of program producers and advertising men obviously was not helpful in unearthing incidents of this kind. What had other students of broadcasting said in this regard? One knowledgeable observer gave the broadcasters more or less a clean bill of health:

> Electronic journalism seems to be completely free
> of any restrictions—save a minor one—that might be
> imposed on it by advertisers. Newsmen have been
> fiercely adamant about keeping advertisers out of their
> act, and management has backed them up. At both net-
> work and station levels, sponsors are dropped before
> being allowed to have any say on what is broadcast
> in the name of news and public affairs. Here and there
> one could find exceptions, and one might well argue
> that the owner who minimizes news on his station might
> be the very one to bow to sponsor pressure, but for
> the most part broadcasting has a fine record on this
> score. One practice which alleviates possible trouble
> is that of permitting an advertiser freedom to remove
> his label from a program of controversy with which he
> may not wish to be identified.[39]

---

*There was some information available on advertisers' attempts to intervene in the editorial policies of television stations. Since the determinants of public affairs programming operated somewhat differently in editorial presentations than in other types of public affairs programs, editorialization has been discussed separately. A discussion of the relationships between advertisers and editorial policies can be found under "The Extent of Editorialization on Television," in Chapter 5, above.

Perhaps the words of another student were closer to the mark. Petersmann writes that "the role of the sponsor in the most potent mass medium never has and never will be clearly defined. He does what he is permitted to do and sometimes what he can get away with.[40]

People within the industry when asked about this problem generally made the distinction between program content per se and what they called "commercial policy." They readily conceded that advertisers should keep out of program content and gave pious assurances that they were indeed kept out. Commercial policy, though, was the area where advertisers were given a role. No neat definition of commercial policy, however, was at hand. Perhaps the words of the FCC's Office of Network Study explain this distinction:

> Advertisers, through their agencies, seek and are accorded a considerable "voice" in the creation, planning, and production of network shows. The agencies assume "responsibility" to the national advertisers whom they represent for the character, quality, and effectiveness as advertising vehicles of the shows put on and paid for by their clients.
>
> Agency control is almost universal over network programming in the area of "commercial policy"—i.e., those elements of program subject matter which may be damaging to, or not in accord with, the advertising or marketing objectives of the sponsor. In addition, the agencies exercise a considerable degree of "creative control" over the subject matter of many programs. These agency functions are performed whether or not a network produces or "controls" the program. However, subject to these limitations, the industry seems in agreement that the ultimate responsibility for network programming must rest with the networks.[41]

Elsewhere in their report the authors added the following: "In the area of nonentertainment programs—news, public affairs, etc.—the advertiser does not have and does not expect to have any creative control of the program, indeed, he plays no part in the creation and production of such programming."[42] The testimony of a network executive vice president before the FCC made the same point. William R. McAndrew stated the following:

> With regard to special documentary or news programs, which vary so much in their range of subject matter, we discuss the type and general subject matter of the programs with sponsors in advance of their sponsorship

commitment, so they will have some idea of what their advertising message will be associated with. However, they are not permitted to determine the program content.[43]

These various statements imply that the line between program content control and commercial policy or creative control was a very narrow one. There was no easy way to locate that dividing line, although it was difficult to find instances of intervention in regularly scheduled news programs. The complexity of the problem was great because it was possible that, when advertising agencies acted, they might not be acting on behalf of the advertisers. So too, network censorship departments may have acted instead of the advertiser or his agency. How could the real relationships be identified?

In order to be fair to all concerned parties, mention should be made of any widely publicized incidents in which advertisers or their agents sought in one way or another to shape programming that they were sponsoring. The following enumeration of incidents is not limited to news and public affairs programs, since the assurance that the process was quite different there could not be accepted at face value. The list of incidents is not presented as representing typical relationships, but it does suggest one kind of relationship that from time to time prevailed between broadcasters and their advertisers.

Presumably, actual incidents of advertiser intervention substantially exceeded the number of publicly reported cases. But, then, there would be no point whatever in reporting the presumably thousands of public affairs programs (or other types of programs) in which there was absolutely no attempt on the part of advertisers or their agents to shape the content in any way. In short, there was no way of knowing how extensive the types of relationships enumerated below really were. Included here are incidents involving not only public affairs programming but programs in general so that the kinds of issues that aroused advertisers will be perfectly clear.

During the final take of an NBC program starring Petula Clark and Harry Belafonte on April 2, 1968, Miss Clark's right hand touched Belafonte's left forearm. The advertising agent for the Plymouth Division of the Chrysler Corporation, sponsor of the program, consulted with his agent, Young and Rubicam. Young and Rubicam then called the producer to say that his client wanted a retake. The producer, Steven Binder, refused. The program went on as originally done. No sanctions appear to have been imposed by the Chrysler Corporation.[44]

The Insurance Company of North America (ICNA), when it learned that NBC in its program "The Pursuit of Happiness," which ICNA was to sponsor, planned to include in the 10:00 p.m. "Special" appearances by publisher Ralph Ginzburg (publisher of Eros and other

controversial magazines) and Dr. Timothy Leary, among others, decided to withdraw its sponsorship from the program. ICNA gave as
its reason that the program was not a proper vehicle for their advertising messages. Two days later it was revealed that the company had
decided to spend most of its television advertising budget in the future
on the sponsorship of major league baseball games.45

The following item appeared in the Columbia Journalism Review:
"The CBS Television Network broke into its rarely interrupted daytime
schedule for a special event on February 14. It was the eighteenth
annual Pillsbury Busy Bake-Off Awards, originating in Los Angeles.
The prizes were presented by Mrs. Phillip W. Pillsbury, wife of the
co-chairman of the board of the Pillsbury Company. The Sponsor?
One guess."46

Television critic Jack Gould noted in June 1966 that NBC had
recently done a program entitled "The Anatomy of Defense," in which
the middle commercial described the General Electric Company's
activities as a defense contractor. Gould further noted that CBS had
scheduled a one-hour documentary on Surveyor I, which was to be
sponsored by the Hughes Aircraft Company, which made Surveyor I.47

On June 14, 1966, CBS televised a Harold Wolper production
called "Wall Street: Where the Money Is." In the course of the
program representatives of brokerage houses and stock exchanges
discussed stocks and bonds. Segments of the documentary were
submitted before the telecast to participants for their approval. One
participant, Gerald Tsai, Jr., who received a preview was president
of the Manhattan Fund. One of the Manhattan Fund's principal holdings
was common stock in the Xerox Company. The Xerox Company was
the sponsor of the program.

A representative of Wolper Productions said that no editing had
been done at the request of the participants. Richard Salant, President
of CBS News, said he himself had only learned these facts three days
before the scheduled telecast and that contracts prevented the program's
cancellation. Salant himself was the person who made known these
facts. Jack Gould, writing of the program, described it as "an invitation
to speculation in general and a plug for Mr. Tsai's Fund in particular."48

During 1966 the Schick Safety Razor Company, whose executive
officer, Patrick J. Frawley, was widely known as active in conservative
political circles, attempted to sponsor on several of CBS's owned-and-
operated stations the program "Up with People," a chorus of whole-
some young people originally associated with the Moral Re-Armament
movement. CBS declined to accept the sponsored program. CBS's
legal department said that the network and its stations did not accept
sponsored entertainment with editorial or ideological viewpoints. The
Schick Company then succeeded in buying time from NBC, and, ultimately, the program appeared in some 30 cities.49

Patrick Frawley's Schick Safety Razor Company sponsored "Hitler in Havana" on WOR-TV in New York on October 25, 1966. This program, described by the New York Times as "virulent anti-communist propaganda," argued that Fidel Castro's propaganda aroused Lee Harvey Oswald and was therefore responsible for the assassination of President John F. Kennedy.[50]

Miss Jean Muir, who in the early 1950s became the symbol of "blacklisting," was in line to appear on ABC's "Girl Talk" program on December 27, 1965. (Fifteen years before, she had been due to take a role in the Henry Aldrich Program when General Foods, the sponsor of the program, insisted on her removal from the cast because of her alleged associations with "subversive" groups.) During the 30-minute interview taped for ABC, Miss Muir spent almost 10 minutes discussing her blacklisting experience, mentioning NBC; Young and Rubicam, the agency involved; and General Foods.

After the taping ABC decided to review the program before allowing it on the air, and broadcast schedules were shifted in order to postpone this particular program. Finally, on January 14, 1966, the program was allowed on the air, but all the sections of controversy were "bleeped out." ABC stated that it risked libel actions if it left the controversial segments intact. As a result there was no mention of the Henry Aldrich program, no mention of General Foods, no mention of NBC, and so forth.[51]

"CBS Reports" did a program on police methods and problems entitled "The Policeman's Lot." During the program the police force in Chicago was shown using computers extensively in its work. The stress was on how these machines made the work of the police so much more effective. The computers "happened" to be made by the International Business Machines Corporation, sponsor of the program. Eric Pace, writing in the New York Times said that "the filmed show served as a come-on for the wares of its sponsors."[52]

The Gulf Oil Corporation was accused by Variety of withdrawing its sponsorship from two NBC programs on racial problems—one on September 2, 1963 ("The American Revolution"), and the other on July 26, 1964 ("Harlem: Test for the North"). The Columbia Journalism Review printed this charge in its fall 1964 issue and received a letter from Craig Thompson, Director of Public Relations of Gulf. In his letter Thompson denied that NBC had ever offered the programs to Gulf. He added the following:

We have sponsored programs dealing with racial and
civil rights events in the past, and possibly will in the
future, but we must do so with a certain amount of
circumspection simply because as a corporation engaged
in retail operation in thirty-seven states it would be

poor business to become identified as a company with
anything that could be called or might be interpreted
as "special pleading."53

On November 11, 1962, Howard K. Smith served as ABC's
commentator on a special program entitled "The Political Obituary
of Richard Nixon." There was great controversy about this program
because of a filmed appearance of Alger Hiss, the former State
Department official convicted of perjury nearly 13 years before, in
great part through the efforts of Nixon. According to reviews of the
program, Hiss's comments on Nixon, although critical, were far more
restrained than had been some of the rhetoric of the 1962 Nixon
campaign for the governorship in California. Hiss accused Nixon of
"political motives" in his original effort to expose Hiss.
       Several ABC advertisers sought to punish the network. The
Schick Safety Razor Company sought without success to cancel about
$1 million worth of contracted advertising, including sponsorship of
"Combat" and "Stony Burke." The Kemper Insurance Company announced that it would withdraw its joint sponsorship of the "ABC Evening
Report," a news program, and this involved approximately $500,000.
A soft drink manufacturer (unidentified) dropped advertising from
ABC in December as a result of the program. Walter H. Annenberg,
publisher of TV Guide, among other publications, and owner of New
Haven and Philadelphia television stations, caused his stations not to
carry the program and deleted all references to his cancellations of
the program from the network news broadcasts.54
       In 1962 Jack Gould reported that sponsors were "dropping out"
of regular and special newscasts about the racial situation in Oxford,
Mississippi. He noted that "apparently they prefer not to be associated
in the public mind with the controversial subject of integration. Aware
of such advertiser sentiments, the networks purpose[ly] have not
pressed the issue."55
       In 1962 CBS also lost three sponsors—Lever Brothers, Brown
and Williamson Tobacco Corporation, and the Kimberly-Clark Corporation—sponsors of "The Defenders" series. This cancellation was
due to one scheduled drama, "The Benefactor," in which a sympathetic
dramatization of a woman seeking an abortion was to be presented in
May. The Speidel Corporation took over sponsorship and announced
that it would also undertake sponsorship of the program for the
following season.56
       In response to the complaints of several school superintendents,
retail store owners, and private citizens in Shreveport, Louisiana,
who promised a boycott of the products of Bell and Howell because of
its sponsorship of ABC's "Close-Up" series, one program of which,
"Walk in My Shoes," presented a cross section of black thought about

the black's place in the United States, the company said that it had
and sought absolutely no control over the content of programs that it
sponsored.[57]

During his visit to the United Nations and the United States
during 1960, Nikita Khrushchev made arrangements to appear on
David Susskind's "Open End," on WNTA, channel 13, in New York. The
day before the broadcast, Sutro Bros. & Co., sponsor of one-half the
program for over two years, announced it would not sponsor its half
of the program due to appear the next day. Rather, it intended to
put on only a message that the company did not endorse the program.
But the brokerage house promised to continue sponsorship in the
future. When WNTA refused to allow such a message to accompany
the program, Sutro canceled its sponsorship permanently. Unhappily,
WNTA replaced the Sutro commercials with spot announcements about
Radio Free Europe![58]

There were also the classic incidents mentioned by former
FCC Chairman Newton Minow in his book Equal Time—for example,
the following:

> A classic tragic example of this lopsided emphasis
> occurred during a showing, sponsored by the natural-
> gas industry. On the program "Playhouse Ninety, "
> there was a drama dealing with the Nuremberg war
> trials, under the title "Judgment at Nuremberg."
> Viewers noticed that a speech by actor Claude
> Rains about the killing through cyanide gas of
> thousands of concentration camp prisoners by Adolf
> Hitler's Third Reich was abruptly interrupted by
> a deletion of words. The editing was done by a
> CBS television network engineer while the videotape
> recording of the drama was on the air. The words
> eliminated were "gas chamber." This editing,
> called "blipping," was done to accommodate the
> sponsor. A broadcasting executive later explained:
> ". . . we felt that a lot of people could not dif-
> ferentiate between the kind of gas up put in the
> death chambers and the kind you cook with."
>
> One of television's finest writers, Rod Serling,
> has also recounted the changes in a script that an
> advertising agency can force. Mr. Serling had based
> a one-hour drama on the lynching of a Negro boy in
> the deep South. By the time the agency had finished
> with the story, the chief character was a former
> convict, living in what one could decide was New
> England.[59]

As noted earlier, there is no suggestion here that these incidents were in any sense typical of advertiser-content relationships
in public affairs programming. Jack Gould of the New York Times
put it all very well when, writing of the program "Wall Street: Where
the Money Is" (mentioned above), he said the following:

> In short, a tradition has grown up where sponsors
> do have a chance to consider the content of a docu-
> mentary before deciding whether to be associated with
> the program in the public eye. That the networks as
> a general rule proceed with a show in any case does
> not negate the reality that the sponsor in effect enjoys
> an option on whether to become involved. . . . the
> consequence of the present situation is for sponsors
> to shop for documentaries that will enhance or at
> least not mar their corporate images. The boys in
> Wall Street were just a little more adept—or lucky—
> than the average sponsor.60

There is virtually no evidence that in regularly scheduled news
programs advertisers have attempted to shape the coverage that
their programs give to specific news stories. This does not mean,
however, that television news coverage in regularly scheduled programs
was a totally self-contained operation. There were pressures from
the outside, but they rarely came from advertisers. Now that the
impact of advertisers upon both the quantity and content of news and
public affairs programming has been considered, the impact of economic pressures upon the individual stations can be examined.

ECONOMIC CONSTRAINTS
AT THE STATION LEVEL

There were those who claimed that no attention had to be paid
to the individual stations because they were the complete captives
of the networks. Anxious to point out how very important the networks
were in American television, these zealots tended to lose perspective.
The following statement by Skornia exemplified this type of analysis:

> Through various types of controls, including the
> power of withholding or withdrawing affiliation contracts
> from stations which show an inclination to become too
> independent, the networks exercise life-and-death
> control over the television stations of the United States.
> Even more important, talent or programs which are

under exclusive contracts to one network will not be
available to areas of the country which that network
may not or does not serve. Networks alone decide
which stations may affiliate with them. The
similarity of this practice to that of patent controls,
which many of the mother corporations exert, is
obvious. Thus, industrial corporation practices,
designed to apply to products, come to control
programming, which comprises ideas.[61]

Skornia should have written that the individual stations exercised
extremely little influence upon network programming in general, except
in the sense that networks, mindful of what affiliates tended to reject
(that is, not to carry), were reluctant to disturb their affiliates more
than was absolutely necessary. The FCC's Office of Network Study
put it more accurately:

The station-licensee plays little or no part in the
production or selection process. He does, of course,
retain his right, under the chain broadcasting rules, to
reject programming, but infrequently does he exercise
that right. He has little opportunity to screen network
programs in advance of broadcast. In practice, he
must rely almost entirely on the judgment of network
managers to choose the network programs he broadcasts in his community. These, of course, are the
staples of his schedule. His responsibility to bring his
influence directly to bear upon all who "have a hand"
in programming his stations has been replaced by
"practical reliance" on the skill, judgment, and
integrity of the managers of his network.[62]

No one has produced evidence to show that the networks are now or
were in the past in a position to influence the quantity and character
of locally produced news and public affairs programming; nor has
anyone made such a claim.
    The character of news public affairs programs that individual
stations put on was in large part a function of the stations' economic
situation. Local public affairs programming typically included news,
editorials, coverage of local public events, interviews or discussions
with local notables, and, occasionally, documentaries on topics of
local or regional interest.
    Virtually all commercial television stations did some local
public affairs programming. But the character and quantity of that
programming varied widely. The single most important variable

associated with these differences in quantity and character was the economics of the individual station. The economics, in turn, were largely a consequence of two factors—the affiliation status of the station and the character and size of the market in which the station was located.

In early 1967 the NAB department of broadcast management made a study of the finances of individual television stations across the country. The study was based on questionnaires sent out to all the stations; 541 replies were received. From these replies the NAB formulated a "financial picture of typical TV station," as follows:

Revenues
24.4% from network time sales and network payments
42.5% from national and regional accounts
33.1% from local advertisers

Expenses
37.1% for programming
34.1% for general administrative costs
16.3% for technical costs
12.5% for sales promotion

The results of this NAB survey show dramatically why the affiliation status of a station was of such importance to its financial standing.[63] Just under 25 percent of the revenues for the typical station derived from the mere fact of affiliation; and this figure, of course, significantly underrepresents the true value of the affiliation, for the "national and regional accounts"—that is, national and regional spot advertising—depended heavily upon the network schedule. The network programs were what drew the audience to which advertisers in turn were drawn. To a similar extent revenue from local advertisers was also dependent upon the network affiliation.

In a sense, all the network affiliate had to do was to "plug in" to the newtork and substantial revenues came in. The network was also the major source of programming. According to the FCC's Office of Network Study, in January 1962 approximately 50 percent of the operating time on all television stations (morning, afternoon, and evening) was devoted to network programs. Between 6:00 p.m. and 11:00 p.m. this figure was 70 percent, and between 7:30 p.m. and 10:30 p.m. it was 90 percent.[64]

The importance of network affiliation was similarly shown in other research by the Office of Network Study. A comparison of two markets, New York and Los Angeles (the first and second market, respectively), was made. In this case, of course, the network

TABLE 22

New York and Los Angeles: Comparison
of Revenues and Income of Network-Owned and
Independent Stations, 1956-62
(million dollars)

Year	Owned-and-Operated Stations	Independents	Total	Owned-and-Operated Stations as % of Total
		Revenues		
1962	90.4	50.6	141.0	64.1
1961	79.1	43.0	122.1	64.8
1960	79.2	41.6	120.8	65.6
1959	75.0	40.1	115.1	65.1
1958	63.9	31.3	95.2	67.1
1957	55.8	32.7	88.5	63.0
1956	53.9	31.2	85.1	63.3
		Income		
1962	43.4	8.3	51.7	84.0
1961	37.1	3.6	40.7	91.3
1960	38.6	2.4	41.0	94.0
1959	37.2	1.7	38.9	95.6
1958	30.8	-2.9	27.9	—
1957	27.3	0.1	27.4	99.6
1956	27.5	-0.3	27.2	—

affiliates in these two markets happened to be network-owned and -operated stations. Nonetheless, the financial data show the superior position of the network affiliates in New York and Los Angeles. (See Table 22.)

The significance of the figures in Table 22 is heightened when it is pointed out that these data were based on the results for six owned-and-operated stations (three in each market) and for eight "independents."[65] In 1969 only 15 percent of affiliated VHF stations reported losses to the FCC, whereas 38 percent of the unaffiliated UMF stations did so.[66]

The single most important fact revealed by these figures is that, although the independents had revenues that were approximately 33 percent of total revenues during 1956-62, they only earned tiny percentages of the total income during the same period. (It ranged from a high of 16 percent in 1962 to less than 1 percent in the years 1956-58.) During two years the independents had no income at all!

It should be pointed out that the most lucrative part of the broadcast business was at the station level. The income from the ownership of these valuable properties was, even for the three networks, the principal source of income to the parent corporations. In 1969 the three networks had a total broadcast income before federal income tax of $92.7 million. Their 15 owned-and-operated stations had a pretax income of $133.4 million.[67]

But, if stations were the most profitable part of the business, the profits were not equally distributed among the station owners. Stations in the larger markets were obviously more profitable than were those in smaller markets. The owned-and-operated stations, located in the largest markets (New York, Chicago, Los Angeles, and so forth), were easily the most profitable stations. FCC figures show that in 1969, whereas these 15 stations made $133.4 million in pretax income, the remaining 489 VHF commercial stations made less than three times as much—$370.7 million.

The dimensions of this unequal distribution of profit were even greater than they appear at first. For the owned-and-operated stations faced keen competition not only with each other but also from some-times as many as four nonaffiliates in the same markets. The stations in the smaller markets, however, usually found themselves with only two VHF competitors, the affiliates of the two other networks. Despite the keener competition in the very largest markets, the owned-and-operated stations were far and away the most profitable outlets.

The fundamental role of the character of the market on a station's profitability is also easily demonstrable. Generally speaking, the larger the market, the larger the profits of stations within that market. For example, the pretax income of the three stations in Raleigh-Durham (the 50th largest market) in 1969 was $1,937,130. The equivalent figure for the three stations in Columbus, Ohio, was $4,654,598.[68] (See Table 3, above, for a list of the 50 largest markets in the United States as of January 1, 1971.) That aggregate profits were higher in markets of larger size did not necessarily mean that each individual station in the large markets would be more profitable than were its counterparts in smaller markets.

The relationship between market size and profitability was striking. It should be obvious, then, that the NAB survey in which it was found that the "typical" television station had in 1966 a pretax income of $332,100 reflected the extreme inequality in the distribution of profit among the nation's stations. The typical station was obviously not located in one of the 50 markets that were of concern here.

It should be pointed out that the affiliation status of a station and its market location did not alone determine the profitability of the station. Other factors played a role. One such factor was the ownership structure of the station—that is, whether its owners had interests in other television stations or not. Those stations that belonged to station groups, such as Metromedia or Westinghouse or Storer, tended to be more profitable than were stations not owned by such groups. The economies of scale attainable by groups were an obvious explanation of this fact. (The impact of ownership structure on public affairs programming, although partly a matter of profitability, was discussed as a separate factor in Chapter 3, above.)

The profitability of a station was important in shaping its decisions with regard to public affairs programming. This was so because many broadcasters saw news and public affairs programming as making no contribution to the profitability of their stations. That being so, stations with comparatively small profits could be expected to have considerably less capacity to engage in this type of programming than did their more prosperous colleagues.

In the 1967 and 1971 questionnaires sent to all commercial VHF stations in the top 50 markets, one question asked whether they regarded news and public affairs programming generally as a basically unprofitable activity. (See Question 2 in both questionnaires in Appendix C, below.) The replies to this question varied considerably. In 1967 35 percent saw it as flatly unprofitable, whereas by 1971 this figure was only 19 percent.

The remaining stations saw this programming as making a contribution to the economic well-being of the station, but either made a distinction between news, which was generally seen as profitable, and public affairs programs, which were not, or saw it all as unprofitable in a narrow sense but profit-generating in the sense that it built an audience for the entertainment side of the station's schedule. Most students of broadcasting have made similar findings. George Darlington wrote the following in Television:

> Public affairs documentaries always result in a loss, station managers report. As the manager of a top-20 market explains it: "We may put $10,000 into the production of an hour public affairs special. If we get a sponsor, and we don't accept participation spots for documentaries, it will probably be a bank or a local utility. We're doing good [sic] if we get $8,000 from the sponsor for the time and production."[69]

Audience size reflected (or caused) the fact that locally originated news was monetarily profitable. Nielsen ratings show that between 1962 and 1965 the homes using television between the hours of 6:30 p.m. and 7:30 p.m. (an hour almost universally reserved for news) rose by 20 percent. The other period for local news, 11:00-11:30 p.m., showed a similar rise. That the audience grew faster during these "news periods" than during other portions of the broadcast day is evidence that local news broadcasts became increasingly popular.[70]

The increased popularity of television news accounted in part for the decision of NBC and CBS to extend the length of their evening news broadcasts (Huntley-Brinkley and Cronkite) from fifteen minutes to one-half hour beginning in September 1963. This was a step for which the news departments of the networks had been pressing for some time. By 1969 there was frequent discussion of the possibility of extending these programs to a full hour in duration. Every indication is that news was continuing to grow in popularity.

A survey as early as 1965 by Television showed that, for just under 60 percent of the television stations, locally originated news was profitable; that something over 20 percent found it to be a break-even operation; and that less than 20 percent found it to be a losing proposition.[71] Questionnaires were sent to the news directors of all the television stations; and 167 responses were received, 135 of which gave the financial standing of their local news operations. Of these, 59.3 percent were operating in the black, 21.5 percent were even, and 19.3 percent were in the red.

Although the profitability of a station clearly influenced its capacity to program news and public affairs shows, there were obviously other factors at work—management's values and notions of responsibility, the interests of the owners, the regulatory environment in which the station operates, the policies of other stations in the same market, and so forth. Nonetheless, in certain types of public affairs programming—most notably, editorials—the economic factor appears to have been the single most dominant influence.

The relationship between the economic resources of a station as measured by gross receipts and the probability that a station would editorialize was very strong. Stations' managers most frequently mentioned economic considerations when asked about their policies with regard to editorializing.[72] (See the end of the analysis under "The Extent of Editorialization on Television," in Chapter 5, above, for a more detailed discussion of the relationships between economic resources and a station's editorializing policies.)

The economic resources of a station, then, appear to have influenced decisions of its managers with regard to public affairs programming. The quantity of such programming and, presumably, the scheduling policies affecting that programming were determined in part by the level of available resources. Since commercial television stations were by definition profit-seeking organizations, the greater the profitability of the stations, the more likely were the stations to make more costly programming decisions.

The role of profitability, then, was very important. It imposed the lower and upper limits on what a station could do. Within those limits, other factors appear to have been more important. Although there was no assurance that a highly profitable station would choose to put on a large amount of news and public affairs programs, the probability that it would was much greater than for a station that was less successful.

Despite the logic of the argument just made and although the NAB had shown the argument to be valid with regard to editorializing, one implication of this argument is questionable. Since, as shown above, the relationship between the size of a market and the profitability of stations was striking, one could logically infer that stations in the larger markets would be likely to engage in more news and public affairs programming than would stations in smaller markets. (See the discussion, above, of market size and profitability.)

The evidence for this generalization is quite mixed, and this inference requires considerable qualification. In general, it was true that stations in New York and Los Angeles engaged in more news and public affairs programming than did their counterparts in Glendive, Montana. The statements of managers of stations in the smaller markets confirm that these stations would be inclined to do more such programming if the impact upon the stations' overall profitability would not be so damaging. But the differences between stations' news and public affairs programming policies and the size of the markets in which those stations were located did not fit any overall pattern.

CONCLUSIONS

In beginning the discussion of economic forces as they operated on the individual station, it was noted that two factors were important in shaping public affairs programming—the stations's profitability and the station's affiliation status. These two factors, of course, were closely related. As the figures for a typical American television station showed, network affiliation was perhaps the single most important source of station revenue (and therefore intimately related to profitability).

Stations that were not affiliated with national networks were invariably less profitable than were stations in the same market that were fortunate enough to be affiliates. The nonaffiliates, or independents, tended to have different programming policies as a result of their lack of affiliation. In general, nonaffiliates tended to do what is called "counter programming"—that is, they tended to put on the type of programming that the affiliates were not putting on.

This policy obviously made great sense. If these stations were to attract an audience, their most promising approach was to do whatever the "big guys" were not doing. When the affiliates were putting on feature films, the nonaffiliates might put on game shows. When the affiliates were putting on daytime game shows, the nonaffiliates were putting on feature films. When the affiliates were putting on public affairs programs—for example, local early evening news—the nonaffiliates were putting on straight mass entertainment programs.

This policy obviously required different policies with regard to news and public affairs programming as well. Although the lower profitability of the nonaffiliates meant that the amount of news and public affairs programming that they could (or were willing to) do was considerably smaller than for the affiliates, it also meant that the scheduling policies for whatever they did in the field were also different.

As pointed out earlier, economics made the networks very reluctant to put on public affairs documentaries, for example, during prime time. The networks also did not broadcast regular news programs during that period. The result frequently was that the nonaffiliates did broadcast public affairs programs, almost exclusively news programs, during the 7:30-11:00 p.m. period. In New York, for example, WPIX (channel 11) put on a full hour of news from 10:00 p.m. to 11:00 p.m.

The results of the survey of programming for the sample stations show that, although the nonaffiliates did very much less news, documentaries, editorializing, coverage of public events, and so forth than the affiliates did, whatever they did do was much more likely to appear during prime time. This finding is mentioned here because it flows directly from economic pressures. (See Chapter 3, above, for a more extensive discussion of this point and the evidence for it.)

By way of summary, then, what were the relationships between the quest for profit, on the one hand, and the quantity and character of public affairs programming, on the other? There can be little doubt that the quantity of such programming was directly dependent upon economic considerations, both at the network and the station levels. Since news programs tended to be the most popular, they tended to be less unprofitable than were documentaries or interviews. It is more difficult to show that the character of news coverage in these news programs was affected by the economic interests of broadcasters, despite the conviction of liberal critics of television that such relationships were clear.

But, when it came to nonnews programs, then the character of these programs did appear to be related to economic considerations.

The advertisers' aversion to controversy was clear, and this made it difficult for contentious issues and problems to reach the air. When they did, the advertisers sought presentations that did not risk offending people. But the public record of advertisers' attempts to intervene in programming was inconclusive. To the extent that advertisers' aims limited programming, they appear to have done so more by their program sponsorship policies than by direct action.

The scheduling practices with regard to news and public affairs programs flowed almost directly out of the question for network and station profit. It was shown that the achievement of profit implied different policies for nonaffiliates than for affiliates, but the role of economics in scheduling was indisputable.

Although it is difficult to show convincingly any relationship between the quest for profit on the part of the networks and the stations and the content of their news programs, it can perhaps be hypothesized that, at the station level, organizations whose economic situation was precarious were unlikely to seek out stories whose coverage would tend to offend influential people who might be in a position to affect the flow of advertising revenue to the station. Certainly, the reluctance of small stations to engage in editorializing fits into such a hypothesis.

In the most general of senses, however, economic pressures played a central role in the whole area of news and public affairs programming. Two of the three other determinants of this type of programming that have been examined—ownership structure and the character of relationships between networks and their affiliates—were partly economic in their character. Virtually all the limits within which news and public affairs programming was done were imposed by economic considerations. That fact alone makes its analysis in this study essential.

7

CONCLUSIONS
AND IMPLICATIONS
OF THE STUDY

Few would dispute the basic argument made here—that the quantity of news and public affairs programming shown, the types of programming offered, the scheduling practices associated with these programs, and even the content of the programming were largely explicable in economic terms. Although stations and networks shared the resource of air time equally, their financial resources and profits varied considerably. The use to which air time was put was basically a function of the quest for profit and only secondarily a function of other factors.

Varying economic pressures on individual stations accounted for most of the differences in public affairs programming policies. For example, the network-owned and -operated stations showed more news and public affairs programming than did stations of any other type. This was largely because they were the richest, most profitable stations in the country and could therefore best afford less lucrative public affairs programming.

That the stations producing the highest profits were, in general, the most likely to editorialize was but another expression of the same overriding significance of economic factors. The more precarious economic situation of unaffiliated stations went far in explaining why nonaffiliates showed less news and public affairs programming than did any other type of station.

Economic pressures largely shaped scheduling practices as well. The meager programming of nonaffiliates tended to be aired during prime time in hopes of capturing some small portion of the affiliates' prime time audiences. Even the willingness of stations to provide air time for those with truly controversial ideas and viewpoints appeared to be related to the resources available to the individual station; those with low profit margins were less prone to risk advertisers' retribution.

At the network level economic pressures were also a principal factor shaping decisions with respect to news and public affairs programming. ABC's network schedule included substantially less public affairs programming than did the schedules of its competitors, CBS and NBC. This fact was largely an expression of ABC's difficulties in achieving profits equivalent to those of CBS and NBC. Documentaries were the rarest form of public affairs programming because they were the most expensive form. The virtual segregation of public affairs programs in the "ghetto" of Sunday schedules was another expression of economic imperatives.

In short, the economic pressures operating on stations and on the networks were critical in shaping the public affairs programming seen by the people of the United States.

The other principal determinant of news and public affairs programming was the regulatory environment in which the television industry operated. That such programs were even shown at all on commercial television may have been the result of FCC regulation. The FCC imposed an obligation on all licensees to offer "balanced programming," of which news and public affairs programs were constitutent elements. Of course, the character of the obligation imposed by the FCC was minimal. One Los Angeles television station broadcast only five minutes of news in 1966 (and ten minutes of weather reports) per day, yet its license renewal was not in jeopardy at the FCC.

The impact of the FCC was clearest in the growth of editorialization in the early 1960s. This development was shown to be nearly a direct response to FCC efforts to encourage that form of public affairs programming. There were other respects in which the regulatory activities of the FCC were found to have had an impact upon public affairs programming.

Through its control over the ownership structure of the industry and through the limits imposed by the FCC on the right of licensees to enter contracts of certain kinds with networks, the FCC did have several indirect effects upon the quantity of news and public affairs programming. The FCC's Fairness Doctrine was widely alleged, however, to discourage broadcasters from including within programs controversial questions on which a fairness issue was likely to arise.

In short, the regulatory environment had proven to be an important determinant in only one sector of public affairs programming—editorialization. The behavior of the regulators generally was shown to be largely verbal posturing accompanied by acquiescence to industry practices in the area of programming.

As for the other determinants examined in the study—ownership structure and affiliation status—there was some reason for seeing these largely as corollaries of the basic economic determinant—the quest for profit. For example, group-owned stations were found to be more likely to editorialize than were single-owner stations. That this was so was probably on account of the greater news-gathering resources (that is, economic resources) available to station groups, as compared to stations owned by parties with no other television interests.

That CBS affiliates appeared to show more news and public affairs programming than did either NBC or ABC affiliates was in large part (although not totally) due to the inclusion by the CBS network, especially in 1966-67, of a larger component of public affairs programming than the other networks included as part of the affiliation program package. That nonaffiliates showed far less news and public affairs programs than did affiliates was almost totally a matter of economics.

SOME IMPLICATIONS OF THE OVERALL FINDINGS

A basic reason for undertaking this study was the examination of the "political behavior" of one "political actor," the television medium. It was postulated that the programming of commercial television had impacts both on the formation of public opinion and on the behavior of other political actors—politicians, interest groups, political parties, bureaucracies, and the like. The factors shaping the quantity of news and public affairs programming shown became the central concern in the study. Another way of stating this same concern is to speak of factors that shaped how active the television industry became in the political system.

Not unexpectedly, it was found that commercial television became active in the political system to the degree permitted by the level of available resources. In this the medium was no different from other political actors. But unlike, say, interest groups and political parties, the medium emerges from this study as a somewhat reluctant actor in the political system. Those in the industry did not generally see themselves as actors in the system.

On the contrary, those at the top levels of management in the station and network organizations saw themselves as business executives primarily, and they saw their task as the building and managing of modern, efficient organizations that would return handsome profits to the stockholders. Those in the news divisions of the networks and those with corresponding functions in the station organizations saw themselves as professional, privileged observers of the political system, not as actors or participants within the system.

Although it is true that all political actors were limited in their political activity by available resources, the television medium was a political actor in a somewhat more limited sense. Whereas the other actors sought resources in order to engage in political activity, the television medium sought resources as a goal in their own right. Then, as a kind of afterthought, the medium entered the political process through public affairs programming. Although for other political actors political activity is the raison d'être, the television medium engaged in the form of political activity called here news and public affairs programming as part of a larger strategy whose primary goal was monetary profit.

Like other major agents of political socialization in the political system (for example, the schools), the media professed an aversion to participation in the political process. They claimed that their impact upon the political system was incidental to the performance of other functions in the society. In one sense, political scientists were right to dismiss such a professed aversion to participation in the political process as little more than a self-serving myth perpetuated by the broadcasters. But in another sense the medium was an actor in the political system in a far more limited and incidental way than were actors such as political parties and interest groups.

The study also has some more practical, less theoretical implications. Although it would be unreasonable to claim that the study substantially advances the general study that political scientists have made of the "independent" regulatory commissions, there is good reason to claim that a new perspective on one dimension of the FCC's policies and practices has been developed here.

Before the completion of this study there was no systematic analysis by political scientists of the FCC's policies in the area of news and public affairs program regulation as a whole. The general regulatory objectives of the FCC in the area of programming were identified as follows: "balanced" programming, individual licensee responsibility for program content, the Fairness Doctrine, and so forth.

The incompatibility of these program regulation objectives with the more general regulatory objectives of the FCC was demonstrated. It was shown that ownership diversification and increased competition in the television industry would, in the absence of direct program regulation, result in less, not more, news and public affairs programming on commercial television.

Furthermore, the record of the FCC in pursuit of both sets of objectives was examined. It was shown that in both cases the commitment of the FCC was largely verbal. Licensees' interests were rarely sacrificed for the achievement of either ownership diversification and increased competition or more balanced programming with a larger amount of public affairs programming.

Even where the FCC had had its greatest success—in encouraging broadcast editorials on commercial television—its "regulation" was largely hortatory. The general accuracy of the argument that the FCC had rarely insisted upon or required compliance with its general regulatory objectives was reflected in the willingness of some broadcasters to state categorically that the FCC had little or no effect upon their programming policies.

Perhaps more interesting than these findings about FCC rhetoric and policies are the implications derived from the sample survey portion of the study. It was shown that the richer and more profitable the station or network, the more likely it was that increased amounts of news and public affairs programming would be shown and the more likely it was that controversial ideas would reach the television screen.

Meanwhile, the FCC was proclaiming its determination to encourage conditions of increased competition in the industry and increased diversification of ownership of television stations. By implication, this objective would require the number of single-owner stations to mount, the number of unaffiliated stations to increase, and, in general, a decrease in the domination of the industry by the three networks.

Such developments, in the absence of direct program regulation by the FCC, would assuredly reduce the amount of news and public affairs programming seen, reduce the number of stations editorializing, and, probably, increase the dependence of individual stations upon advertisers, with a consequent increased aversion to controversy on the part of station management. And yet, the FCC could not be persuaded by its vocal minority to move to direct program regulation.[1]

The reluctance of the FCC even to follow the meager rules that it had itself established to achieve some of its regulatory objectives— for example, the rule limiting ownership of top 50 VHF stations to three per party—did not augur well for FCC attempts at direct program regulation. Theodore Lowi has pointed out that the general character of administrative regulation in the United States since the New Deal has meant that regulatory bodies have eschewed formal rule-making wherever possible and have proceeded on a case-by-case basis where bargaining and accommodation become the norm.[2]

This practice has been shown to have prevailed at the FCC in the area of television licensing. Lowi's prescription of more direct regulation by what he calls the general application of the "rule of law" is consistent with the recommendation made here, even though it would be anathema to what Lowi calls "interest group liberalism."

One further matter on which some members of the FCC have spoken out has been illuminated by this study. The FCC has evidenced a recurrent fear that the news and public affairs programming on commercial stations might serve the wider interests of parent corporations and their managers. Virtually no evidence in support of such allegations was uncovered.

Commissioner Nicholas Johnson fairly accurately described the pattern of ownership in the television industry when he wrote of the "media barons," but the occasions on which the barons used their power to shape news and public affairs programming were few and far between.[3] At least, systematically assembled evidence to support such accusations was not available. Of course, it may well be that occasional allegations of this type by members of the FCC and by critics of the television industry contributed to the apparent absence of such practices.

Another possible implication of the study is that those at the FCC and outside who hoped to increase the quantity of news and public affairs programming on commercial television should abandon their efforts. In view of the economic situation in the industry—where mass audiences, not usually available for public affairs programs, were required for survival—efforts to induce greater amounts of such programming were bound to be marginal in their effect.

Short of a decision to abandon attempts to increase such programming on commercial television, three possibilities remained: first, the FCC could move to direct program regulation by enforcing rules by which licensees would be required to present a certain proportion of programming each day; second, technological and promotional efforts could be made to facilitate the creation of larger audiences for news and public affairs programming; or, third, the structure of the television industry could itself be changed so that it would be economically possible to appeal to smaller audiences.

By the end of the 1960s it was clear that these options were being pursued simultaneously. Congress, under pressure from the FCC and television critics, established the Corporation for Public Television and began to inject federal funds into noncommercial television as a device for generally improving the quality of television programming available. A significant portion of the new programming that would result from the Corporation for Public Television would be public affairs programming.[4] In a sense, the decision to begin governmental financing of noncommercial television reflected a recognition that efforts to improve the quantity and to diversify the character of commercial television fare were unlikely to bear fruit.

At the same time, advances in the development of Community Antenna Television Systems (CATV) were proceeding rapidly, and many believed that mass audience broadcasting might well give way to broadcasting for more specialized audiences as it became technologically possible to construct audiences for specific programs. In a review of a book by media student Ben H. Bagdikian, Elie Abel wrote the following:

> It is, however, in the broadcast area that Bagdikian finds the most immediate technological challenge to existing forms. With commendable clarity he traces the extraordinary potential of cable television to undermine, perhaps to shatter, the television networks as we have known them. Because cable offers the advertiser an opportunity to pre-select a particular segment of what used to be called One Big National Audience—at a tiny fraction of what the big networks charge. [sic] There is at least a hint, though Bagdikian stops short of outright prophecy, that mass audience broadcasting could go the way of the mass-circulation magazines like Collier's and the Saturday Evening Post.[5]

That is, at the same time that efforts at the creation of a public television network were being made, the development of CATV raised the possibility that larger audiences for public affairs and other specialized programming on commercially sponsored outlets could be reached at costs far lower than those that were possible in the late 1960s. As noted above, the FCC in early 1971 for the first time indicated an inclination to begin direct program regulation as a device to expand the amount of public affairs programming available on commercial television.

Finally, the study has some implications about the degree to which the mass media support and reinforce existing values within American society—that is, the degree to which they support the prevailing ideology within the political system. Political scientists have long pointed to the media as one agent of political socialization whose function is to support the values and premises of existing social, economic, and political institutions. For example, Robert A. Dahl has written as follows:

> What is essentially correct, however, is that the amount of time and space devoted by the mass media to views openly hostile to the prevailing ideology is neglible. An American who wishes to find criticisms of the basic

social, economic, and political structures can indeed find
them, but he will have to search outside the mass media.
And naturally, the number who are strongly motivated
enough to do so is relatively small. Hence, the general
effect of the mass media is to reinforce the existing
institutions and ideology.[6]

Although this study was not explicitly concerned with the degree
to which commercial television programming did generally support
or reinforce prevailing norms and values, some data connected with
this question were assembled. It will be recalled that many stations
in their responses to the questionnaires meant by "controversy"
something far short of views critical of the fundamental social,
political, and economic arrangements in the United States. (See the
discussion under "The Content of Editorials," in Chapter 5, above.)
In 1969 Elmer Lower, president of ABC News, commissioned
a study of ABC's 1969 newscasts to discover the degree to which
ABC's news had a particular slant. This study contained the following
findings: 14 hours, 35 minutes, of news supported the Administration's
viewpoint on political matters; 9 hours, 35 minutes, opposed the
Administration's viewpoint; and 13 hours, 37 minutes, were found to
be neutral. The words and faces of pro-Administration figures and
opponents of the Administration were present in a four-to-one ratio.[7]
In short, ABC's news was heavily biased in favor of official political
views. Also, there is no reason to believe that those opposing official
views held positions in opposition to the prevailing norms, values,
and ideology of American society.
This study helps to explain how programming generally sup-
portive of prevailing norms and values found its way to the television
screen. Through a focus on the relationships between advertisers,
networks, and stations, some of the mechanisms of the process were
described. It is clear from this study that the quest for sponsorship
of public affairs programming, the objectives of sponsors and their
agencies, and the fear on the part of networks that programs might
be rejected by affiliates all conspired to make it difficult for views
openly hostile to the prevailing ideology to gain access to the commercial television screen.
There were, however, several reasons to believe that commercial television's public affairs programming was becoming increasingly hospitable to views hostile to the prevailing ideology.
First, the increased role of spot advertising and the marked decrease
in advertising associated with specific programs (for example, the
Hallmark Hall of Fame) made it likely that programmers could
become more independent of advertisers.

Second, the verbal encouragement of some at the FCC presumably was leading some broadcasters to be more open to controversial views, although the Fairness Doctrine presumably made some hesitant. Third, the appearance, at least, that views hostile to prevailing norms were themselves more common and were therefore reflected in public affairs programming—covering such stories as Black Panther trials and shoot-outs, occupations of buildings by the Young Lords, speeches and demonstrations associated with the Chicago Seven, and the like—reinforced the belief that such programming was becoming more open.

The dependence of the stations and the networks upon advertising was obvious to even the most casual student of television. But the limited extent to which this dependence affected programming was perhaps less obvious. Most people probably overestimated the degree to which this dependence shaped the program content, especially in the field of public affairs programming.

Although far more systematic study of the content of news and public affairs programming is required, it appears that views hostile to prevailing norms were not more prevalent on commercial television for a host of reasons unrelated to the dependence on advertising. These may have had largely to do with the segments of society from which television personnel were recruited and with the organizational characteristics of the stations and the networks producing the bulk of news and public affairs programs.

FUTURE INDUSTRY PROSPECTS AND FURTHER RESEARCH

Many would argue that the underlying principle of commercial television—that the programming on commercial television largely reflects the views, tastes, and values of the mass audience—is bound to require modification in the near future. Certainly, it is an open question whether it is in the public interest for the quantity and character of news and public affairs programming available to most people on television to be almost totally dependent upon the financial success of the stations and the networks.

Although some would see in this reality some basically "democratic" element, in the sense that programming ultimately reflects the felt needs of the overwhelming majority of the country's population, others are deeply worried by leaving the gathering and dissemination of information and opinion about public events to the vagaries of marketplace forces.

At the beginning of the 1970s it appeared that advancing broadcast technology, largely in the form of community antenna systems
(cable TV), and the prospect of increased involvement of the federal
court system in the regulation of television would significantly alter
the shape of the television industry's practices as described here.
The development of "public interest law firms," ready to represent
television viewers in the processes of license renewal, had already
begun to force changes in regulatory policies at the FCC.

The success of the United Church of Christ's Everett Parker
in transferring the license of WLBT-TV in Jackson, Mississippi, to
a group more prepared to serve black audiences in that city, the
success of John Banzhaf in eliminating cigarette advertising from
commercial television, and the growth of "strike" applications from
local groups claiming that licensees were not keeping promises made
in renewal applications were quite possibly harbingers of what is to
follow. In addition, changes in the "political culture" of the United
States could also effect considerable changes in the regulatory policies
of the FCC, probably in the direction of more aggressive regulation.

There can be little doubt that commercial television is at an
important crossroad in its history. Broadcast executives, students
of the television medium, and those with regulatory responsibility
over the industry would all be well advised to proceed cautiously and
on the basis of systematic analysis of the medium's behavior; and a
great deal of research remains to be done.

What has been done in this study makes a great deal clearer
what remains to be done:

1. Content analysis of public affairs programming in relation
to the determinants identified in this study, as well as others

2. Decision-making studies of specific public affairs programming processes

3. Analysis of managerial attitudes as a variable affecting the
quantity of public affairs programming shown and the content of
programming resulting

4. Analysis of attitudes of journalistic professionalism among
reporters, producers, editors, cameramen, and others involved in
the public affairs programming process

5. Analysis of network and station news divisions as separate
actors within broadcasting organizations.

The need for such studies is apparent. The fifth suggestion, above,
merits particular attention. In this study, the unit of analysis adopted
was that of the firm—the network and the station organization. The
character of the conclusions in the study in large part reflects that
choice.

When one speaks of the media as actors in the political system, does one necessarily speak about CBS or ABC? Or does one speak about the news divisions of those networks? Had the news divisions been taken as the primary unit of analysis, economic pressures and the regulatory environment might well have appeared far less important than were some other factors in shaping news and public affairs programming. It might even have been possible to identify the media as zealous participants in the political process rather than as reluctant tag-alongs.

A great deal of political science research into television and into the media generally remains to be done. Hopefully, a beginning has been made here.

CHAPTER 1

1. For an excellent discussion of this issue, see Kurt Lang and Gladys Engel Lang, Politics and Television (Chicago: Quadrangle Books, 1968).

2. Vice President Agnew's much-disputed speech on the media in Des Moines on November 13, 1969, was, in part, an assertion of this basic truth. The media reacted with predictable hostility. (See the transcript of this speech in Marvin Barrett, ed., Survey of Broadcast Journalism 1969-70 (New York: Grosset & Dunlap, 1970), pp. 131-38.

3. See David Easton, The Political System (New York: Alfred A. Knopf, 1953), pp. 129-41.

4. Walter Lippmann, Public Opinion (New York: Macmillan, 1960).

5. Paul F. Lazarsfeld, Bernard Berelson, and Hazel Gaudet, The People's Choice (New York: Duell, Sloan & Pearce, 1944).

6. V. O. Key, Politics, Parties, and Pressure Groups (4th ed.; New York: Thomas Y. Crowell, 1968), pp. 521-27.

7. Daniel Lerner, The Passing of Traditional Society—Modernizing the Middle East (New York: The Free Press of Glencoe, 1958).

8. Bernard C. Cohen, The Press and Foreign Policy (Princeton: Princeton University Press, 1963).

9. See Gabriel Almond and Bingham Powell, Comparative Politics: A Developmental Approach (Boston: Little, Brown, 1966); and Richard R. Fagen, Politics and Communication (Boston: Little, Brown, 1966).

10. Jay G. Blumler and Denis McQuail, Television in Politics: Its Uses and Influences (Chicago: University of Chicago Press, 1969).

11. Lang and Lang, Politics and Television.

12. Herbert I. Schiller, Mass Communications and American Empire (New York: August M. Kelley, Publishers, 1969).

13. Bryce Rucker, The First Freedom (Carbondale: Southern Illinois University Press, 1968).

14. See Marvin Barrett, ed., Survey of Broadcast Journalism 1968-69 (New York: Grosset & Dunlap, 1969), Survey of Broadcast Journalism 1969-70, and Survey of Broadcast Journalism 1970-71 (New York: Grosset & Dunlap, 1971).

15. See Fred W. Friendly, Due to Circumstances Beyond Our Control . . . (New York: Random House, 1967); John Hohenberg, The

News Media: A Journalist Looks at His Profession (New York: Holt, Rinehart & Winston, 1968); Robert MacNeil, The People Machine: The Influence of Television on American Politics (New York: Harper & Row, 1968); Nicholas Johnson, How To Talk Back To Your Television Set (Boston: Atlantic-Little, Brown, 1969); and Les Brown, Television, The Business Behind the Box (New York: Harcourt, Brace Jovanovich, 1971).

16. Marshall McLuhan, Understanding Media: The Extensions of Man (New York: Signet Books, 1964).

17. See American Political Science Association, Program, 64th Annual Meeting, September 3-7, 1968, Panel 16-Hl, p. 39.

18. A useful place to begin this survey was a bibliography published by the National Association of Broadcasters, Television Information Office, Television and Politics—A Bibliography (New York, 1964).

19. In addition to books referred to above, several periodicals were useful. The major trade publication of the broadcast industry was a weekly, Broadcasting. Other periodicals with good coverage of programming matters included a monthly, Television; the newspaper of the entertainment industry, Variety; the Columbia Journalism Review; the Television Quarterly; the Journal of Broadcasting; and the Alfred I. DuPont-Columbia University broadcast surveys, an annual first published in 1969.

20. The FCC reported that in August 1965 the percentage was 33.8 percent and that by June 1967 it had increased to 42.1 percent, using Census Bureau statistics. See 33rd Annual Report, Fiscal Year 1967, U.S. Federal Communications Commission (Washington, D.C., 1968), p. 38.

21. 36th Annual Report, Fiscal Year 1970, U.S. Federal Communications Commission (Washington, D.C., 1971), p. 3.

22. See "In the Matter of Amendment of Section 73.636(a) of the Commission's Rules Relating to Multiple Ownership to Television Broadcast Stations," U.S. Federal Communications Commission, FCC 65-537, Docket 16068, June 21, 1965, p. 1612.

CHAPTER 2

1. See transcript of Agnew's speech in Marvin Barrett, ed., Survey of Broadcast Journalism 1969-70 (New York: Grosset & Dunlap, 1970), p. 131.

2. American Research Bureau and Television Digest, Inc., Television Factbook, No. 41 (1971-72 ed.; 2 vols.; Washington, D.C.). Data for the period 1966-67 were derived from American Research Bureau and Television Digest, Inc., Television Factbook, No. 37 (1967 ed.; 2 vols.; Washington, D.C., 1967).

3. Television Factbook, No. 41, II, 4b ff.

4. See, for example, "Notice of Proposed Rule Making and Memorandum, Opinion and Order Proposing Amendment of Section 73.636(a) of the Commission's Rules Relating to Multiple Ownership of Television Broadcast Stations," U.S. Federal Communications Commission, Docket No. 18110, August 1, 1968. There ARB rankings are referred to as the best ones available.

5. See Frank Wolf, "Some Determinants of Public Affairs Programming on Commercial Television in the United States" (unpublished Ph.D. dissertation, Columbia University, 1971).

6. The extent to which newspapers owned television stations in the smaller markets with one or two stations was a recurring concern to the FCC. Frequently in these markets the one or two stations were owned by one or two papers published in the same community. In November 1967 the FCC compiled data on the extent to which newspapers owned television stations. In the country as a whole it was found that 25 percent of all the commercial stations, both UHF and VHF, were owned by newspapers, and these figures excluded the 15 network-owned and -operated stations. This trend was even more marked in the larger markets. Excluding the three largest markets (where the three affiliates were all network-owned and -operated stations), 35 percent of the stations in the top 25 markets were owned by newspapers. For more detailed data, see Statistical Material on Newspaper-Broadcast Joint Interests as of November, 1967, U.S. Federal Communications Commission, prepared for the Antitrust and Monopoly Subcommittee of the Committee on the Judiciary, U.S. Senate, (Washington, D.C., 1968), particularly Tables 6 and 13.

Mindful of this trend, the FCC proposed on March 25, 1970, new rules that would limit the holdings of mass communications media in any market to one or more daily newspapers, or one television broadcast station, or one AM-FM combination. The proposed rule also involved provisions for the divestiture of holdings within five years of its effectiveness. See 36th Annual Report, Fiscal Year 1970, U.S. Federal Communications Commission (Washington, D.C., 1971), pp. 35-36.

7. Harry J. Skornia, Television and Society: An Inquest and Agenda for Improvement (New York: McGraw-Hill, 1965), pp. 19-20.

8. Cf. Warren Breed, "Social Control in the News Room: A Functional Analysis," Social Forces, XXXIII (May 1955), 326-35.

9. For a more professional and technical discussion of this general point, see Amitai Etzioni, Modern Organizations (Englewood Cliffs, N.J.: Prentice-Hall, 1964), chs. 2, 6, 7, and 10.

10. See Broadcasting, XXV, 5, (July 29, 1968), 9.

11. See New York Times, March 21, 1969, p. 94.

12. Interview with FCC Commissioner Nicholas Johnson, Washington, D.C., 1969.

13. See Mark Lane, A Citizen's Dissent: Mark Lane Replies (New York: Holt, Rinehart & Winston, 1968), p. 28.

14. See Victor S. Navasky, "One Man's Doubt," New York Times, July 14, 1968, Book Review Section, p. 32. (Review of Mark Lane's A Citizen's Dissent.)

15. See Fred W. Friendly, Due to Circumstances Beyond Our Control . . . (New York: Random House, 1967); and Robert MacNeil, The People Machine: The Influence of Television on American Politics (New York: Harper & Row, 1968).

16. Friendly, Due to Circumstances Beyond Our Control . . ., pp. 132 and 208-9.

17. MacNeil, The People Machine, p. 63.

18. Ibid., p. 64.

19. United Research, Inc., The Implications of Limiting Multiple Ownership of Television Stations, Prepared for the Council for Television Development (2 vols.; Cambridge, Mass., 1966), Vol. I; sec. 2, par. 8; sec. 8, par. 12; and sec. 8, par. 19; respectively.

20. "In the Matter of Applications by American Broadcasting Companies, Inc. . . . ," U.S. Federal Communications Commission, FCC 66-1186 and 92762, Docket No, 16828, December 21, 1966, p. 14, par. 30. (Majority Opinion.)

CHAPTER 3

1. See United Research, Inc., The Implications of Limiting Multiple Ownership of Television Stations, Prepared for the Council for Television Development (2 vols.; Cambridge, Mass., 1966), Vol. I, sec. 8, par. 29.

2. Quoted from "Sample Form of NBC Affiliation Contract," made available by NBC in August 1968, p. 2, clause 4.

3. See Columbia Journalism Review, VI, 4 (Spring 1967), 3.

4. New York Times, January 10, 1958, p. 47.

5. Figures provided directly by CBS.

6. Figures supplied by NBC's Audience Measurement Department.

7. Jack Gould, New York Times, January 10, 1958, p. 47.

CHAPTER 4

1. 36th Annual Report, Fiscal Year 1970, U.S. Federal Communications Commission (Washington, D.C., 1971), p. 31.

2. See William K. Jones, "Licensing of Major Broadcast Facilities by the Federal Communications Commission" (unpublished paper prepared for the Administrative Conference of the United States, Committee on Licenses and Authorizations, Columbia University School of Law, September 1962), pp. 174-76.

    3. Former FCC Chairman Newton N. Minow was, of course, particularly adept in the use of his position to mobilize others to seek changes in broadcast programming. More recently, Commissioner Nicholas Johnson made particular use of his position to publish critical views of the industry's programming. See, for example, Nicholas Johnson, "The Media Barons and the Public Interest. An FCC Commissioner's Warning," Atlantic, CCXXI, 6 (June 1968), 43-51; and Nicholas Johnson, How to Talk Back to Your Television Set (Boston: Atlantic-Little, Brown, 1969). Johnson had also used television itself as a platform for his views, making occasional appearances on late-night "talk shows," such as ABC's "Dick Cavett Show."

    4. Testimony of E. William Henry, Chairman of the FCC, on July 15, 1963, in U.S. Congress, House, Committee on Interstate and Foreign Commerce, Broadcast Editorializing Practices, Hearings, before a subcommittee of the Committee on Interstate and Foreign Commerce, House of Representatives, 88th Cong., 1st sess., 1963. p. 87.

    5. Quoted in Television Network Program Procurement, U.S. Federal Communications Commission, Office of Network Study, Second Interim Report, Part I (Washington, D.C., 1962), pp. 269-70. See also Roscoe L. Barrow, "The Attainment of Balanced Program Service in Television," Virginia Law Review, LII, 4 (May 1966), 633-66.

    6. Television Network Program Procurement, Second Interim Report, Part I, p. 168.

    7. See FCC Form 301, p. 1, secs. IV-V. According to the FCC, "news programs" include "reports dealing with current local, national, and international events, including weather and stock market reports; and when an integral part of a news program, commentary, analysis, and sport news." (See p. 8, secs. IV-V, item [c].) "Public affairs" programs include "talks, commentaries, discussions, speeches, editorials, political programs primarily concerning local, national, and international public affairs." (See p. 8, sec. IV-B, item [d].) In this study an effort was made to exclude sports and weather reports where the amount of minutes devoted to them could be ascertained.

    8. See Broadcasting, LXXIII, 12 (September 18, 1967), 73.

    9. See New York Times, January 24, 1966, p. 95.

    10. See New York Times, June 3, 1968, p. 53.

    11. See New York Times, February 22, 1971, p. 59.

    12. Bernard Schwartz, The Professor and the Commissions (New York: Alfred A. Knopf, 1959), pp. 76-77.

    13. Harry J. Levin, Broadcast Regulation and Joint Ownership of Media (New York: New York University Press, 1960), p. 174.

    14. "In the Matter of Applications by American Broadcasting Companies, Inc. . . . ," U.S. Federal Communications Commission,

FCC 66-1186 and 92762, Docket No. 16828, December 21, 1966, p. 19, par. 40. (Memorandum, Opinion, and Order.)

15. See Broadcasting, LXXIV, 2 (January 8, 1968), editorial; and New York Times, January 2, 1968, p. 1.

16. See 32nd Annual Report, Fiscal Year 1966, U.S. Federal Communications Commission (Washington, D.C., 1967), p. 95.

17. Television, XXIV, 8 (August 1967), 92. (Editorial.)

18. Broadcasting, LXXIII, 13 (September 25, 1967), 60.

19. New York Times, February 10, 1968, p. 67.

20. Bryce Rucker, The First Freedom (Carbondale: Southern Illinois University Press, 1968), p. 237. Rucker adds that the percentage was fairly stable throughout the 1960s and that most of the reduction took place prior to 1960. This change resulted largely from the policy of giving preference, all other matters being equal, to nonnewspaper transfers and new license applicants.

21. See 36th Annual Report, Fiscal Year 1970, pp. 35-37.

22. Ibid.

23. Anthony Lewis, New York Times, December 6, 1959, sec. iv, p. 9.

24. Ibid.

25. 36th Annual Report, Fiscal Year 1970, p. 15.

26. James M. Landis, Report on the Regulatory Agencies to the President-Elect (Washington, D.C., December, 1960), p. 53.

27. Ibid., p. 71.

28. Newton N. Minow, Equal Time: the Private Broadcaster and the Public Interest, ed. Lawrence Laurent (New York: Atheneum, 1964), p. 7.

29. Marver H. Bernstein, Regulating Business by Independent Commission (Princeton: Princeton University Press. 1955).

30. Ibid., p. 90.

31. Ibid., pp. 86-90.

32. Ibid., p. 90.

33. 36th Annual Report, Fiscal Year 1970, p. 32.

34. For details on the NAB budget and membership see Broadcasting, LXXIII, 1 (July 3, 1967), 32. See also U.S., Congress, House, Committee on Interstate and Foreign Commerce, Public Television Act of 1967, Hearings, before a subcommittee of the Committee on Interstate and Foreign Commerce, House of Representatives, 90 th Cong., 1st sess.,1967, p. 715.

35. Leonard Zeidenberg, "Is the FCC Obsolete?," Television, XXIII, 10 (October 1966), 27.

36. Nan Robertson, New York Times, August 1, 1965, p. 63.

37. Dave Berkman, "A Modest Proposal: Abolishing the FCC," Columbia Journalism Review, IV, 3 (Fall 1965), 34.

38. Lawrence Laurent, in Minow, Equal Time, p. 46.

39. Broadcasting, LVIII, 77 (February 15, 1960), 88 and 91.

40. Columbia Journalism Review, IV, 3 (Fall 1965), 38.

41. John Gardiner, "The New and Ominous Mood of Capitol Hill," Television, XXIV, 6 (June 1967), 55.

42. Stan Opotowsky, TV: The Big Picture (New York: E. P. Dutton, 1961), p. 102.

43. Drew Pearson and Jack Anderson, "Television's 'Ethics,'" New York Post, July 26, 1968, p. 38. It should be noted that the second point above was obviously not a verifiable statement in that form although its basic assertion that the NAB was extremely well organized was, obviously, well taken.

44. Berkman, "A Modest Proposal," p. 34.

45. Schwartz, The Professor and the Commissions, pp. 139-40.

46. Charles E. Doyle, "Newton Minow in the 'Vast Wasteland': Attempts at Innovation in a 'Mature' Agency" (unpublished doctoral seminar paper prepared for Government G9241x-G9242y, Columbia University, November 23, 1966).

47. Ibid., pp. 50 ff.

48. Ibid., pp. 145-46.

49. Ibid., pp. 147-48.

50. Television, XXII, 8 (August 1965), 126. (Editorial.)

51. Robert MacNeil, The People Machine: The Influence of Television on American Politics (New York: Harper & Row, 1968),

52. Ibid.

CHAPTER 5

1. "In the Matter of Editorializing by Broadcast Licensees," U.S. Federal Communications Commission, FCC 49-422, Docket No. 8516, June 1, 1949.

2. National Association of Broadcasters, "Editorializing on the Air" (Washington, D.C., 1963), p. 7. (Pamphlet.)

3. New York Times, May 2, 1959, p. 49.

4. New York Times, June 22, 1966, p. 95.

5. George W. Darlington, "The Many Worlds of Local TV," Television, XXIV, 8 (August 1967), 33 ff. The percentages cited above were extracted from a chart on p. 41 of this article.

6. National Association of Broadcasters, "Radio and Television Editorializing" (Washington, D.C., 1967), p. 7. (Pamphlet.) For an account of the major findings of the study, see Broadcasting, LXXIII, 6 (August 7, 1967), 58 ff.

7. "Radio and Television Editorializing," p. 7.

8. See "In the Matter of Editorializing by Broadcast Licensees." In the earlier decision in 1938 involving the Mayflower Broadcasting Company of Boston, whose radio station had endorsed a political

candidate, the FCC had said, "Radio can serve as an instrument of democracy only when devoted to the communication of information and the exchange of ideas fairly and objectively presented. A truly free radio cannot be used to advocate the causes of the licensee. It cannot be used to support the candidacies of his friends. It cannot be devoted to the support of principles he happens to regard most favorably. In brief, the broadcaster cannot be an advocate." U.S., Congress, House, Committee on Interstate and Foreign Commerce, Broadcast Editorial Practices, Hearings, before a subcommittee of the Committee on Interstate and Foreign Commerce, House of Representatives, 88th Cong., 1st sess., 1963, p. 151.

9. See New York Times, August 27, 1954, p. 8.

10. See the following sources for more details: New York Times, January 10, 1958, p. 47; New York Times, July 22, 1959, p. 57; New York Times, June 1, 1961, p. 55; and Mary Ann Cusack, "Editorializing in Broadcasting" (unpublished Ph.D. dissertation, Wayne State University, 1960), pp. 57 ff.

11. Harry J. Skornia, Television and Society: An Inquest and Agenda for Improvement (New York: McGraw-Hill, 1965), pp. 62-63.

12. William A. Wood, Electronic Journalism (New York: Columbia University Press, 1967), p. 62.

13. John C. Doerfer, "Editorially Speaking—A Time for Action," Broadcasting, LIV, 19 (May 5, 1958), 40-41.

14. New York Times, May 16, 1959, p. 54.

15. New York Times, May 4, 1959, p. 29.

16. "Report and Statement of Policy Re: Commission En Banc Programming Inquiry," U.S. Federal Communications Commission, FCC 60-970, Docket No. 12103 July 29, 1960.

17. See ibid.; or Responsibility for Broadcast Matter, U.S. Federal Communications Commission, Office of Network Study, Interim Report (Washington, D.C., 1960), p. 213.

18. See Minow's March 1, 1962, speech before the Public Affairs Editorializing Conference of the NAB; see also Charles E. Doyle, "Newton Minow in the 'Vast Wasteland': Attempts at Innovation in a 'Mature' Agency" (unpublished doctoral seminar paper prepared for Government G9241x-G9242y, Columbia University, November 23, 1966), pp. 124 ff.

19. Doyle, "Newton Minow in the 'Vast Wasteland," pp. 146-47.

20. Laurence Laurent in Newton N. Minow, Equal Time: The Private Broadcaster and the Public Interest, ed. Lawrence Laurent (New York: Atheneum, 1964), pp. 114-15.

21. "Radio and Television Editorializing," especially p. 4.

22. Ibid., p. 12.

23. Ibid., p. 11.

24. See the account of NAB President Harold E. Fellows' speech to the NAB in Chicago in 1959, in New York Times, May 16, 1959, p. 54.

25. "Radio and Television Editorializing," p. 10.

26. Ibid., p. 2.

CHAPTER 6

1. See "In the Matter of Applications by American Broadcasting Companies, Inc. . . . ," U.S. Federal Communications Commission, FCC 66-1186 and 92762, Docket No. 16828, December 21, 1966, p. 36. (Dissenting Opinion of Commissioner Nicholas Johnson.) (This was the case involving the proposed merger of IT&T with ABC.)

2. Mary Ann Cusack, "Editorializing in Broadcasting," (unpublished Ph.D. dissertation, Wayne State University, 1960), p. 16.

3. National Labor Relations Board, "Decision and Order," Case No. 10-CC-452, Chattanooga, Tenn., Local No. 662, Radio and TV Engineers, IBEW, AFL-CIO v. Middle South Broadcasting Company, Radio Station WAGC, 133 NLRB No. 165, as quoted in Harry J. Skornia, Television and Society: An Inquest and Agenda for Improvement (New York: McGraw-Hill, 1965), p. 100.

4. Skornia, Television and Society, p. 99.

5. The complexities of advertising and commercials on television are well explained in a FCC study. See Television Network Program Procurement, U.S. Federal Communications Commission, Office of Network Study, Second Interim Report, Part II (Washington, D.C., 1965).

6. See 36th Annual Report, Fiscal Year 1970, U.S. Federal Communications Commission, (Washington, D.C., 1971), p. 153, for further statistical detail.

7. See Television Network Program Procurement, Second Interim Report, Part II, pp. 45-48, for a discussion of these points. See also Chapter 3, above, for further discussion.

8. See ibid., p. 48.

9. Quoted in Newton N. Minow, Equal Time: The Private Broadcaster and the Public Interest, ed. Lawrence Laurent (New York: Atheneum, 1964), p. 18.

10. See Television Network Program Procurement, U.S. Federal Communications Commission, Office of Network Study, Second Interim Report, Part I (Washington, D.C., 1962), especially pp. 363-94.

11. See New York Times, March 7, 1962, p. 43.

12. Dirk Petersmann, "Anatomy of a Sponsor" (unpublished paper prepared at Columbia University School of Journalism, May 12, 1968), p. 21.

13. Ibid., pp. 13-14.

14. These Nielsen ratings were reported in the New York Times, October 16, 1966, sec. ii, p. 17.

15. New York Times, January 24, 1962, p. 67.

16. New York Times, September 12, 1967, p. 94.

17. Broadcasting, LXXVI, 2 (January 13, 1969), 49.

18. Skornia, Television and Society, p. 125.

19. See Television, XXIV, 3 (March 1967), 28-29, for a complete list of ratings and audience shares for the 1966-67 season.

20. See Loomis C. Irish, "Monday Memo," Broadcasting, LXXIII, 20 (November 13, 1967), 18.

21. See New York Times, September 12, 1967, p. 94.

22. See New York Times, June 9, 1965, p. 74.

23. William A. Wood, Electronic Journalism (New York: Columbia University Press, 1967), p. 5.

24. See the account of Salant's speech before the Advertising Club of Hartford in the New York Times, April 22, 1961, p. 51.

25. See Albert R. Kroeger, "News, News, News, News," Television, XXII, 2 (February 1965), 28 ff.

26. Responsibility for Broadcast Matter, U.S. Federal Communications Commission, Office of Network Study, Interim Report (Washington, D.C., 1960), p. 327.

27. See Roscoe L. Barrow, "The Attainment of Balanced Program Service in Television," Virginia Law Review, LII, 4 (May 1966), 633-66, especially 662 ff.

28. See ibid., p. 636.

29. See Responsibility for Broadcast Matter, pp. 638-39.

30. New York Times, July 16, 1967, p. 55.

31. Paul F. Lazarsfeld and Robert K. Merton, "Mass Communication, Popular Taste and Organized Social Action," in Wilbur Schramm, ed., Mass Communications (Urbana: University of Illinois Press, 1960), p. 503.

32. Responsibility for Broadcast Matter, p. 390.

33. See Broadcasting, LXXV, 26 (December 23, 1968), 46.

34. Part of testimony in John Henry Faulk v. AWARE, Vincent Hartnett, and Laurence Johnson, quoted in John Henry Faulk, Fear on Trial (New York: Simon and Schuster, 1964), p. 239.

35. Broadcasting, LXXV, 26 (December 23, 1968), 43.

36. Ibid.

37. For an excellent account of television's treatment of the question of smoking and health, see the Columbia Journalism Review, II, 2 (Summer 1963), 6-12.

38. See "Murrow's Indictment of Broadcasting," First publication of the text of a speech before the Chicago convention of the Radio and Television News Directors Association on October 15, 1958, in the

Columbia Journalism Review, IV, 2 (Summer 1965), 27-32; this
quotation can be found on pp. 27-28.

39. Wood, Electronic Journalism, p. 129.

40. Petersmann, "Anatomy of a Sponsor," p. 2.

41. Responsibility for Broadcast Matter, p. 226.

42. Ibid., p. 324.

43. Testimony of William R. McAndrew, Executive Vice President, NBC News, in Television Network Program Procurement,
Second Interim Report, Part II, p. 345.

44. Petersmann, "Anatomy of a Sponsor," p. 12.

45. New York Times, May 4, 1967, p. 79, and May 6, 1967, p.
63.

46. Columbia Journalism Review, V, 4 (Winter 1966-67), 3-4.

47. Jack Gould, New York Times, June 17, 1966, p. 21.

48. New York Times, June 16, 1966, p. 95, and June 17, 1966,
p. 90.

49. New York Times, June 30, 1966, p. 79.

50. New York Times, October 28, 1966, p. 83.

51. Broadcasting, LXX, (January 3, 1966), 124; and New York
Times, December 25, 1965, p. 29, and January 15, 1966, p. 55.

52. Columbia Journalism Review, V, 2 (Summer 1966), 3.

53. Variety, July 29, 1964; Columbia Journalism Review, III, 3
(Fall 1964), 3; and Columbia Journalism Review, IV, 1 (Spring 1965),
53.

54. New York Times, November 17, 1962, p. 49, November 20,
1962, p. 24, and December 7, 1962, p. 38; Columbia Journalism Review,
I, 4 (Winter 1963), 2; and Television, XXIII, 12 (December 1966), 9.

55. New York Times, October 5, 1962, p. 67.

56. New York Times, April 20, 1962, p. 52.

57. New York Times, September 26, 1961, p. 78.

58. New York Times, October 8, 1960, p. 46; October 9, 1960,
p. 34; and October 11, 1960, p. 15.

59. Minow, Equal Time, pp. 14 and 16-17, respectively.

60. Jack Gould, New York Times, June 17, 1966, p. 91.

61. Skornia, Television and Society, p. 59.

62. Television Network Program Procurement, Second Interim
Report, Part I, p. 59.

63. The results of this survey were published in Broadcasting,
LXXIII, 5 (July 31, 1967), 41.

64. Television Network Program Procurement, Second Interim
Report, Part I, pp. 42-43.

65. Ibid., p. 55.

66. 36th Annual Report, Fiscal Year 1970, p. 159.

67. Ibid., p. 152.

68. Ibid., pp. 166-67.

69. George W. Darlington, "The Many Worlds of Local TV," Television, XXIV, 8 (August 1967), 42.

70. Wood, Electronic Journalism, p. 42.

71. See Kroeger, "News, News, News, News."

72. For documentation of these assertions see National Association of Broadcasters, "Radio and Television Editorializing" (Washington, D.C., 1967), pp. 10 ff. (Pamphlet.)

CHAPTER 7

1. On February 19, 1971, the FCC made public a potentially revolutionary decision (proposed rule-making) to require stations in the 50 largest markets to devote at least 15 percent of their programming to locally originated materials and at least 15 percent to news and public affairs programming. By a vote of five to two, the FCC for the first time displayed a willingness to regulate programming in a direct way. This rule may tend to increase the amount of public affairs programming shown by some top 50 market stations, although many such stations were already including that amount of public affairs programming in their regular schedules. See New York Times, February 22, 1971, p. 59.

2. See Theodore Lowi, The End of Liberalism—Ideology, Policy, and the Crisis of Public Authority (New York: W. W. Norton, 1969), especially pp. 29-54 and 299-303.

3. Nicholas Johnson, "The Media Barons and the Public Interest—An FCC Commissioner's Warning," Atlantic, CCXXI, 6 (June 1968), 43-51.

4. See the report of the Carnegie Commission on Educational Television, Public Television: A Program for Action (New York: Bantam Books, 1967).

5. Elie Abel, "An Inside Look at the Media by a Critical Eye," Washington Post, February 24, 1971, p. B5. (A Review of Ben H. Bagdikian, The Information Machines: Their Impact on Men and the Media [New York: Harper & Row 1971].)

6. Robert A. Dahl, "The American Oppositions: Affirmation and Denial," in Robert A. Dahl, ed., Political Oppositions in Western Democracies (New Haven: Yale University Press, 1966), pp. 47-48.

7. See Edward W. Barrett, "One Juror's Observations," in Marvin Barrett, ed., Survey of Broadcast Journalism 1969-70 (New York: Grosset & Dunlap, 1970), pp. 92-96, for an account of this study.

THE CONSTRUCTION OF
THE STATION SAMPLE

The original sample of stations was drawn from data accurate as of January 1, 1967. This was done as follows. For each class of station (classes according to affiliation statuses and ownership types) at least one-sixth of the total membership of the class was included in the sample. (See Appendix Table 1.)

APPENDIX TABLE 1

Nature of Sample by Station Type

Station Type	Total	Number in Sample	%
Network-owned stations	15	6	40.0
Single-owner affiliates	36	7	16.7
Group-owned affiliates	86	14	16.5
Group-owned nonaffiliates	15	6	40.0
Single-owner nonaffiliates	3	3	100.0
Total Top 50 Stations	155	36	23.5
Nonnetwork-owned affiliates	122	21	17.2
Unaffiliated stations	18	9	50.0
Separate markets	50	34	68.0

In the cases where markedly more than 16 percent of the members of a class were included in the sample, the small absolute number of such stations in existence accounts for the seeming imbalance. Six stations of each class seemed an absolute minimum number of representatives for even a modest attempt at generalization.*

---

*Appendix Table 1 shows that certain "classes" should perhaps not have been treated as classes at all. For example, there were only three single-owner nonaffiliates in the 155 stations in the 50 largest

To achieve a fair distribution of markets of various ranks, stations were selected from among the smallest and largest of the 50 markets. But the sample nevertheless slightly overrepresented stations in the larger markets. Ideally, the mean of market ranks in the sample would be 25 (midway between 1 and 50), but the actual mean was 21.7. This inclusion of more stations from markets with ranks above 25 than stations from markets ranked 26 through 50 reflected the character of two classes of stations—the network-owned and -operated stations and those stations that were not affiliated with any networks. The network-owned and -operated stations were all located in the very largest markets—in New York, Los Angeles, Chicago, Philadelphia, Detroit, San Francisco, Cleveland, Washington, and St. Louis. These markets were among the 13 largest ones in 1967. So too, 11 out of the 18 unaffiliated stations were located in these very large markets.

If this overrepresentation of stations from the larger markets was to have been eliminated, it would have meant the virtual exclusion of stations in the remaining classes located in these largest markets. Had stations located in these largest markets not been included in the sample of other classes (for example, group-owned affiliates), there could have been no assurance whatever that variations between programming on various stations had to do with ownership structure rather than with market size. Therefore, the overrepresentation of stations from the larger markets was accepted as a necessary evil. The ranks of markets in the sample resulted then in the following distribution:

Ranks	1-10	10 stations
Ranks	11-20	9 stations
Ranks	21-30	6 stations
Ranks	31-40	6 stations
Ranks	41-50	5 stations

---

markets. This fact implies that either the 155 stations were too few to represent the various classes adequately and that the total population should have been larger or that classes such as single-owner nonaffiliates should not have been identified.

In fact, the commercial VHF stations in markets with ranks from 51 to 223 were, with two exceptions, group-owned or single-owner affiliates. That is, the small classes were almost exclusively located in the 50 largest markets—that is, among the 155 stations in the population. Especially in the case of the unaffiliated stations owned by parties with no other television interests, the class should be thought of merely as three unusual stations and not as a group representing a larger number of such entities.

In addition to the criterion of market rank, the geographical location of markets was another factor to be balanced in the sample. There were no top 50 markets located in the prairie states and only one in the Rocky Mountain states. Thus, the stations in these areas were absent from the sample. The largest number of major markets was in the Mid-West, followed by the South and the Middle Atlantic states, and finally by the border states, the West, and New England. An attempt was made to have the proportions in the population as a whole reproduced in the sample. This was largerly achieved, save for a slight underrepresentation of stations in the border states. (See Appendix Table 2.)

Not only was it necessary to balance the geographical distribution of the sample as a whole; but it was also important that the affiliates of each of the three networks in the sample represent a fair cross section of the markets in which the networks had affiliates. For example, had the ABC affiliates been drawn largely from the northeast and had the ABC stations then been found to pursue markedly different policies with regard to public affairs programming than those of CBS and NBC affiliates, then it would have been impossible to distinguish between what might have been regional variations rather than differences among the three groups of affiliates. The network stations in the sample, including both owned-and-operated stations and ordinary affiliates not owned by the networks, were as follows:

ABC	CBS	NBC
San Francisco	Philadelphia	Chicago
Detroit	St. Louis	Huntington-Charleston
Hartford	Charlotte	Atlanta
Tampa	Boston	Sacramento
Cincinnati	Buffalo	Syracuse
Indianapolis	Nashville	Memphis
Albany	Pittsburgh	Cleveland
Toledo	Baltimore	Lansing
Manchester	Houston	Louisville

As far as the ownership of stations in the sample was concerned, again an attempt was made to reproduce the approximate distribution of various types of owners in the total population of top 50 market stations. The owners of station groups varied in the extent of their holdings—some owned five top 50 VHF stations; others owned only one (they owned additional stations in markets outside the top 50.)

An effort was made to include group owners with different numbers of top 50 stations in their possession. No more than one station represented each owner in the sample. The following is a list of group owners of top 50 VHF stations, at least one of which was in

Number and Location of Markets

Region	Number of Markets in Top 50	Number of Markets in Sample	Location of Markets in Sample
New England	4	3	Boston Hartford-New Haven Manchester
Middle Atlantic	8	6	Philadelphia Albany-Schenectady-Troy Pittsburgh Buffalo Syracuse New York
South	9	6	Memphis Nashville Tampa-St. Petersburg Houston Atlanta Dallas-Fort Worth
Border	7	4	Louisville Baltimore Charlotte Huntington-Charleston
Mid-West	15	9	Cleveland St. Louis Detroit Lansing-Onondaga Cincinnati Indianapolis Toledo Minneapolis-St. Paul Chicago
West	5	4	San Francisco Los Angeles Sacramento-Stockton Seattle-Tacoma
Rocky Mountain	1	1	Denver
District of Columbia	1	1	Washington, D.C.
Total	50	34	

the sample. (The numbers in parentheses indicate how many groups
there were owning that number of stations in the 50 largest markets—
for example, there were 20 group owners owning only a single top 50
station.)

Owners of Five Stations (5)	Owners of Two Stations (9)
Group-W	WKY
Taft	WGN-Chicago Tribune
Storer	Corinthian
RKO-General	
Cox	Owners of One Station (20)
	Gene Autrey
Owners of Four Stations (4)	Jefferson Standard
Metromedia	Sunpapers
Capital City	Eaton
Avco	WAVE
Newhouse	

Owners of Three Stations (5)
Triangle
Chris-Craft
Scripps-Howard

It should be apparent, then, that the construction of the station
sample involved the simultaneous balancing of a number of factors.
Obviously, no attempt to collect data about public affairs programming on these sample stations was made until the sample as a whole
had been constructed.

In 1971 the validity of the generalizations originally made in
1967 was tested again. In order to do this the very same sample
stations used in 1967 were employed. This was done largely for purposes of convenience and comparability. Although there had been
some changes in the 50 markets in the intervening period—for example, St. Louis had become the 15th market rather than the 13th—the
basic configuration of stations in the 50 largest markets was almost
identical.

Likewise, there had been some minor changes in the ownership
of individual stations and of the affiliation status of individual stations,
but, again, these changes were marginal in significance. Two of the
stations in the 1967 sample were in markets that were in 1971 below
the top 50 markets (Lansing and Manchester). One NBC station in
1971 had been and ABC station in 1967. These changes explain the
slightly different character of the 1971 sample as compared with the
1967 one. For example, this is why there is a slight underrepresentation of ABC affiliates in the 1971 group.

Nonetheless, there is no reason to doubt the general accuracy of the 1971 findings. In almost every respect they were consistent with those of 1967. The major difference was that the total quantity of news and public affairs programming offered had increased substantially in the four-year period. NBC affiliates were offering comparatively more such programming in 1971 than in 1966-67 as well. But in virtually all other respects the 1967 findings were substantiated by the 1971 data.

PROBLEMS IN PROCURING THE
PROGRAM DATA

A variety of problems arose in the collection of program schedules. Obviously, the most reliable way of assembling the schedules
would have been to examine the program logs at each station's headquarters. But a small budget and limited time made this procedure
impossible. The next best source of this information was the daily
program schedules published in local newspapers. In general, the
daily newspaper schedules were found to be more accurate than were
the common weekend television supplements that often printed television program schedules for the forthcoming week.

Last-minute schedule changes were more frequently reflected
in the daily listings. Such last-minute changes were potentially important in this study, since the coverage of unanticipated public events
might well be involved. Because the regional editions of TV Guide
published schedules with the same lack of last-minute accuracy,
schedules published in daily newspapers in the cities where the stations
were located were taken as the primary source of program data.

Where daily papers published by two different organizations
were available within the same market, both schedules were consulted.
When program schedules had been assembled from these sources, they
were then checked against the schedules that appeared in the various
regional editions of TV Guide. For each station, then, there were at
least two independent sources of program information. In some cases,
there were as many as four.

There were, nonetheless, very difficult problems to resolve.
For example, the published schedules, unlike program logs, did not
show how much time was devoted to commercial messages. Although
there were generally observed maxima in this regard, the variation
could be quite considerable. Furthermore, where a station presented,
for example, a weeknight early evening news program from 6:00 p.m.
to 7:00 p.m., it was rarely clear from the published schedules how
many minutes of these broadcasts were devoted to weather and sports
reports. Where the schedules did not report this information, it was
assumed for all stations that five minutes of a 15-minute broadcast
would be devoted to nonpolitical materials (weather and sports) and
that 15 minutes of a one-hour broadcast could be expected to be of
this nature. It was assumed that 10 minutes of a 30-minute broadcast was devoted to nonnews material.

Even with these rules of thumb, there were still ambiguities. In some cases newspaper strikes in individual cities meant that for one week or part of a week in a particular market there was only one source of program information—TV Guide. In a few instances there were inconsistencies between listings in the city's two newspapers. In these cases, the evening paper was taken as authoritative because of its later deadline. But, in general, this rather elaborate method of cross-checking did facilitate the acquisition of reasonably reliable program information, with the limitations, of course, that have been mentioned.

One piece of information for each station—the percentage of each station's broadcast day that was devoted to public affairs programming of various types—proved to be elusive. Since there was no way of knowing how long each station's broadcast day was, these percentages could not be computed. Some stations operated around the clock; others signed off sometime after midnight; others began broadcasting only in midafternoon. Therefore, there was no option but to compute the total number of minutes of various types of programming and then to compare the absolute amounts. For purposes of comparison, it was arbitrarily decided that a broadcast day began at 5:00 a.m., or whenever the first program after that hour went on the air.

Despite these various difficulties, the resulting data did prove useful for general comparative purposes, although limitations were imposed by these problems. Although four weeks of programming in 1966 were used for the 1967 sample, 14 days chosen at random across the calendar year were used for 1971. Then the results for 1971 were multiplied by two in order to have figures that were comparable to the four weeks of 1966. The same procedures and rules of thumb were used for analysing both periods.

THE QUESTIONNAIRES AND
THEIR CIRCULARIZATION

Wherever possible the questionnaires were sent to the "public affairs director," if there was someone at the station with this or a comparable title. It was sometimes necessary, however, to address the questionnaire to the "news director," or even to the "program director." Some of the smaller station organizations did not even have this degree of labor division. In such cases the questionnaire was sent to the chief executive officer, whose title usually was "vice president and general manager."

In both 1967 and in 1971 two circularizations were conducted. Those stations not replying to the first communication were sent a second copy of the questionnaire. Although the results of this procedure were helpful, it was nonetheless disappointing that, whereas 78 stations replied in 1967, only 58 replies were received in 1971.

The 1967 responses were broadly representative of the entire population of top 50 stations, with stations in 44 of the 50 markets replying. In 1971 stations in 40 of the 50 markets replied. With the exception of the two small classes of stations—owned-and-operated stations and single-owner nonaffiliates—substantial representation of each ownership type was secured. A wider geographic distribution than was possible within the station samples was also obtained. The questionnaire reponses also reduced the chances that the overrepresentation of stations in larger markets in the sample would skew the overall results of the study. The following data provide additional information by ownership type about responses received:

	Total Number of Stations in Top 50 Markets, 1967	Total Number of Replies, 1967	Total Number of Replies, 1971
Owned-and-operated stations	15	5	1
Group-owned affiliates	86	47	29
Single-owner affiliates	36	18	18
Group nonaffiliates	15	7	9
Single nonaffiliates	3	1	1
Total	155	78	58

	Number of Stations in Sample, 1967	Number of Replies, 1967	Number of Replies, 1971
Owned-and-operated stations	6	3	0
Group-owned affiliates	14	9	8
Single-owner affiliates	7	4	4
Group nonaffiliates	6	4	4
Single nonaffiliates	3	1	1
Total	36	21	17

The study as a whole was then based on some data from 93 of the 155 stations in the 50 largest markets in 1967 and on data from 75 of the 158 stations in these markets in 1971. These stations were located in 48 of the 50 markets. The following data make this clearer:

	Number of Stations in Top 50 Markets, 1966-67	Number in Sample or Questionnaire Responses, or Both, 1967	Number in Sample or Questionnaire Responses, or Both, 1971
Owned-and-operated stations	15	8	7
Group-owned affiliates	86	52	35
Single-owner affiliates	36	21	19
Group nonaffiliates	15	9	11
Single nonaffiliates	3	3	3
Total	155	93	75

Appendix Tables 3 and 4 show the sources of questionnaire responses, market by market, and the number of stations in each market responding. Copies of the questionnaires sent in 1967 and 1971 can be found below. It seems reasonably clear that the smaller response in 1971 is because the 1971 questionnaire sought direct information about the profitability of stations, a highly sensitive matter. Only one of the 58 respondents gave any information at all in this regard, and several respondents indicated their irritation at this request for information.

APPENDIX TABLE 3

Stations Responding to Questionnaire, by Market,
Arranged in Order of Market Rank, 1967

Market	Number of Stations Responding	Market	Number of Stations Responding
New York	2	Dayton	0
Los Angeles	2	Sacramento	3
Chicago	1	Columbus	2
Philadelphia	2	Harrisburg	0
Boston	0	Charlotte	1
Detroit	3	Syracuse	2
San Francisco	1	Tampa	1
Cleveland	2	Wheeling	1
Pittsburgh	2	Portland	1
Washington, D.C.	1	Memphis	3
Baltimore	2	Grand Rapids	1
Providence	1	Toledo	2
St. Louis	1	Johnstown	0
Hartford	1	Birmingham	2
Dallas	4	Albany	2
Cincinnati	2	Denver	2
Minneapolis	2	Greenville	2
Indianapolis	4	New Orleans	3
Atlanta	1	Nashville	3
Miami	2	Flint	1
Seattle	1	Huntington	2
Buffalo	0	Greensboro	1
Kansas City	2	Lansing	1
Milwaukee	2	Manchester	0
Houston	1	Louisville	1

APPENDIX TABLE 4

Stations Responding to Questionnaire, by Market,
Arranged in Order of Market Rank, 1971

Market	Number of Stations Responding	Market	Number of Stations Responding
New York	2	Milwaukee	1
Los Angeles	2	Buffalo	0
Chicago	0	Dayton	1
Philadelphia	1	Columbus	1
Boston	2	Portland	1
Detroit	1	Tampa	1
San Francisco	1	Charlotte	1
Cleveland	1	Memphis	0
Washington, D.C.	1	Greenville	2
Pittsburgh	2	Johnstown	2
Miami	2	Birmingham	2
Baltimore	0	Nashville	1
Dallas	1	Denver	2
Hartford	0	Toledo	0
St. Louis	2	Harrisburg	0
Cincinnati	2	Grand Rapids	2
Minneapolis	3	Syracuse	0
Atlanta	1	Wheeling	1
Providence	0	Greensboro	0
Indianapolis	2	Albany	1
New Orleans	2	Flint	1
Houston	2	Louisville	0
Sacramento	1	Huntington	1
Seattle	2	Raleigh	2
Kansas City	1	Oklahoma City	2

QUESTIONNAIRE (1967)

Call Letters of Station _____

Location of Station _____

Network Affiliation, if any _____

1. Why does your station present public affairs programming?
   (Please make a short statement.)
2. Do you regard public affairs programming generally as a basically
   unprofitable activity?
3. What percentage of air time in a typical broadcast week on your
   station would you estimate is devoted to public affairs programming?
   (Circle one.)
   (a) 5% or less   (c) 10-15%   (e) more than 20%
   (b) 5-10%   (d) 15-20%
4. What percentage of your public affairs programming is devoted to
   programs other than news broadcasts? (Circle one.)
   (a) 10% or less   (c) 20-30%   (e) more than 50%
   (b) 10-20%   (d) 30-50%
   IF YOUR STATION IS NOT AFFILIATED WITH A NATIONAL
   NETWORK, PLEASE PROCEED TO QUESTION # 7.
5. Have you from time to time during the last several years decided
   not to carry network public affairs programs (either series or
   individual programs) of one kind or another?
                   Yes _____   No _____
6. If you answered question # 5 with a "yes," (i.e., you have sometimes
   NOT carried network public affairs programs) how would you
   characterize the reasons for these actions? (Circle one.)
   (a) concern with program content   (b) sponsor-related
                                             concerns
   (c) reluctance to forego larger audiences available for alternative
       programs
   (d) all of these   (e) (other) _____
7. Does your station currently broadcast editorials?
                   Yes _____   No _____
8. Was your station broadcasting editorials during February, May,
   August, and November, 1966?
                   Yes_____   No _____
9. If you are currently broadcasting editorials, or you were broadcasting editorials during the 1966 months mentioned above, how
   many times on average were editorials presented per week? At
   what time or times? On what days (weekdays, Saturdays, or
   Sundays)?

10. If you were broadcasting editorials during 1966, or are at present broadcasting editorials, how would you characterize the topics of these editorials? (Circle one.)
    (a) more on local and regional issues than on national matters
    (b) more on national matters than on local and regional issues
    (c) evenly distributed between local/regional and national issues

11. In your opinion does the Federal Communications Commission have an impact upon your decisions with regard to public affairs programming?

    Yes _____   No _____
    If "yes," in what way? _____

    _____

12. Have the FCC's recommendations with respect to broadcast editorializing had any impact upon your policies in this regard?

    Yes _____   No _____

13. Would you characterize your station as willing to allow politically controversial ideas or personnages to appear in your programs?

    Yes _____   No _____
    If "yes," could you give a few examples of such controversial persons or ideas? _____

    _____

    _____

14. Does your station face a VHF educational station in the same market?

    Yes _____   No _____

15. If you answered question # 14 with a "yes," how would you characterize the impact of the presence of such a competing station upon your public affairs programming policies? (Circle one or more.)
    (a) has little or no impact
    (b) induces you to engage in some MORE EXTENSIVE PUBLIC AFFAIRS PROGRAMMING to compete for audiences interested in such programs
    (c) induced you to engage in somewhat LESS EXTENSIVE PUBLIC AFFAIRS PROGRAMMING because the educational station presents a fair amount of such programs, thus sharing the responsibility of keeping the public informed
    (d) induces you to engage in somewhat MORE EXTENSIVE PRIME TIME PUBLIC AFFAIRS PROGRAMMING
    (e) induces you to engage in somewhat LESS EXTENSIVE PRIME TIME PUBLIC AFFAIRS PROGRAMMING
    (f) (other) _____

ANY ADDITIONAL COMMENTS YOU MAY WISH TO MAKE ABOUT THIS QUESTIONNAIRE OR ITS CONCERNS WILL BE MOST WELCOME

QUESTIONNAIRE (1971)

Call Letters of Station _____

Location of Station _____

Network Affiliation, if any _____

Ownership of Station _____

Gross Revenues, last fiscal year _____

Pre-tax Profit, last fiscal year _____

1. Why does your station present news and public affairs programs?
   (Please make a short statement)
2. Do you regard news and public affairs programming generally as
   a basically unprofitable activity?
3. What percentage of air time in a typical broadcast week on your
   station would you estimate is devoted to news and public affairs
   programming? (Circle one)
   (a) 5% or less   (c) 10-15%   (e) more than 20%
   (b) 5-10%   (d) 15-20%
4. What percentage of your broadcast week is devoted to regularly
   scheduled news broadcasts?
   (a) 5% or less   (c) 10-15%   (e) more than 20%
   (b) 5-10%   (d) 15-20%

IF YOUR STATION IS NOT AFFILIATED WITH A NATIONAL NET-
WORK PLEASE PROCEED TO QUESTION NO. 7

5. Have you from time to time during the last several years decided
   not to carry network news or public affairs programs (either series
   or individual programs) of one kind or another?
                    Yes _____   No _____
6. If you answered question No. 5 with a "yes," for what reason or
   reasons did you not carry the network programming? (Make
   brief statement)
7. Does your station currently broadcast editorials?
                    Yes _____   No _____
8. If you do broadcast editorials, how are they scheduled?
   (a) on a regular basis (how many times per week? _____)
   (b) from time to time (how often per month? _____)
9. If you do not now broadcast editorials, do you intend to begin doing
   so within the next six months?
                    Yes _____   No _____

10. Was your station editorializing in 1966?
    Yes _____   No _____

11. If you do now or have in the past editorialized, how would you
    characterize the topics of these editorials? (Circle one)
    (a) more on local and regional issues than on national matters
    (b) more on national matters than on local and regional issues
    (c) evenly distributed between local/regional and national issues

12. Does the Federal Communications Commission have an impact
    upon your decisions with regard to news and public affairs pro-
    gramming?
    Yes _____   No _____
    If "yes," in what ways? _____
    _____
    _____

13. Have the FCC's recommendations with respect to broadcast
    editorializing had any impact upon your policies in this regard?
    Yes _____   No _____

14. Would you characterize your station as willing to allow politically
    controversial ideas or persons to appear in your programs?
    Yes _____   No _____
    If "yes," could you give a few examples of such controversial
    persons or ideas? _____
    _____
    _____

15. Do you believe the Nixon Administration has been attempting to
    control, censor, or "muzzle" the press to any extent? (Please
    comment)

NEWSPAPER AND PUBLISHER INTERESTS IN THE
TOP 50 MARKET TELEVISION STATIONS

Newspapers Owning Commercial VHF Television
Stations in 50 Largest Markets,
as of January 1, 1967

New York News
> WPIX,   New York
>> (Interlocking ownership with WGN-TV, Chicago, and
>> KWGN-TV, Denver.)

Triangle Publications
> WFIL-TV,   Philadelphia
> WNHC-TV,   Hartford-New Haven
> WFBG-TV,   Johnstown-Altoona
>> (Published Philadelphia Inquirer, among other news-
>> papers.)

Boston Herald-Traveler
> WHDH-TV, Boston

Detroit News
> WWJ-TV,   Detroit

San Francisco Chronicle
> KRON-TV,   San Francisco

Cox Broadcasting Corporation
> WHIO-TV,   Dayton
> WSB-TV,   Atlanta
> WSOC-TV,   Charlotte
> WIIC-TV,   Pittsburgh
> KTVU,   Oakland-San Francisco
>> (Owned Dayton News and Dayton Journal Herald,
>> Atlanta Journal, Atlanta Constitution, Miami News,
>> and other newspapers in Ohio.)

Scripps-Howard Broadcasting Company
> WEWS,   Cleveland
> WCPO-TV,   Cincinnati
> WMC-TV,   Memphis
>> (Published the following top 50 market newspapers:
>> Cleveland Press, Cincinnati Post, Cincinnati Times-
>> Star, Columbus Citizen-Journal, Pittsburgh Press,

Washington Daily News, Memphis Commercial Appeal
and Press-Scimitar, Fort Worth Press, Denver Rocky
Mountain News, Birmingham Post-Herald, Hollywood
Sun-Tatler, and one-third interest in New York World
Journal Tribune.)

The Hearst Corporation
    WBAL-TV,   Baltimore
    WISN-TV,   Milwaukee
    WTAE-TV,   Pittsburgh
       (Published the following top 50 market newspapers:
       Baltimore News-American, Los Angeles Herald-
       Examiner, San Francisco Examiner, Boston Record-
       American, Boston Sunday Advertiser, Albany Times-
       Union, Knickerbocker News, Seattle Post-Intelligencer,
       and one-third of New York World Journal Tribune.)

Washington Evening Star
    WMAL-TV,   Washington, D.C.

Newsweek, Inc.
    WTOP-TV,   Washington, D.C.
       (Published the Washington Post.)

Baltimore Sunpapers
    WMAR-TV,   Baltimore
       (Published the Baltimore Sun.)

Newhouse Broadcasting Corporation
    WSYR-TV,   Syracuse
    WAPI-TV,   Birmingham
    KTVI,   St. Louis
    KOIN-TV,   Portland (50 percent)
       (Published the following top 50 market newspapers:
       Syracuse Post Standard, Syracuse Herald Journal,
       Birmingham News, Portland Oregonian and Oregon
       Journal, St. Louis Globe-Democrat, New Orleans
       Times-Picayune and States Item, and newspapers in
       Newark, Long Island, and Staten Island.)

St. Louis Post-Dispatch
    KSD-TV,   St. Louis

Dallas Times-Herald
    KRLD-TV,   Dallas-Fort Worth

Dallas Morning News
    WFAA-TV,   Dallas-Fort Worth

Oklahoma City Oklahoman and Times
    KTVT,   Dallas-Fort Worth
    WTVT,   Tampa-St. Petersburg

Fort Worth Star Telegram
    WBAP-TV,   Dallas-Fort Worth

Cowles Communications
    WREC-TV, Memphis
    WCCO-TV, Minneapolis-St. Paul (47 percent)
        (Published Minneapolis Star and Tribune and San
        Fernando Valley Times.)
Tribune Publishing Company
    KTNT-TV, Seattle-Tacoma
        (Published Tacoma News Tribune.)
Buffalo Evening News
    WBEN-TV, Buffalo
Houston Post
    KPRC-TV, Houston
Corinthian Broadcasting Corporation
    KHOU-TV, Houston (86 percent)
    KXTV, Sacramento-Stockton
    WISH-TV, Indianapolis
        (Subsidiary of Whitney Communications, whose interests
        included one-third of the New York World Journal
        Tribune.)
McClatchy Newspapers
    KOVR, Sacramento-Stockton
        (Newspapers include the Sacramento Bee.)
Columbus Dispatch
    WBNS-TV, Columbus
Lancaster New Era and Intelligencer-Journal
    WGAL-TV, Harrisburg-Lancaster-York
    WTEV, Providence
        (Steinman Family owned all these properties.)
Tampa Tribune and Times
    WFLA-TV, Tampa-St. Petersburg
Dix Family
    WTRF-TV, Wheeling-Steubenville
        (Published newspapers in Ohio and Kentucky.)
Johnstown Tribune-Democrat
    WJAC-TV, Johnstown-Altoona
Greenville News-Piedmont
    WFBC-TV, Greenville-Spartanburg-Asheville
        (Greenville News-Piedmont Co. published the News-
        Piedmont and Asheville Citizen-Times and owned
        49.8 percent of the television station.)
Greensboro News and Record
    WFMY-TV, Greensboro-Winston/Salem-High Point
Louisville Courier-Journal and Times
    WHAS-TV, Louisville

Piedmont Publishing Company
    WSJS-TV,   Winston/Salem-Greensboro-High Point
        (Published Winston/Salem Journal and Twin City Ga-
        zette.)
WGN Broadcasting
    WGN-TV,   Chicago
    KWGN-TV, Denver
        (WGN Broadcasting was owned by Tribune Co., pub-
        lisher of the Chicago Tribune, Chicago American, and
        Sunday American, among other newspapers—interlocking
        ownership with WPIX, New York, owned by the New
        York News.)

Magazine Publishers Owning Commercial VHF Television Stations in 50 Largest Markets, as of January 1, 1967

Prairie Farmer Publishing Company
    WABC-TV, New York
    KABC-TV, Los Angeles
    WBKB, Chicago
    WXYZ-TV, Detroit
    KGO, San Francisco
        (This firm was a subsidiary of ABC, and published
        agricultural periodicals, including Prairie Farmer,
        Wallace's Farmer and Iowa Homestead, and the
        Wisconsin Agriculturist. The stations above were
        owned and operated by ABC.)
Triangle Publications
    WFIL-TV, Philadelphia
    WNHC-TV, Hartford-New Haven
    WFBG-TV, Johnstown-Altoona
        (In addition to its newspaper interests shown above,
        this firm published TV Guide and Seventeen.)
The Hearst Corporation
    WBAL-TV, Baltimore
    WISN-TV, Milwaukee
    WTAE-TV, Pittsburgh
        (In addition to its newspaper interests shown above,
        this firm owned Avon Books, several British magazines,
        and published the following: House Beautiful, Good
        Housekeeping, Cosmopolitan, Motor, Motor Boating,
        Town and Country, Harper's Bazaar, Bride and Home,
        Sports Afield, Popular Mechanics, the American Drug-
        gist, and Science Digest.)

Newsweek, Inc.
 WTOP-TV, Washington, D.C.
  (In addition to its newspaper interests shown above,
  this firm published Newsweek.)
Samuel Newhouse
 WSYR-TV, Syracuse
 WAPI-TV, Birmingham
 KTVI, St. Louis
 KOIN-TV, Portland
  (In addition to its newspaper interests shown above,
  this firm controlled organizations publishing the fol-
  lowing: Vogue, Mademoiselle, House and Garden,
  Glamour, The Bride's Magazine, Analog Science Fiction/
  Science Fact, American Modeler, and Air Progress.)
Cowles Publications
 WREC-TV, Memphis
 WCCO-TV, Minneapolis-St. Paul
  (In addition to newspaper interests shown above, this
  firm had a 50 percent interest in Harper's and pub-
  lished Family Circle, Venture, and Look.)
Whitney Communications
 KHOU-TV, Houston
 KXTV, Sacramento-Stockton
 WISH-TV, Indianapolis (86 percent)
  (In addition to newspaper interest shown above, this
  firm owned Corinthian Broadcasting whose stations are
  listed above. The magazines published by Whitney
  included the Sunday supplement Parade, Interior Design,
  and Harvest Years.)
Time-Life Inc.
 WOOD-TV, Grand Rapids
 KLZ-TV, Denver
 WFBM-TV, Indianapolis
  (Published Time, Life, Fortune, and Sports Illustrated.)
Meredith Publishing Company
 WHEN-TV, Syracuse
 KCMO-TV, Kansas City
  (Published Better Homes and Gardens and Successful
  Farming, and owned Appleton-Century-Crofts.)
United Technical Publications
 WHIO-TV, Dayton
 WSB-TV, Atlanta
 WSOC-TV, Charlotte
 KTVU, Oakland-San Francisco
 WIIC-TV, Pittsburgh

(Owned 80 percent by Cox Broadcasting, this publisher
published Radio Electronics Master Catalogue, Office
Master Catalogue, Electronics Products Magazine,
and the American Journal of Medical Electronics.)

Newspapers Owning Commercial VHF Television Stations in 50 Largest Markets, as of January 1, 1971

New York News
        WPIX, New York
                (Interlocking ownership with WGN-TV, Chicago, and
                KWGN-TV, Denver.)
Boston Herald-Traveler
        WHDH-TV, Boston
Detroit News
        WWJ-TV, Detroit
San Francisco Chronicle
        KRON-TV, San Francisco
Cox Broadcasting Corporation
        WHIO-TV, Dayton
        WSB-TV, Atlanta
        WSOC-TV, Charlotte
        WIIC-TV, Pittsburgh
        KTVU, Oakland-San Francisco
                (Owned Atlanta Journal, Atlanta Constitution, Miami
                News, and Dayton News and Dayton Journal Herald.)
Scripps-Howard Broadcasting Company
        WEWS, Cleveland
        WCPO-TV, Cincinnati
        WMC-TV, Memphis
                (Published the following top 50 market newspapers:
                Cleveland Press, Cincinnati Post, Cincinnati Times-
                Star, Columbus Citizen-Journal, Pittsburgh Press,
                Washington Daily News, Memphis Commercial Appeal
                and Press-Scimitar, Fort Worth Press, Denver Rocky
                Mountain News, Birmingham Post-Herald, and Holly-
                wood Sun-Tatler.)
The Hearst Corporation
        WBAL-TV, Baltimore
        WISN-TV, Milwaukee
        WTAE-TV, Pittsburgh
                (Published the following top 50 market newspapers:
                Los Angeles Herald-Examiner, San Francisco Examiner,
                Boston Record-American, Boston Sunday Advertiser,

Albany Times-Union, Knickerbocker News, and Seattle
Post-Intelligencer.)
Post-Newsweek Stations
    WTOP-TV,   Washington
    WPLG-TV,   Miami
        (Published Washington Post.)
Washington Evening Star
    WMAL-TV,   Washington
Baltimore Sun
    WMAR-TV,   Baltimore
Newhouse Broadcasting Corporation
    WSYR-TV,   Syracuse
    WAPI-TV,   Birmingham
    WTPA-TV,   Harrisburg
    KTVI, St. Louis
    KOIN-TV,   Portland (50 percent)
        (Published the following top 50 market newspapers:
        Syracuse Post Standard, Syracuse Herald Journal,
        Birmingham News, Portland Oregonian and Oregon
        Journal, St. Louis Globe-Democrat, New Orleans
        Times-Picayune and States Item, Harrisburg Patriot
        and News, and newspapers in New Jersey, Long Island,
        and Staten Island.)
St. Louis Post-Dispatch
    KSD-TV, St. Louis
Fort Worth Star-Telegram
    WBAP-TV,   Dallas-Fort Worth
Dallas Morning News
    WFAA-TV,   Dallas-Forth Worth
Dallas Times-Herald
    KDFW-TV,   Dallas-Fort Worth
Oklahoma City Oklahoman and Times
    WKY-TV,   Oklahoma City
    WTVT,   Tampa
    KTVT,   Fort Worth
    KHTV,   Houston
    WVTV,   Milwaukee
Cowles Communications
    WCCO-TV,   Minnaepolis-St. Paul (47 percent)
        (Published Minneapolis Star and Tribune.)
Houston Post
    KPRC-TV,   Houston
Sacramento Bee
    KOVR,   Sacramento-Stockton

Tacoma News Tribune
    KTNT-TV,   Tacoma-Seattle
Milwaukee Journal and Sentinel
    WTMJ-TV,   Milwaukee
Buffalo Evening News
    WBEN-TV,   Buffalo
Columbus Dispatch
    WBNS-TV,   Columbus
Tampa Tribune and Times
    WFLA-TV,   Tampa-St. Petersburg
Greenville News and Piedmont
    WFBC-TV,   Greenville-Spartanburg-Asheville
          (Also published Asheville Citizen-Times.)
Johnstown Tribune-Democrat
    WJAC-TV,   Johnstown-Altoona
Lancaster New Era and Intelligencer-Journal (Steinman)
    WGAL-TV,   Lancaster
    WTEV,   Providence
Greensboro News and Record
    WFMY-TV,   Greensboro
Louisville Courier-Journal and Times
    WHAS-TV,   Louisville
WGN Continental Broadcasting Co.
    WGN-TV,   Chicago
    KWGN-TV,   Denver
   (Interlocks with WPIX, New York; published Chicago Tribune
   and Chicago Today.)

Magazine Publishers Owning Commercial VHF
Television Stations in 50 Largest Markets,
as of January 1, 1971

Triangle Publications
    WFBG-TV,   Johnstown-Altoona
    WSUS-TV,   Winston/Salem-Greensboro-High Point
          (Published TV Guide and Seventeen.)
Prairie Farmer Publishing Co.
    WABC-TV,   New York
    WLS-TV,   Chicago
    KABC-TV,   Los Angeles
    KGO-TV,   San Francisco
    WXYZ-TV,   Detroit
          (Subsidiary of ABC, which published Prairie Farmer,
          Wallace's Farmer, and Wisconsin Agriculturist.)

The Hearst Corporation
    WBAL-TV,   Baltimore
    WISN-TV,   Milwaukee
    WTAE-TV,   Pittsburgh
          (Published House Beautiful, Good Housekeeping, Cos-
          mopolitan, Motor Boating and Sailing, Town and Country,
          Harper's Bazaar, Sports Afield, Popular Mechanics,
          American Druggist, and Science Digest.)
Fairchild Publications Inc.
    WTVD,   Durham
    KTRK-TV,   Houston
    WKBW-TV,   Buffalo
    WFIL-TV,   Philadelphia
    WNHC-TV,   New Haven-Hartford
          (Subsidiary of Capital City Broadcasting Corporation
          which published Women's Wear Daily, Home Furnishings
          Daily, Daily News Record, Footwear News, Electronic
          News, Metalworking News, Supermarket News, and
          Men's Wear Magazine.)
Newsweek, Inc.
    WTOP-TV,   Washington
    WPLG-TV,   Miami
    WCKY,   Cincinnati
          (Published Newsweek.)
Samuel Newhouse/Conde Nast Publications, Inc.
    WSYR-TV,   Syracuse
    WTPA,   Harrisburg
    WAPI-TV,   Birmingham
    KTVI,   St. Louis
    KOIN-TV,   Portland (50 percent)
          (Conde Nast, controlled by Newhouse family published
          Vogue, Mademoiselle, House and Garden, Glamour,
          The Bride's Magazine, Analog Science Fiction/Science
          Fact, and Air Progress.)
Cowles Communications Inc.
    WCCO-TV,   Minneapolis
          (Published Look and Venture.)
Time, Inc.
    KLZ-TV,   Denver
    WOOD-TV,   Grand Rapids
    WFBM-TV,   Indianapolis
          (Published Time, Life, Fortune, and Sports Illustrated.)
Meredith Corporation
    WHEN-TV,   Syracuse

KCMO-TV,   Kansas City
WNEM-TV,   Bay City-Saginaw
    (Published Better Homes and Gardens and Successful
    Farming.)
United Technical Publications
    WHIO-TV,   Dayton
    WSB-TV,   Atlanta
    WSOC-TV,   Charlotte
    KTVU,   Oakland-San Francisco
    WIIC-TV,   Pittsburgh
        (Subsidiary of Cox Broadcasting, which published Radio
        Electronics Master Catalogue, Electronic Engineers
        Master Catalogue, and Office and Electronic Products
        Magazine.)

ADVERTISING ON NETWORK TELEVISION

APPENDIX TABLE 5

Advertising Budgets of Network Public Affairs Advertisers, 1965-66
(dollars)

Firm	Network Public Affairs Advertising, 1965	Total Network Advertising, 1966	Total Spot Advertising, 1966	Total Television Advertising, 1966
American Home Products	14,400,000	45,215,300	11,887,890	57,103,190
Philip Morris	4,415,000	23,908,800	9,246,520	33,155,320
General Mills	3,252,500	22,021,500	17,103,020	39,124,520
Prudential Insurance Co.	3,100,000	3,327,200	n.a.	n.a.
Warner-Lambert	3,080,800	20,913,800	20,381,430	41,295,230
J. B. Williams Co.	3,006,600	14,998,400	854,520	15,852,920
Block Drug	3,005,600	12,483,800	464,170	12,947,970
Westinghouse	2,706,500	4,288,200	745,890	5,626,090
General Cigar	2,600,000	3,304,700	n.a.	n.a.
Gulf Oil Corporation	2,575,700	2,327,200	4,641,410	6,968,610
Bristol-Myers	1,840,400	68,070,600	25,531,770	93,602,370
Aluminum Co. of America	1,708,500	5,327,000	1,031,540	6,358,540
Colgate-Palmolive	1,640,500	36,879,100	30,236,270	67,115,370
Brown and Williamson	1,618,000	21,960,200	7,810,810	29,771,010
Purex	1,467,200	3,618,000	3,430,410	7,048,410
General Motors	1,405,500	34,300,300	4,136,430	38,436,730
Savings and Loan Foundation	1,398,300	881,000	n.a.	n.a.
Standard Brands	1,346,000	6,922,300	8,622,500	15,544,800
Shell Oil	1,303,800	5,478,600	7,904,420	13,383,020
Wilkinson Sword	1,300,000	1,579,000	n.a.	n.a.
Kendall Co.	1,300,000	2,130,500	n.a.	n.a.
John Hancock	1,300,000	1,579,000	n.a.	n.a.
S. C. Johnson and Sons	1,266,200	17,776,800	5,178,560	22,955,360
3M Company	1,200,000	3,878,600	n.a.	n.a.
Xerox	1,131,000	3,195,500	n.a.	n.a.
American Dairy Assoc.	882,000	747,000	n.a.	n.a.
Eastern Airlines	867,800	1,091,700	n.a.	n.a.
Shulton, Inc.	840,100	5,360,700	662,740	6,023,440
Armour and Co.	795,700	6,905,700	1,141,270	8,046,970
International Business Machines	744,600	1,832,200	n.a.	n.a.
Sunbeam	712,200	7,885,000	3,531,660	11,416,660
General Foods	704,800	49,712,800	43,600,330	93,313,130
B. F. Goodrich	657,300	2,708,000	n.a.	n.a.

(Continued)

Firm	Network Public Affairs Advertising, 1965	Total Network Advertising, 1966	Total Spot Advertising, 1966	Total Television Advertising, 1966
Hunt Foods	649,000	6,919,500	2,713,320	9,632,820
Stanley Warner (International Latex)	599,200	15,954,700	131,130	16,985,830
Hazel Bishop	596,100	610,900	n.a.	n.a.
Smith, Kline, and French	563,200	7,669,600	n.a.	n.a.
American Motors	502,440	4,902,400	1,024,780	5,927,180
Campbell Soup Co.	493,200	7,321,000	7,418,420	15,088,020
Institute of Life Insurance	452,000	1,921,800	n.a.	n.a.
Liggett and Myers	447,700	21,434,600	11,538,150	32,972,750
Carnation Co.	444,800	15,638,000	3,222,900	18,860,900
Miles Laboratories	443,100	16,759,500	15,959,500	32,719,000
Norwich Pharmacal	429,700	7,266,800	310,850	7,577,640
Carter-Wallace	392,700	4,483,000	5,249,210	9,732,210
Continental Insurance	392,100	1,434,400	n.a.	n.a.
Union Carbide	382,900	5,763,700	639,900	6,403,600
P. Lorillard	379,200	18,307,900	7,714,500	26,022,440
Reynolds Metals	347,400	n.a.	n.a.	n.a.
U.S. Plywood	316,900	642,400	n.a.	n.a.
Polaroid	307,500	7,466,500	0	7,466,500
Proctor and Gamble	269,100	101,251,200	77,905,760	179,156,960
Sherwin Williams	225,700	2,674,200	n.a.	n.a.
Florists Telegraph Delivery	220,300	1,934,900	n.a.	n.a.
Alberto-Culver	209,000	12,759,200	8,310,550	21,069,750
Charles Pfizer	186,700	4,189,100	2,465,680	6,654,780
Kayser Roth Corporation	177,000	1,362,300	n.a.	n.a.
Kaiser Industries	177,000	1,212,800	n.a.	n.a.
Andrew Jergens	172,000	4,491,300	1,086,120	5,577,420
Richardson-Merrell	157,300	7,606,300	4,447,680	12,053,980
SCM Corporation	150,000	n.a.	n.a.	n.a.
Revlon	144,000	2,210,500	n.a.	n.a.
Johnson and Johnson	143,200	6,749,500	9,919,870	16,669,370
Quaker Oats	135,000	10,423,000	8,722,660	19,145,660
Black and Decker Management Co.	130,200	1,171,600	n.a.	n.a.

Firm	Network Public Affairs Advertising, 1965	Total Network Advertising, 1966	Total Spot Advertising, 1966	Total Television Advertising, 1966
ing-Seeley Thermos	126,000	209,700	n.a.	n.a.
ennen	123,700	2,287,000	n.a.	n.a.
hanel, Inc.	118,000	1,300,500	n.a.	n.a.
aymond Research Corp.	115,100	n.a.	n.a.	n.a.
terling Drug	114,100	21,125,100	6,797,200	39,032,300
assey Ferguson	114,000	n.a.	n.a.	n.a.
nderson-Clayton	105,100	5,332,500	2,506,640	7,839,140
cripto, Inc.	105,000	1,400,100	n.a.	n.a.
lin Mathieson	105,000	2,266,700	n.a.	n.a.
ord Motor Co.	103,000	23,347,400	4,643,080	27,990,480
artz Mountain Products	95,000	902,700	n.a.	n.a.
nheuser-Busch	87,700	1,944,000	4,470,390	6,414,390
ever Brothers	86,200	32,740,600	25,296,400	58,037,000
oodyear Tire and Rubber	77,000	5,389,000	1,426,500	6,815,500
alston-Purina	71,000	9,055,500	11,316,310	20,371,810
.S. Rubber	66,000	n.a.	n.a.	n.a.
n Oil	61,700	1,690,300	n.a.	n.a.
ardley of London	57,000	1,103,200	n.a.	n.a.
exaco	56,500	2,455,000	n.a.	n.a.
allace and Tiernan	50,000	2,461,000	n.a.	n.a.
iller Brewing	49,200	n.a.	n.a.	n.a.
ational Plastics Products	48,500	n.a.	n.a.	n.a.
merican Cyanimid	46,000	7,025,500	571,500	7,597,000
perry Rand	43,000	3,798,000	n.a.	n.a.
chick Electric	39,000	906,700	n.a.	n.a.
orton International	37,000	3,085,500	n.a.	n.a.
illette	33,000	33,485,500	8,366,900	41,852,400
ath Packing	32,000	405,400	n.a.	n.a.
hesebrough-Ponds	31,500	6,986,700	4,381,290	11,367,990
.S. Steel	29,500	n.a.	n.a.	n.a.
uxton, Inc.	28,500	422,100	n.a.	n.a.
enith	25,000	3,086,100	n.a.	n.a.
cott Paper	25,000	1,880,700	n.a.	n.a.
otorola	25,000	4,974,800	32,750	5,007,550

(Continued)

Firm	Network Public Affairs Advertising, 1965	Total Network Advertising, 1966	Total Spot Advertising, 1966	Total Televisio Advertising, 19*
General Electric	25,000	8,590,900	1,266,490	9,857,390
Twentieth Century Fox	22,000	183,600	n.a.	n.a.
DuPont	21,800	6,482,900	581,000	7,063,900
Lanvin	21,700	514,600	n.a.	n.a.
Beltone Electronic Corp.	21,700	n.a.	n.a.	n.a.
Sta Nu	20,000	n.a.	n.a.	n.a.
Walt Disney Productions	20,000	1,847,400	n.a.	n.a.
Dr. Pepper Co.	19,000	1,174,100	n.a.	n.a.
Koret of California	18,000	356,700	n.a.	n.a.
Dow Chemical	17,100	2,767,600	n.a.	n.a.
Chrysler Corporation	17,000	25,691,700	2,362,160	28,053,860
Abbott Laboratories	17,000	1,637,600	n.a.	n.a.
North American Philips	15,000	2,722,100	n.a.	n.a.
Dow Jones and Company	13,000	182,300	n.a.	n.a.
Ocean Spray Cranberries	12,000	2,312,600	n.a.	n.a.
American Photography Equip- ment Co.	8,500	n.a.	n.a.	n.a.
Heublein, Inc.	8,500	1,314,000	5,532,620	6,846,620
Mentholatum Company	8,500	n.a.	n.a.	n.a.
Rubber Maid	8,500	485,000	n.a.	n.a.
Singer	8,500	4,155,700	n.a.	n.a.
United Fruit	8,500	n.a.	n.a.	n.a.
CIBA Corporation	8,000	369,700	n.a.	n.a.
William Underwood Co.	8,000	1,231,000	n.a.	n.a.
Eversharp	7,500	609,500	n.a.	n.a.
International Minerals and Chemicals	7,000	1,350,900	n.a.	n.a.
R. J. Reynolds	7,000	42,515,600	7,311,730	49,827,330
National Cotton Council	6,000	n.a.	n.a.	n.a.
PepsiCo	6,000	11,570,200	15,922,540	27,492,740
Plough, Inc.	6,000	3,806,100	1,850,210	5,656,310
Golden Grain Macaroni	4,000	1,438,300	n.a.	n.a.
Mayer, Oscar, and Co.	3,000	2,776,300	n.a.	n.a.
Mead Johnson	3,000	2,258,200	5,051,900	7,310,100

Note: The abbreviation "n.a." stands for "not available."

Sources: See the discussion under "Notes on Sources of Data for 1965-66," below.

APPENDIX TABLE 6

Advertising Budgets of Top 50 Advertisers Not Sponsoring Public Affairs
Programming During the 1965 Season
(dollars)

Firm	Rank (out of 50)	Total Network Advertising, 1966	Total Spot Advertising, 1966	Total Television Advertising, 1966
American Tobacco	10	31,470,700	9,356,490	40,827,190
Coca-Cola Co.	13	4,638,900	34,120,410	38,759,310
Kellogg	15	18,648,300	16,442,350	35,090,650
William Wrigley Jr.	24	937,000	22,654,630	23,591,630
National Dairy Products	30	12,839,100	5,361,490	18,200,590
National Biscuit	36	10,091,800	4,533,350	14,625,150
Corn Products	37	3,126,900	10,540,570	13,667,470
Continental Baking	38	429,400	13,117,220	13,546,620
Ford Motor Dealers	41	0	12,448,260	12,448,260
Pillsbury	43	8,846,400	2,789,600	11,636,000
Eastman Kodak	47	9,119,500	1,709,210	10,828,710
J. Schlitz Brewing	48	2,943,200	7,340,650	10,283,850
General Motors Dealers	49	0	10,173,360	10,173,360
Menley and James Labs	50	7,321,000	2,801,410	10,122,410

Sources: See the discussion under "Notes on Sources of Data for 1965-66," below.

Advertising Budgets of 25 Largest Network Advertisers, 1970

(dollars)

Firm	Network Advertising	Spot Advertising	Total Television Advertising
Proctor and Gamble	128,476,300	50,799,800	179,276,100
Bristol-Myers	57,078,600	23,329,100	80,407,700
R. J. Reynolds	52,416,500	14,404,900	66,821,400
Colgate-Palmolive	46,518,400	38,863,300	85,381,700
Warner-Lambert	46,210,900	17,855,900	64,066,800
General Foods	41,642,000	46,774,900	88,416,900
Sterling Drug	41,324,000	12,934,700	54,258,700
American Home Products	40,844,900	26,357,500	67,202,400
Lever Brothers	38,581,400	20,869,100	59,450,500
Philip Morris	36,685,800	11,491,800	48,177,600
General Motors	32,972,300	8,963,200	41,935,500
Ford Motor Co.	31,377,600	7,544,800	38,922,400
Miles Laboratories	28,953,500	9,591,600	38,545,100
S. C. Johnson and Sons	28,803,700	n.a.	n.a.
American Brands	28,042,600	n.a.	n.a.
Gillette	27,479,300	16,320,800	43,800,100
Kellogg	24,966,500	8,539,500	33,506,000
General Mills	24,152,400	17,935,600	42,098,000
British-American Tobacco	23,131,100	7,832,800	30,963,900
J. B. Williams Co.	22,467,800	n.a.	n.a.
Chrysler Corporation	21,541,600	3,927,600	25,469,200
Ralston-Purina	18,739,100	6,354,100	25,083,200
Kraftco	18,359,300	13,164,600	31,523,900
PepsiCo	16,864,300	13,425,400	30,289,700
Rapid American Corporation	16,242,200	n.a.	n.a.

Note: The abbreviation "n.a." stands for "not available."

Sources: Broadcasting, LXXX, 12 (March 21, 1971), 38-43, and LXXX, 18 (May 3, 1971), 30-31.

NOTES ON SOURCES OF DATA FOR 1965-66

The figures in Appendix Tables 5 and 6 were extracted from
Broadcasting, LXX, 8 (April 25, 1966), 28-32, which published a list
of 137 sponsors who had advertised on network public affairs programs
during 1965. Unfortunately, no such figures were subsequently published for either 1966 or 1967. It was therefore necessary to use
the 1965 figures. This was no great misfortune since the magnitudes
were what were of interest, and these did not vary greatly from year
to year.

According to Broadcasting, advertising budgets increased by
7-10 percent from 1965 to 1966. With the exception of those advertisers who changed their basic advertising strategy between 1965 and
1966, it can safely be assumed that their investments in public affairs
programming in 1966 were approximately 10 percent greater than those
in 1965. (The 10 percent figure is probably more nearly correct
than 7 percent, since there were indications that advertising support
for public affairs programming was increasing relative to other types
of programs.)

The statistics on 1965 public affairs program advertising were
collected for the Television Bureau of Advertising and published in
Broadcasting in somewhat more raw form than those that appear in
Appendix Tables 5 and 6. The 137 advertisers were listed with their
respective expenditures to each network, and these figures were
further broken down into types of public affairs programming supported—for example, news, documentaries, specials, space shots,
and so forth. The network totals for public affairs advertising in 1965
represent the computed totals of these separate figures, advertiser
by advertiser.

The remaining figures on advertising in Appendix Tables 5 and
6 were available for 1966, the year during which public affairs programming was examined in this study. These figures, if reduced by
approximately 10 percent, would approach the 1965 figures. Total
advertising expenditures and network television advertising for 1966
were taken directly from Broadcasting, LXXII, 12 (March 20, 1967),
40B-40D.

The breakdowns of advertising expenditures into network and
spot advertising in 1966, as well as gross figures for television advertising in 1966, were taken from a chart published in Broadcasting,
LXXII, 16 (April 17, 1967), 34. This chart gave the figures for the
100 largest advertisers during 1966. Therefore, in many cases, the
spot and total figures were not available for some of 1965's major
public affairs sponsors.

There was one apparent error in the Broadcasting data. In the March 20, 1967, issue, Smith, Kline, and French was shown to have spent $7,669,600 on network advertising in 1966. Nonetheless, in the April 17, 1967, issue of the same magazine, Smith, Kline, and French was not listed as one of the top 100 advertisers. The nearly $7.7 million spent on network advertising during 1966 would have made the firm rank 66th in 1966.

BOOKS

Almond, Gabriel, and Bingham Powell. Comparative Politics: A Developmental Approach. Boston: Little, Brown, 1966.

Balk, Alfred, and James Boylan, eds. Our Troubled Press. Boston: Little, Brown, 1971.

Barnouw, Erik. A History of Broadcasting in the United States. Vol. II. New York: Oxford University Press, 1968.

Barrett, Marvin, ed. Survey of Broadcast Journalism 1968-69. New York: Grosset & Dunlap, 1969.

_____. Survey of Broadcast Journalism 1969-70. New York: Grosset & Dunlap, 1970.

_____. Survey of Broadcast Journalism 1970-71. New York: Grosset & Dunlap, 1971.

Bernstein, Marver H. Regulating Business by Independent Commission. Princeton: Princeton University Press, 1955.

Bluem, William A.; John F. Cox; and Gene McPherson. Television in the Public Interest. New York: Hastings House, 1961.

Blumler, Jay G., and Denis McQuail. Television in Politics: Its Uses and Influences. Chicago: University of Chicago Press, 1969.

Brown, Les. Television: The Business Behind the Box. New York: Harcourt, Brace Jovanovich, 1971.

Clark, David G., and Earl R. Hutchison. Mass Media and the Law. New York: John Wiley & Sons, 1970.

Cohen, Bernard C. The Press and Foreign Policy. Princeton: Princeton University Press, 1963.

Coons, John E. Freedom and Responsibility in Broadcasting. Evanston, Ill.: Northwestern University Press, 1961.

Dahl, Robert A., ed. Political Oppositions in Western Democracies. New Haven: Yale University Press, 1966.

Easton, David. The Political System. New York: Alfred A. Knopf, 1953.

Emery, Walter Byron. Broadcasting and Government: Responsibilities and Regulations. East Lansing: Michigan State University Press, 1961.

Etzioni, Amitai. Modern Organizations. Englewood Cliffs, N.J.: Prentice-Hall, 1964.

Fagen, Richard R. Politics and Communication. Boston: Little, Brown, 1966.

Fainsod, Merle. Government and the Economy. 3d ed. New York: W. W. Norton, 1959.

Faulk, John Henry. Fear on Trial. New York: Simon and Schuster, 1964.

Friendly, Fred W. Due to Circumstances Beyond Our Control . . . New York: Random House, 1967.

Friendly, Henry J. The Federal Administrative Agencies: The Need for Better Definition of Standards. Cambridge, Mass.: Harvard University Press, 1959.

Goldman, Eric F., ed. Broadcasting and Government Regulation in a Free Society. Santa Barbara: Center for the Study of Democratic Institutions, 1959.

Head, Sydney W. Broadcasting in America: A Survey of Television and Radio. Boston: Houghton Mifflin, 1956.

Hohenberg, John. The News Media: A Journalist Looks at His Profession. New York: Holt, Rinehart & Winston, 1968.

Jenkins, Clive. Power Behind the Screen: Ownership Control and Motivation in British Commercial Television. London: Mac-Gibbon and Kee, 1961.

Johnson, Nicholas. How to Talk Back to Your Television Set. Boston: Atlantic-Little, Brown, 1969.

Key, V. O. Politics, Parties, and Pressure Groups. 4th ed. New York: Thomas Y. Crowell, 1968.

_____. Public Opinion and American Democracy. New York: Alfred A. Knopf, 1961.

Krislov, Samuel, and Lloyd D. Musolf, eds. The Politics of Regulation. Boston: Houghton Mifflin, 1964.

Lane, Mark. A Citizen's Dissent: Mark Lane Replies. New York: Holt, Rinehart & Winston, 1968.

Lang, Kurt, and Gladys Engel Lang. Politics and Television. Chicago: Quadrangle Books, 1968.

Lazarsfeld, Paul F.; Bernard Berelson; and Hazel Gaudet. The People's Choice. New York: Duell, Sloan & Pearce, 1944.

Lerner, Daniel. The Passing of Traditional Society—Modernizing the Middle East. New York: The Free Press of Glencoe, 1958.

Levin, Harry J. Broadcast Regulation and Joint Ownership of Media. New York: New York University Press, 1960.

Lippmann, Walter. Public Opinion. New York: Macmillan, 1960.

Lowi, Theodore. The End of Liberalism—Ideology, Policy, and the Crisis of Public Authority. New York: W. W. Norton, 1969.

McConnell, Grant. Private Power and American Democracy. New York: Alfred A. Knopf, 1966.

McLuhan, Marshall. Understanding Media: The Extensions of Man. New York: Signet Books, 1964.

MacNeil, Robert. The People Machine: The Influence of Television on American Politics. New York: Harper & Row, 1968.

Mailer, Norman. The Armies of the Night. New York: New American Library, 1968.

Mendelsohn, Harold, and Irving Cuspi. Polls, Television, and the New Politics. Scranton: Chandler Publishing Co., 1970.

Minow, Newton N. Equal Time: The Private Broadcaster and the
    Public Interest. Edited by Lawrence Laurent, New York:
    Atheneum, 1964.

Opotowsky, Stan. TV: The Big Picture. New York: E. P. Dutton, 1961.

Paul, Eugene. The Hungry Eye: An Inside Look at Television. New
    York: Ballantine Books, 1962.

Rubin, Bernard. Political Television. Belmont, Calif.: Wadsworth
    Publishing Co., 1967.

Rucker, Bryce. The First Freedom. Carbondale: Southern Illinois
    University Press, 1968.

Sayre, Wallace S., ed. The Federal Government Service. 2d ed.
    Englewood Cliffs: Prentice-Hall, 1965.

Schiller, Herbert I. Mass Communications and American Empire.
    New York: August M. Kelley, Publishers, 1969.

Schramm, Wilbur. Responsibility in Mass Communication. New York:
    Harper & Row, 1957.

_____, ed. Mass Communications. Urbana: University of Illinois
    Press, 1960.

Schwartz, Bernard. The Professor and the Commissions. New York:
    Alfred A. Knopf, 1959.

Siepmann, Charles Arthur. Radio, Television, and Society. New York:
    Oxford University Press, 1950.

Skornia, Harry J. Television and Society: An Inquest and Agenda for
    Improvement. New York: McGraw-Hill, 1965.

_____. Television and the News: A Critical Appraisal. Palo Alto:
    Pacific Books, 1968.

_____, and Jack William Kitson. Problems and Controversies in
    Television and Radio. Palo Alto: Pacific Books, 1968.

Steiner, Gary A. The People Look at Television. New York: Alfred
    A. Knopf, 1963.

Truman, David. The Governmental Process: Political Interests and Public Opinion. New York: Alfred A. Knopf. 1951.

Weinberg, Mayer. TV in America. New York: Ballantine Books, 1962.

Wood, William A. Electronic Journalism. New York: Columbia University Press, 1967.

ARTICLES IN JOURNALS AND PERIODICALS

Abel, Elie. "An Inside Look at the Media by a Critical Eye," Washington Post, February 24, 1971, p. B5.

Barrow, Roscoe L. "The Attainment of Balanced Program Service in Television," Virginia Law Review, LII, 4 (May 1966), 633-66.

Berkman, Dave. "A Modest Proposal: Abolishing the FCC," Columbia Journalism Review, IV, 3 (Fall 1965), 34-36.

Breed, Warren. "Social Control in the Newsroom: A Functional Analysis," Social Forces, XXXIII (May 1955), 326-35.

Bryant, Ashbrook P. "Responsibility for Broadcasting Matter," Journal of Broadcasting, V (Summer 1960), 3-16.

Coase, R. H. "Economics of Broadcasting and Government Policy," American Economic Review, LVI (May 1966), 440-47, 467-75.

Darlington, George W. "The Many Worlds of Local TV," Television, XXIV, 8 (August 1967), 33 ff.

_____. "The Many Worlds of Local TV," Television, XX, 8 (August 1963), 31 ff.

_____. "The Many Worlds of Local TV," Television, XIX 8 (August 1962), 37 ff.

Drew, E. B. "Is the FCC Dead?," Atlantic, CCXX (July 1967), 29-36.

Eck, R. "Real Masters of Programming," Harper's, CCXXXIV (March 1967), 45-52.

Gardiner, John. "The New and Ominous Mood of Capitol Hill," Television, XXIV, 6 (June 1967), 32 ff.

Gilman, Morris J. "Going It Alone—Life Without Networks, "Tele-vision, XX, 6 (June 1963), 24 ff.

Irish, Loomis C. "Monday Memo," Broadcasting, LXXIII, 20 (November 13, 1967), 18.

Johnson, Nicholas. "The Media Barons and the Public Interest: An FCC Commissioner's Warning," Atlantic, CCXXI, 6 (June 1968), 43-51.

Klapper, Joseph T. "What We Know about the Effects of Mass Communication: The Brink of Hope," Public Opinion Quarterly, XXI, pp. 453-74.

Kroeger, Albert R. "How Things Stand with the Groups," Television, XXIII, 3 (March 1966), 29 ff.

_____. "News, News, News, News," Television, XXII, 2 (February 1965), 28 ff.

Levin, Harvey J. "Antitrust Laws and Mass Media," Challenge, XI (July 1963), 11-13.

Loevinger, Lee. "The Games People Play Over Television," Tele-vision, XXIV, 11 (November 1967), 49 ff.

_____. "The Issues in Program Regulation," Federal Communications Bar Association Journal, XX (March 1966), 142-58.

Murrow, Edward R. "Murrow's Indictment of Broadcasting," Columbia Journalism Review, IV (Fall 1965), 27-32.

Navasky, Victor S. "One Man's Doubt," New York Times, July 14, 1968, Book Review Section, pp. 32 ff.

Pearson, Drew, and Jack Anderson. "Television's 'Ethics,' " New York Post, February 26, 1968, p. 38.

Roseburg, Herbert H. "Program Content," Western Political Quarterly, II, 4 (December 1949), 375-401.

Winick, Charles E. "The Television Station Manager," Advanced Management Journal, XXXI, 1 (March 1967), 53-60.

Zeidenberg, Leonard. "Is the FCC Obsolete?," Television, XXIII, 10 (October 1966), 31 ff.

NEWSPAPERS AND PERIODICALS

Broadcasting

Columbia Journalism Review

Journal of Broadcasting

New York Times

Television

TV Digest

Television Quarterly

TV Guide

Variety

Washington Post

OFFICIAL SOURCES

U.S. Congress. House. Committee on Interstate and Foreign Com-
    merce. Broadcasting Editorializing Practices. Hearings before
    a subcommittee of the Committee on Interstate and Foreign
    Commerce, House of Representatives, 88th Cong., 1st sess.,
    1963.

_____. Network Broadcasting. Report of the Committee on Inter-
    state and Foreign Commerce pursuant to section 136 of Legis-
    lative Reorganization Act of 1946, Public Law 601, 79th Congress
    and House resolution 99, 85th Cong., 1958.

_____. Public Television Act of 1967. Hearings before a subcom-
    mittee of the Committee on Interstate and Foreign Commerce,
    House of Representatives, 90th Cong., 1st sess., 1967.

_____. Television Network Program Procurement. Report of Federal Communications Commission, Office of Network Study, First Interim Report, 88th Cong., 1st sess., 1963.

_____. Committee on the Judiciary. "Television," in Monopoly Problems in Regulated Industries, Part II, Vols. 1-4. Washington, D.C.: U.S. Government Printing Office, 1957.

U.S. Congress. Senate. Committee on Interstate and Foreign Commerce. Political Broadcasts—Equal Time. Hearings before a subcommittee of the Committee on Interstate and Foreign Commerce, Senate, 86th Cong., 1st sess., 1959.

_____. The Television Inquiry—Network Practices and UHF-VHF Problems. Hearings before a subcommittee of the Committee on Interstate and Foreign Commerce, Senate, 84th Cong., 2d sess., 1956.

U.S. Federal Communications Commission. 31st Annual Report, Fiscal Year 1965. Washington, D.C.: U.S. Government Printing Office, 1966.

_____. 32nd Annual Report, Fiscal Year 1966. Washington, D.C.: U.S. Government Printing Office, 1967.

_____. 33rd Annual Report, Fiscal Year 1967. Washington, D.C.: U.S. Government Printing Office, 1968.

_____. 34th Annual Report, Fiscal Year 1968. Washington, D.C.: U.S. Government Printing Office, 1969.

_____. 35th Annual Report, Fiscal Year 1969. Washington, D.C.: U.S. Government Printing Office, 1970.

_____. 36th Annual Report, Fiscal Year 1970. Washington, D.C.: U.S. Government Printing Office, 1971.

_____. The Communications Act of 1934, with Amendments and Index Thereto. Washington, D.C.: U.S. Government Printing Office, 1968.

_____. "In the Matter of Amendment of Section 73.636 (a) of the Commission's Rules Relating to Multiple Ownership of Television Broadcast Stations," FCC 65-537, Docket No. 16068, June 21, 1965.

_____."In the Matter of Applications by American Broadcasting Companies, Inc. . . . ," FCC 66-1186 and 92762, Docket No. 16828, December 21, 1966.

_____. "In the Matter of Editorializing by Broadcast Licensees," FCC 49-422, Docket No. 8516, June 1, 1949.

_____. "Notice of Proposed Rule Making and Memorandum, Opinion and Order Proposing Amendment of Section 73.636(a) of the Commission's Rules Relating to Multiple Ownership of Television Broadcast Stations," Docket No. 18110, August 1, 1968.

_____. "Report and Statement of Policy Re: Commission En Banc Programming Inquiry," FCC 60-970, Docket No. 12103 July 29, 1960.

_____. Report on Chain Broadcasting. Docket No. 5060, May 1941.

_____. Statistical Material on Newspaper-Broadcast Joint Interests as of November, 1967. Prepared for the Antitrust and Monopoly Subcommittee of the Committee on the Judiciary, U.S. Senate. Washington, D.C.: U.S. Government Printing Office, 1968.

_____. Office of Network Study. Network Broadcasting. 2 vols. Washington, D.C.: U.S. Government Printing Office, 1957.

_____. Responsibility for Broadcast Matter. Interim Report. Washington, D.C.: U.S. Government Printing Office, 1960.

_____. Television Network Program Procurement. Second Interim Report, Part I. Washington, D.C.: U.S. Government Printing Office, 1962.

_____. Television Network Program Procurement. Second Interim Report, Part II. Washington, D.C.: U.S. Government Printing Office, 1965.

MONOGRAPHS, REPORTS, PAMPHLETS, AND OTHER PUBLICATIONS

American Research Bureau and Television Digest, Inc. Television Factbook. No. 37. 1967 ed., 2 vols. Washington, D.C., 1967.

_____. Television Factbook. No. 41. 1971-72 ed. 2 vols. Washington, D.C., 1971.

Arthur D. Little, Inc. Television Program Production, Procurement, and Syndication—An Economic Analysis. Report Relating to the FCC's Proposed Rule in Docket 12782. 2 vols. Cambridge, Mass., 1966.

Carnegie Commission on Educational Television. Public Television, a Program for Action. New York: Bantam Books, 1967.

Cusack, Mary Ann. "Editorializing in Broadcasting." Unpublished Ph.D. dissertation, Wayne State University, 1960.

Doyle, Charles E. "Newton Minow in the 'Vast Wasteland': Attempts at Innovation in a 'Mature' Agency." Unpublished doctoral seminar paper prepared for Government G9241x-G9242y, Columbia University, November 23, 1966.

Jones, William K. "Licensing of Major Broadcast Facilities by the Federal Communications Commission." Unpublished paper prepared for the Administrative Conference of the United States, Committee on Licenses and Authorizations, Columbia University School of Law, September 1962.

Landis, James M. Report on the Regulatory Agencies to the President-Elect. Washington, D.C., December, 1960.

National Association of Broadcasters. "Editorializing on the Air." Washington, D.C., 1963. (Pamphlet.)

_____. "Radio and Television Editorializing." Washington, D.C., 1967. (Pamphlet.)

_____. "The Television Code." 9th ed. Washington, D.C., 1964. (Pamphlet.)

_____. Television Information Office. Television and Politics— A Bibliography. New York, 1964.

_____. Television: Freedom, Responsibility, Regulation, a Bibliography. New York, 1962.

Petersmann, Dirk. "Anatomy of a Sponsor." Unpublished paper prepared at Columbia University School of Journalism, May 12, 1968.

Stonesifer, Richard J. "The FCC and Broadcasting." Unpublished
    paper, 1964.

United Research, Inc. The Implications of Limiting Multiple Owner-
    ship of Television Stations. Prepared for the Council for Tele-
    vision Development. 2 vols. Cambridge, Mass., 1966.

Wolf, Frank. "Some Determinants of Public Affairs Programming on
    Commercial Television in the United States." Unpublished Ph.D.
    dissertation, Columbia University, 1971.

ABOUT THE AUTHOR

FRANK WOLF is Assistant Professor of Political Science at Drew University and is currently Resident Director of Drew's London Semester program.

Dr. Wolf received B. A. degrees from Williams College and Oxford University and a Ph. D. in political science from Columbia University. Since 1966 he has been an editorial associate for <u>Foreign Affairs</u>.